Out of the Wild

SEVEN YEARS IN THE WILDERNESS
JAMESTOWN BAY, FIORDLAND NATIONAL PARK

Charlie Paterson

DEDICATION

To my lovely patient wife, Bronny

Published by Charlie Paterson, New Zealand Email: charliewilderness@hotmail.com

Copyright 2017© Charlie Paterson

ISBN: 978-1-980-24554-4

Design by Craigs Design & Print Ltd
PO Box 99, Invercargill 9840, New Zealand
07640

Contents

NEW ZEALAND

MARTINS BAY

JAMESTOWN BAY

LAKE MCKERROW

LAKE ALABASTER

MILFORD SOUND

HOLLYFORD VALLEY

(Geographx)

Introduction

AWAY IN A VERY REMOTE AND QUIET LOCATION where the annual rainfall is recorded in metres and the age of the encompassing tall forest trees are recorded in centuries, is a very special piece of wilderness. To walk there from the nearest road end will take you a two or three day trek through lowland temperate rainforest being situated deep inside New Zealand's largest and most scenic National Park. It's a place where timid Red deer graze silently in the back yard during the still winter nights and hide in the thick secure forest during the day. Where you read at night by the flickering light of a wax candle and cook lean venison stew on a wood burning range during the day. Where it might take months for you to get your mail or your next lot of supplies. Where your only communication to the outside world is twice a week on Tuesdays and Fridays via an old green metal encased SSB radio – but only if the 12 volt battery is up to charge and if the changeable atmospheric conditions are okay for the radio waves to bounce over the mountains to civilization and if, of course, you haven't forgotten what day of the week it is!? Where your only transport is by foot, boat or kayak, there being no roads or cars in this dense rainforest. Where soft, wilderness romantics often visit and quickly lose interest due to the constant bite of the sandfly during the day and their cousins the mosquitos during the night. Where your venison is hung in the old traditional fashion to store because there is no regular electricity for a freezer. Where the surrounding rainforest, mountains, lakes and rivers create many special treats and interesting challenges few ever get to discover, experience or even comprehend in their very busy little worlds.

A piece of rainforest wilderness that chewed up seven years of my life.

DON'T BE FOOLED INTO THINKING this is some sort of romantic wilderness novel extolling the virtues of a wilderness lifestyle; it is not. It is more my story, with all its ugly warts, describing seven years of constant challenges and tribulations, big, small and imagined, in order to survive in this idyllic little spot and achieve what others said I could not do.

I have struck many problems and made many mistakes in this very special location, mostly of my own making, stupidity and arrogance. I could have easily done without them at the time, they almost broke me physically, mentally, spiritually and financially. They did though force upon me a change in my life's outlook which remoulded it for the better. Problems are nothing but 'challenges' to overcome and mistakes are nothing other than 'learning curves' to avoid repeating, not a philosophy I invited but one I've inherited in life and can recommend to others. This tale has heaps of both.

'Physical Challenges' against nature in river, forest and lake and when it comes to nature we may win the day to day battles but, ultimately, we all will lose the war with nature and time.

It involves 'Financial Challenges' of having no money while being the poor kid building unwanted sandcastles in the rich kids' sand pit (Fiordland National Park).

It involves 'Challenges of Loneliness' spending one winter in the wild where I didn't see anybody for three months and when I finally did see some trampers, trekking through 'my' patch of wilderness, I hid and watched these intruders in their uncomprehending trespassing!

It involves 'Challenges of Ill Health', my runty body not being designed for the stress and work I put it through to achieve this mad endeavour among the ancient and twisted podocarps. Splattering my white porcelain bowel in shocking red for three secret years being too embarrassed by my bloody bowel motions to seek help; too fatalistic to really care.

It involves 'Mental Challenges' of depression, where dark rainy days accompany lonely dark thoughts and the rifle perched beside the wood range whispers a fool's release from all the worries and unfairness in life.

It involves silly 'Bureaucratic Challenges' fighting the jealous 'have nots' and worse still the greed of those very few people who do have it but say, "you can't have it."

It involves a 'Belief Learning Curve', being very reluctant to accept that a God actually does exist, a very scary concept to digest in full. Discovering that you can try running from the fact but you can never hide from the evidence and knowledge once it's been revealed.

All these unwanted Challenges and Learning Curves changed my life and forced me to come "Out of the Wild" so to speak, in a very literal sense. To come out of a New Zealand forest and mountain wilderness that consumed seven years of my life, a wilderness I both love and hate with a real passion and probably will till my dying day.

I am writing this not only because friends tell me that I should but also because it's a productive way to spend quiet evenings or fill in rainy days of which Fiordland has quite a few.

THE BOOK IS WRITTEN IN A ROUGH TIME LINE from 1995 to 2002. However, each chapter tends to start and finish with either a short description of my surroundings at the time of writing or some small memory, event, character or historical note associated to the overall tale of my life and battles here in the misty, green rainforest of Fiordland. To preserve people's privacy – an important commodity – and also, to avoid possible embarrassing recounts of their antics, I have changed the odd name and with those well-known companies that may get a bit upset with my accounts of certain events I have also given them new names.

To start this tale I'll copy straight from my messy notes compiled over the years and describe a content moment to set the scene, it is one of the few you will find in this book. Through these pages you will meet some interesting people, maybe even learn from my mistakes and hopefully have an interesting read.

My Wilderness Home in Jamestown Bay, Lake McKerrow, Fiordland National Park.

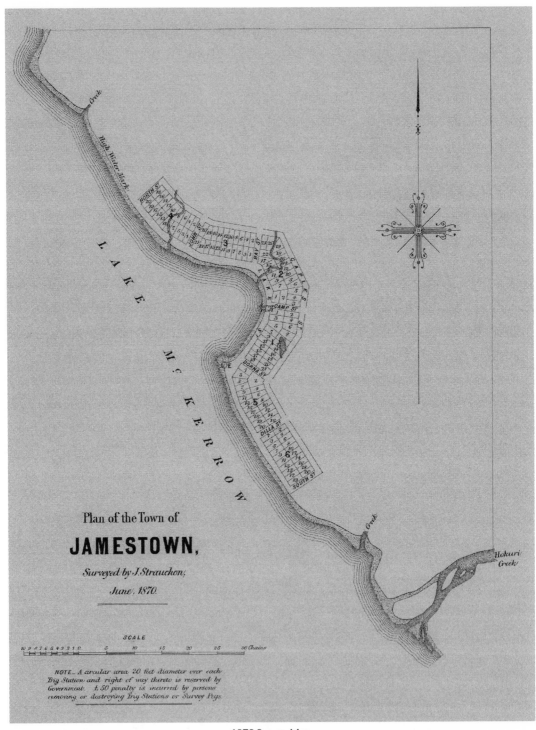

Plan of the Town of

JAMESTOWN,

Surveyed by J. Strauchon;

June, 1870.

SCALE

1870 Survey Map.
Strauchon, John, 1848-1934. Plan of the town of Jamestown [electronic resource] / surveyed by J. Strauchon, June, 1870; W. Spreat, Lith. Ref: 834.51bje 1870. Alexander Turnbull Library, Wellington, New Zealand.

Chapter One | # HISTORY

THE PRESENT: There is the sound of a simmering kettle on my grey, cast iron, wood range, a happy, content noise of water in readiness to boil. Its quiet hum in peaceful competition with the sound of light Fiordland raindrops gently caressing my roof of iron above. Rivalling both these faint background sounds is the distant and intermittent chorus of some happy, green feathered Bellbird outside, unperturbed by his or her moist rainforest surrounds.

Nice smells abound. There is a slight odour of Kamahe wood smoke intermixed with the pleasant aroma of baking bread. Homemade bread that will need to be extracted shortly from the wood range on which that happy simmering kettle has its domain.

Such peaceful sounds and lovely smells are common in my life, they give me a sense of simplicity, well-being and security for they tell my subconscious that I am not wet, nor cold, nor hungry, having experienced all three at times here in the wilderness.

However, it is the sense of sight that will need the most description, the natural beauty of which cannot be done justice with my short and limited ability of the written word. The dwelling in which I sit has been built over and off an ancient lake terrace in the rainforest with the back of the house being almost ground level, the front of the house elevated almost a full story above the forest floor so the vista I can see is through sub-storey Fiordland Podocarp rainforest. From my writing platform, a hick kitchen table made of native white and red pine, recycled timbers, out through floor to ceiling windows I can see a living breathing rainforest in all its special grandeur.

This dense rainforest is not classified as a tropical rainforest with monkeys swinging in the treetops and snakes in the undergrowth but a forest classified as a 'temperate' rainforest having snow and ice on the surrounding granite mountaintops and thick furred possums hiding in the dark hollows of very old trees.

There are a hundred shades of green, one of nature's favourite colours made brilliant in a magnificent and innumerable array of plants. The forest floor is literally drowning in an emerald carpet of ferns, the most common being the Crown ferns and baby tree ferns, heavy moisture bending their frail fronds and dripping off their tips in large persistent drops. Breaking through the green depths of fern are a multitude of small native shrubs, bushes and juvenile trees, all in a permanent battle for any life-giving sunlight that is not already stolen by the larger rainforest trees overhead. The parent trees themselves are nature's wonderful art, covered in mosses, vines and many other epiphyte and parasitic plants. Some are bent and twisted being centuries old, while others are young saplings straight and true, no two alike in the three million acres of adjoining forest. The trees around the house are predominantly blotch barked Kamahe, however, I can see a very tall and straight Rimu near the southwest corner of my veranda. Out front an old, large, weathered Matai fights off large Rata vines as thick as a man's forearm which entangles its trunk, a battle which the old Matai will eventually lose to the strangling, parasitic Rata and finally to Newton's law of gravity. A couple of small paper bark Fuchsia trees hold the middle ground in my green vista, their trunks showing the claw mark signs of those furry little mammals, the Australian brush tailed possum introduced by unwise men, whose consuming hunger is slowly killing this very special forest. All this is visible through those large windows of mine, making up the wonderful creation, just one of God's little gardens, a New Zealand Podocarp rainforest. Windows that badly need a clean.

Directly at my front and in between those forest trees I can see the still waters of Lake McKerrow, flat as a sheet of blue tinted glass, which is a common occurrence, her clean waters being sheltered from the predominate winds by a beautiful half-moon shaped bay. A bay no more than 500 yards across its mouth; its sandy beaches are overhung with yellow flowered Kowhai trees. Yellow, juicy, spring flowers that are being greedily consumed by large and fat native wood pigeons.

This beautiful Bay I call home is known on the map as Jamestown Bay. There is of course no town here, the population most of the time being one. Just me.

Jamestown Bay and her lake is inside a New Zealand National Park of some three million acres, being the largest, most spectacular and rugged of New Zealand's many Parks, and she has quite a few of them. This one is a World Heritage Park and called Fiordland National. It forms my surrounding forest garden.

Mountainous Fiordland is a majestic sort of place, overflowing with awe-inspiring scenery in the form of abrupt granite mountains, topped with clean, white snow and aged, blue ice. Mountains into whose hard rock both time and ancient ice has carved deep, glacial, U-shaped valleys, some of which have become long beautiful fiords flooded by the Tasman Sea. Where the snow, ice, rock and sea do not dominate this natural geological wonderland – rainforest, river and lake does, filling in the many gaps. There being literally hundreds of turbulent water courses, peaceful mountain tarns and pristine lakes in Fiordland, a park famous for water.

McKerrow being a long narrow lake, just one of many, whose shape is dictated by the steep valley slopes of the surrounding mountain mass. All this natural beauty is a huge draw card to overseas visitors who flock to our island shore to gaze on only a very small section of this Park, mainly because the rest is so wild and inaccessible. Milford Sound being one of those few accessible places. A beautiful, special place spoilt through the greed for the tourist dollar. Milford Sound being my closest port of call, is fifteen minutes over the mountains by helicopter or, if you wish to walk there, about five or six days up the Kaipo and around the alpine Lake Never-Never and down the steep bluffs into Milford. Milford being a very busy place with cattle truck style tourist boats, shunting back and forth in this scenic Fiord to get the optimum bums on seats ratio and dollars in the bank. While my little Bay is a very, very, very quiet one in comparison. No easy access here.

Jamestown Bay is in North Fiordland very near the West Coast and the Tasman Sea. The terrain hereabouts is less severe and less dramatic than further South where the mountain masses rise directly out of the sea; Milford Sound for example has the highest and deepest sea cliffs in the world. However, standing at the edge of my little Bay you can just see the jagged and snowy peak of Mount Madeline, a mother of a mountain, being the second highest in the Park. Her bigger neighbour, Mount Tutoko, Fiordland's highest is obscured behind Madeline's granite buttresses. Both these royal mountains dominate the skyline scenery of the Hollyford Valley; that is when it's not raining or hidden in cloud or mountain mist. Lake McKerrow and my little Jamestown Bay is situated towards the northern end of the valley, close to the distant sound of the Tasman. This location I call home is a remote and wild place. A place I have grown to love and hate. It is three days walk from the nearest road end, the Hollyford road. This road is an offshoot of the longest no exit road in New Zealand, the Milford Road, so we are talking a very quiet piece of New Zealand countryside.

I have lived here over five years with no TV, radio, phone or freezer. My chosen location and resulting simple lifestyle may to some appear romantic and at times it does have those very special qualities but, there is a dark flip side to every coin.

To some the fact I can live in and own a piece of land inside a World Heritage Park is a bone of contention, the marrow of which is the issue of that unique land ownership. At times it is an emotive one, stimulated mainly by that human vice, jealousy. Others may assume that being able to live here must be based on a mixture of some good luck or inherited fortune. It is a very incorrect assumption and maybe after you read this, that is if you continue to read, you will discover that my path to this point in time has not been a very easy or pleasant one to travel. In fact, I have worked very hard to exist here. In hindsight I have worked harder than warrants my achievements here amongst the ancient Podocarps, as well as having made sacrifices in life that probably do not warrant those achievements.

This three bedroom, 150 square metre kit-set log home has involved 43 seven hundred kilogram loads (30 tonnes) trucked to the end of the Hollyford Road, helicoptered to the head of Lake McKerrow, floated down 17.7 kms of lake to Jamestown Bay to be then carried by hand onto site. A process of material cartage that took me, with the help of others, three months! I spent seven weeks living in a tent in the rainforest before I had the opportunity to sleep under a tin roof. I have floated building materials down the Hollyford River, while at other times I have brought them around by sea from Milford Sound mainly because I did not have the money to bring them in any other way. I spent four years where my annual income was less than a single male gets on our welfare system and yet still kept my project going forward. There were times when money was so tight I spent long periods when my only food was rolled oats and deer meat. Where my diet was so inadequate, the stress so extreme and the work hard that I developed colitis but still kept my project alive. I have been the subject of ridicule, cultivated rumour and even bureaucratic blackmail from the mayor herself but, I always kept moving ahead, albeit very, very slowly at times. I have seen drowning and dealt with death, up close and personal beside the cold, dark waters of the Pyke River. I have lived with oppressive loneliness and dark depression. I have foolishly sunk boats, dealt with storms, floods and mis-mothered, distressed trampers on the Hollyford Track on a regular basis and even helped to save some lives.

Those are some of the bad things which have happened due to my existence and life here but there are of course some good experiences as well. Living in a three million acre garden where nature has many special treats for those who take the time to look for them. Meeting lots of good and healthy minded people tramping the Hollyford Track. Having the freedom few ever get to experience. And, of course, satisfying the male ego of achieving a goal that others told me I could not do.

To understand how I have come to live in such a special location you need to have an idea of the history. Mainly to understand why freehold land (Deeded Title) can exist in a National Park. Without these uniquely positioned blocks of land, I would not have a story to tell. I am not a historian, nor shall I pretend to be. The information is all freely available in such interesting books as 'Martins Bay' by John Hall-Jones and by other notable historians and authors. So here goes a short history lesson and the start of my story.

THE PAST: It all started back in the mid-1880s when the goldfields of Central Otago were in their heyday. Our forefathers were discovering a new measure of prosperity from the shiny, yellow metal hidden in the hills, vales and rivers of that beautiful golden tussock country, Central Otago, forming in the process instant towns like Arrowtown and Queenstown. There was, however, an issue of access to those goldfields and their entombed riches. Those tough, industrious miners had to travel by foot, horse, coach or cart from Queenstown to the east coast of the South Island, then embark on a sailing ship at the busy port of Dunedin to sail around the bottom of the Island through the unpleasant Foveaux Strait into the Tasman Sea and then on to Australia. Quite a time consuming and hazardous trip in those days. It didn't take long before those pioneer fathers of ours started looking at the new maps being drafted by hardy explorers of the time. Explorers such as Caples, Alabaster, Hector and others who entered that unknown wilderness region of Fiordland, discovering new rivers, lakes, valleys, mountains and most importantly of all, passes over the Southern Alps. The Southern Alps formed a serious barrier, dissecting Queenstown, her miners and their precious gold from the West Coast and the Tasman Sea. The West Coast, as a crow flies, is a lot closer to the gold fields than the east coast and Dunedin's port. It was just over that snow-capped mountain range, the Southern Alps, but that word 'just' can be a very deceptive one.

So was born the theory of the West Coast Port. A port to service the thriving gold fields of Central Otago and give a closer economic link to our neighbour in the colonies, Australia. Sydney being the outpost of the then civilised world.

Such was the dream of one James MacAndrew who helped formulate and promote the idea with some vigour. He had of course some opposition to this proposal. Concerns were raised, such as the Hollyford Bar and the cost of a road over the Southern Alps etc. but he didn't let such little details stop his grand plan. Finally convincing the Government to dispatch a survey party with the aim of surveying off a port and township for settlement. Basically, everything from now on was a disaster.

On the 26th February 1870, the *Charles Edward*, a government paddle streamer, carrying a survey party lead by John Strauchon, steamed and paddled her way around the wild and remote West Coast to Martins Bay, a long, sandy bay which is just up the coastline from Milford Sound and into which the Lower Hollyford River finishes its journey to the sea.

The Lower Hollyford River, for description purposes, is a tidal river that is both very wide and shallow. A river which at times has a very Amazonian feel to it with the rainforest trees hanging over the slow, swirling waters. A river having only a very short life from being born and fed by Lake McKerrow, my home lake. It travels only a few short miles and then has its demise as it empties into the Tasman Sea over the Hollyford Bar at Martins Bay. The Upper Hollyford River on the other hand is the complete opposite being long, turbulent and scenic but I'll describe her later as she plays a major part in my story.

On the *Charles Edward's* first attempt at crossing the Hollyford Bar she ran into problems, hitting rocks on the northern side of the entrance, then, on the second attempt, she touched bottom with the sand spit on the southern side of the entrance. She wasn't the first, nor was she the last, to have unpleasantries with this wild, West Coast bar. Over the years this bar has claimed the lives of both man and vessels, mind you, most of the West Coast bars have evil reputations supplying the local cemeteries with additional tombstones and sadness. Further up the Lower Hollyford she ran aground a third time, this time on a sand bar midstream. Not a good beginning for a waterway that was supposed to service a busy West Coast port. After some river side chit-chat in which the skipper, a Captain Holmes, no doubt had quite a bit to say and then with the probable assistance of a change of tide, the *Charles Edward* was under way yet again and paddled her way into Lake McKerrow. It was not long before Captain Holmes landed his cargo of surveyors and their stores onto a sandy beach in what John the surveyor later described as, "a very pretty half-moon shaped bay." A bay he was to name Jamestown. This of course is the sheltered little Bay I can see between the forest trees from my dining room table.

The poor old *Charles Edward* returned down the Lower Hollyford River where it hit another snag and sunk. By now the reader can probably gather that James MacAndrew's West Coast port wasn't off to a good start. The tale gets even more depressing.

John got stuck into the task at hand and by June 1870 had surveyed off a township of some 124 quarter acre sections, complete with streets with such simple names as North Street for the north end of town, South Street for the south end, Lake Street which obviously bordered the lake following the shoreline around the bay. He even showed some recognition to one of those notable explorers of the area, Caples Street, these streets only being totara pegs in the forest and straight lines on a map, a copy of which I have on my living room wall. When looking at John's survey map, one can only admire the man. This hardy surveyor and party with their 1870s gear were dumped into this wilderness, surrounded by snow-capped mountains, rainforest and the very persistent sandflies, yet this industrious team set up camp and surveyed through the moist bush to create a paper township. Tremendous calculations of trigonometry must have been done on ink and parchment by flickering candle light under damp canvas while outside the kiwi and Morepork would be ruling the night air with their weird and wonderful sounds.

How would John feel now if he was transported back through time and placed on the beach in the exact spot where he was landed back on the 26th of February 1870? He would not see streets, shops, hotels, churches or any other evidence of a town or port. He would see much the same sight that greeted him all that time ago, a small tranquil bay, surrounded by the ancient forest and a mountainous backdrop. He would wonder, "What happened?" and I'm sure he would probably note the absence of those noisy and friendly birds which once thrived in this forest and made it alive with their presence but which are now sadly gone. He may even observe the tracks of the introduced deer on the sandy beach. But, if he had objectively observed the world since his departure, with all its destruction of the natural environment and extinction of a large portion of her species, he may even rejoice at the failure of his remote township in the wilderness.

July 1870 saw yet another mishap with the sinking of the *Esther Ann* on the Hollyford Bar. She was bringing Jamestown's first settlers. There was no loss of life but there was a great loss of property, including a sawmill for the new town and probably a greater loss of enthusiasm by the new settlers with no real supplies or tools to start a town from scratch in the wilderness. In December the *Tairoa* made its way up the river, her skipper reporting seven or eight houses with cultivated gardens in the township. But things went from bad to worse for this fledgling settlement.

Skippers started refusing to bring their valuable vessels over the Hollyford Bar, who could blame them. Shipping around that part of the coast was rare back in the 1800s and isn't that common even now, so passing visits were not measured in days nor weeks but in months; even then the weather had to be right to land supplies for the new settlement. As a result food for the new settlers at Jamestown became an issue and the little settlement started to starve. But that's a story for later.

Soon the settlers realised that this pretty little bay had no future, they began to drift away. By 1879 James' little wilderness town was reported as "deserted" by a visiting skipper.

Although Jamestown was deserted, John's survey map and the legal titles of land survived. In 1902, the Fiordland National Park was formed. It was seen as a wild land of mountains, fiords, forests, lakes and rivers and was just too rugged and remote to have any productive use, so the government of the day wisely made Fiordland into a National Park. Any parcel of land or title which was not owned or was deemed as 'abandoned' was gazetted and formed into the new national park, the 'abandoned land' being classified as land which people had stopped paying rates on. So a majority of the land or legal titles surveyed off for settlement in the 1800s were incorporated into the Park. The land was remote and the past owners probably did not see any point in continuing to pay rates on land they couldn't do anything with, common sense really. This is where it gets interesting, a few individuals still held hope for this remote part of south-west New Zealand and continued to pay their rates and dues to the necessary authorities. As a result, those thoughtful people retained their legal title to the land. Those people passed the titles on to the next generation, then the next, then the next, etc. and the land maintained its freehold title status as long as each generation paid the rates. If they didn't their land became 'Abandoned Land' and was formed into the Park.

By the time I became aware that some of these freehold deeded titles still existed 120 years after their conception, there were only five freehold titles left from the original 126 titles at Jamestown, all surrounded by a World Heritage Park and beautiful virgin rainforest. In fact, in the three million acres of Fiordland National Park there are only 25 or 26 freehold deeded titles.

THE PRESENT: It has stopped raining outside, the solitary notes of the Bellbird have gone to be replaced with a great quiet with absolutely no noise except for an ever slight hum from the evening invasion of blood-starved sandflies trying to gain access through my open windows but being foiled in their ever constant attempts by the thin, black, alloy insect mesh that covers such openings. A nice, calm evening in the Bay without a breath of wind to disturb the flat, pure waters of this beautiful Fiordland lake, not even a wood pigeon feather, lost from up high, would have any given direction as it descended to the ferny forest floor. Such calm and quiet evenings and mornings are very common here in this sheltered little Bay. A great night for a hunt up the Hokuri Flats. But there is no need as I already have a yearling and its mother hind hanging under my veranda, the results of last evening's walk in the bush out back, a blessing of sorts as I don't normally get onto my staple diet (deer) that easily only fifteen minutes' walk from my doorstep.

The bread that was baking in my Wagner wood range at the beginning of this chapter is now long gone having been consumed several days ago as this book writing project is only as mood and time permits. But because it is the start of my six month season my pantry is full to overflowing with tinned goods such as baked beans, sliced peaches, etc. With dry goods like flour, rolled oats, sugar, etc. and with a variety of other basic foods. Items that don't need freezing as I do not have the luxury of a freezer. I wish I did but the operating costs of a diesel generator and the

flying in of the fuel is well beyond my frugal existence. For this reason I plan and budget to get in and store all such dry and tin goods only once at the beginning of my six months season.

Anyway, back to that bread or not having any on the table. It is of no real concern as I have plenty of fresh flour and live active yeast in the walk-in pantry to make some more. This well stocked pantry, however, hasn't always been so full.

During my first two years its shelves became a little bare. Money was non-existent and keeping afloat meant bouncing off my tip toes so my nostrils would clear the water surface to enable me to take a breath. Any limited money went towards getting a house built under somewhat challenging circumstances, not towards feeding and looking after myself properly. But all that is for the telling later.

It's time to light a candle, to stop writing and maybe hide my mind away in a Wilbur Smith novel.

Chapter Two | # ACQUISITION

THE PRESENT: The single candle emits a flickering golden glow, creating an atmosphere of old age charm and giving me enough light to illuminate the dining room table but leaving the rest of the room in semi-twilight darkness. There is enough light to write by. The candle is perched atop a Timora Merlot bottle of green glass which some friendly guest has brought in, drunk and probably enjoyed. The wax from several previous candles has formed a dead cascade of white around its mouth and stem. Molten wax frozen in time.

Outside a lone Morepork voices its eerie call, a sound clearly transmitted through the surrounding rainforest in which this small owl has its nightly domain. On other still nights such as this, his chorus is normally greeted by others in this dark little Bay of ours, but not tonight. Maybe his neighbours are otherwise engaged in the hunt and pursuit of prey, like a large, juicy weta or a small, succulent rat, much too engrossed to respond to his distinctive calls of "Hello".

I haven't written for a while and it is now near the end of my season and there is a touch of frost in the air. The night outside is clear, cool and very still. It is a typical Fiordland autumn night with bright, clean stars in the cloudless sky above. A nice night for an outside bath or, if I had guests, a walk down the beach for a bonfire and a bottle of cheap Port, there being no artificial light or sound to pollute the feeling of well-being. Fiordland nights such as this are very special, only being bettered when a harvest moon is out to give the bush a silvery glow. On such nights I feel a little lonely, as these are the sort of nights one can easily share with someone special.

The coolness of the weather has brought on the Rut or Roar with the stags advertising their presence in groans of sexual frustration. All keen and driven by nature to enjoy the comforts only a hind can give and willing to fight off any competitor for those wonderful releases. Some won't survive the Roar as their drive to reproduce will dull their normally acute sense of survival.

I meet the first of the annual influx of hunters today, of no real concern to the local deer population. Big 'talkers', all decked out in new and expensive camouflage gear and associated bits and pieces mostly unnecessary for the task at hand. New gear normally donates a lack of use and hence experience, the expense normally donates a softness of life in the wealthier, professional classes not really used to the hard options of serious stalking in the thick, damp, Fiordland bush, the reality of which hold no romance. The deer hereabouts being very educated to such influxes when all that human scent makes them migrate into the thick, secure bush where only the very keen seek them out as prey. It's those hunters of few spoken words with old, well-worn gear from some labouring or trade background that go beyond the 'comfort zone' of most who will knock over their animals; they tend not to be the 'talker' sort but the 'doer' sort.

THE STORY: How and why I came to live in such a remote wild spot requires a back track to another time and place. Stewart Island is the southern-most and smallest of New Zealand's three main islands. Only a very small section of the island is developed, the rest is all forest, swamp, quiet coastal inlets, rocky exposed shoreline or cold wind-swept beaches. The weather is dictated by cold fronts sweeping off the Antarctic so it's not a South Pacific island one gets a tan on. However, it is a great place if you are into hunting, fishing, diving, tramping and escaping – but very boring if you are not. It's a masculine sort of place where most of the locals wear white gumboots, woollen Swandris and talk fishing, hunting and steamy, sexual exploits in the old South Seas Hotel.

1994 found me the 'Stewart Island Manager' for an aquaculture company called Royalty Salmon [1]. I was responsible for two sea-cage farms with twenty-six staff and an annual output of 700 tonnes of King Salmon. At the time we were getting $14 a kilogram for the pink flesh fish which related to a turnover of $9.8 million. To add to the situation we had enough fish in the water to go to a production of 2000 tonnes in the coming year. It was heady, responsible stuff for a mere 27 year old, but it also found me very stressed, negative and unhappy.

It hadn't always been that way, in fact when I started in the industry four years previously I was quite content, although I probably didn't realise it at the time. I was just a 23 year old boy labouring on the sea-cages, working on a shift basis of seven days on and seven days off, living with four other blokes on a barge in Big Glory Bay, off Paterson's Inlet. When the work was done we went playing, either fishing, diving or hunting. All very handy to the barge being moored in a nice wee cove and only a couple of chains from the shore, bush and whitetail deer. Life was good with easy access to seafood like crayfish, paua, scallops, oysters, blue cod and flounder. This ocean smorgasbord did not last long as the aquaculture industry was mushrooming and the influx of workers off all the farms engaged in a general rape and pillage of the local ocean basically fished the area out. Sad but typical of human greed and I was part of it. In my seven days off the company would fly me to Invercargill and I would return to Queenstown to a small house in Fernhill which I had bought while stoking the boilers of the T.S.S *Earnslaw* prior to my employment with Royalty.

This, in hindsight, was a fun part of life. Men living and working in remote areas away from society's watchful eyes tend to have boyish moments and are likely to get up to a lot of mischief and mayhem. Mischief which at times had

---

1   Not the real name of the company.

Home on the Sea, Little Glory Bay.

One of the two Seacage Salmon Farms I managed – Stewart Island.

spectacular results, like blowing up old 44-gallon drums by placing them on top of driftwood bonfires on some remote, quiet and uninhabited beach. The most memorable result was a fireball of some fourteen metres in diameter, leaving no trace of the once roaring bonfire on the Stewart Island sand and achieved with only five litres of petrol. Hollywood special effects New Zealand style. Each drum was different and very unpredictable in result with the expectation of course of a big bang and nervous audience hiding behind barnacle encrusted rocks at the end of the sandy beach. Occupational Health & Safety (OHS) and the Conservation Department (DOC) would have had kittens if they knew of these antics but remote locations tend to hold many similar secrets of men playing away from watchful eyes. It was dangerous stuff to play at and stopped after a couple of close calls.

Male home economics also got to shine brightly through when intense boredom struck. Five men living on a small barge tend to explore all sorts of avenues to escape boredom. A favourite was to place five eggs on a plate, each egg initialed on the white shell with a felt pen before being inserted in the microwave which was turned on high. Five grown adults would intensely watch through the microwave door the exploding yellow and white results, each hoping that theirs was not the last egg to burst as the last one to pop gets the un-enviable job of cleaning the inside of the microwave. Unpleasant because the time difference between the first and last egg bursting meant the first one became reasonably encrusted and hardened on the white interior by the time the last one had its demise. Memorable times.

With the aquaculture industry taking off, I was soon offered a job of Shift Supervisor responsible for four others on my seven day, 24-hour shift. That was okay, we were a tight little team and all got on a treat.

After a further six months with still more rapid growth I was offered the Farm Manager's job which I grabbed, male ego and all, responsible for not only ten men but production of around 350 tonnes of salmon. In general I fitted the job very well, taking the challenges on with youthful enthusiasm. The only downfall was that I was no longer on a seven day on, seven day off roster and started to spend almost all my time living on the barge at Stewart Island with hardly any days off. However, I did a good job as manager. Too good as it turns out because in another twelve months, after only a short time in the industry, I was offered the job of Stewart Island Manager and everything basically went to custard.

My rise in the management ladder wasn't associated with any great intelligence, far from it, but because I was practically minded, held old-fashioned work ethics and was in on the ground floor of a new industry which didn't have a pool of experienced people to fish from, anybody who had been on the sea cages a couple of months was deemed experienced as a result.

At its height Royalty Salmon was a very buoyant and healthy company to invest in with strong production, processing and marketing arms. As a result Royalty was soon in a position to take over one of our competing operators, New Zealand Salmon, whose marine licenses and its fish in the water were of value, but their sea cage operation in Big Glory were not, being very outdated, over-staffed and inefficient. A liability.

Obviously to make this operation profitable for the new shareholders there had to be change. People in general hate change in their work environment which they haven't instigated themselves. First we had to make operational changes, second we needed to reduce staff numbers and third we had to bring their salaries into line with Royalty's salaries. To give the reader an idea, their labourers were earning the same as a farm manager for Royalty two rungs up the management ladder. With a complete change in the theory of production, a reduction of staff numbers and a major cut in salary, the new owners weren't well liked by the staff, all of which were employed from the small Stewart Island Community. I was the front line for Royalty at Stewart Island and it was my unpleasant job to instigate this change.

As a consequence I went from being a well-liked manager of ten staff to a very unpopular manager of twenty six staff. I no longer got smiles and friendly ribbing from my efficient little team while out on the cages, instead I now got dark scowls and biting sarcasm from a large group of unhappy men. At 27 my skin wasn't quite tough enough to handle the thorns of hate which resulted from this new situation thrown into my path by Royalty. I got through on pure bluff and hard work but this new burden took the stuffing out of me as a manager and a human being.

Other stresses compounded. There was the issue of 'bounce diving' (diving and surfacing multiple times over a short period) with the industry in general misreading recreational dive tables and the resulting nitrogen levels in a diver's blood stream. As a diver, I and others were doing up to fifteen bounce dives down to 55 feet in an hour, doing so once a week in winter and sometimes twice a week in summer. For a long time I was the only Class 4 diver Royalty had at Stewart Island until others were trained. We read the dive tables as taught, being only one dive, down to a depth of 55 feet for 60 minutes, an easy calculation at the time. After these long dives I was feeling unwell so, after some advice from the Dive Practitioner and an approach to the Navy Dive Hospital, I discovered that this type of diving was called 'Bounce Diving' and deemed "Not good" because the nitrogen compounded in the blood stream each time you went down to 55 feet. Basically put, I and the other divers under my employ were subject to mild forms of decompression sickness (the Bends) each time they did large multiple dives to clean away the dead salmon in the sea cages. Misreading our dive tables that were not designed for commercial bounce diving. I took the new-found results to my bosses and was told to, "not make a rod for my back." Basically, if I wanted to keep my job then I was to keep quiet on the whole issue of bounce diving as it was in the too hard basket for Royalty to solve at the time. However, my conscience got the better of me and I went to a friend in OSH on the quiet to explain the sticky situation my employer had put me in. He came up with a great plan, approaching the other operators in surprise audits of dive practices and in the process formulating a safer bounce diving procedure for the industry as a whole. All this was done prior to him coming to Royalty with it so, to my employers, it didn't look like I was the instigator of the issue.

Another major stress was associated to the New Zealand fur seal, a protected species and a known scourge to salmon farmers the globe over. Up to a point Royalty was the choir boy in our dealing with seals. Where we used such things as Number 8 detonators, tuna bombs and even underwater ultra-sonic scarers to keep the nightly raiders away from our precious livelihoods, our competitors in the Bay simply shot them and then did a very poor job of hiding the fact. However, after our acquisition of New Zealand Salmon, the mortality rates associated to seal attack started to get out of hand and my boss told me to solve it very quickly, telling me very directly how he wanted me to deal "permanently" with these problems. "But don't document the solutions, no faxes, memo's, diary entries etc."! He was basically asking me to break the law, to preserve the shareholder's investment and, of course, the jobs of my twenty six staff.

Seals are intelligent animals and learnt to raid the farms mainly at night to obtain what for them was an easy feed. To describe the process of an attack, the submerged seal would charge the side of the sea cage net compressing the side without breaking through, making the salmon swim denser in the enclosed cage, an easier target for them to bite individually. Then they would simply chew and suck the omega rich flesh through the net, so the seal didn't actually end up inside the cage. In the morning when you pulled the mortality rings to the surface you tended to find either just the heads or dead fish with bite marks or sometimes carcasses with very neat half-moon sections chomped cleanly out of them. The odd fish lost to this nocturnal approach wasn't really the problem. The real problem was the stress of the attack would force the remaining frightened fish in the cage under attack to rub violently against the side of the confined nets in their attempts to avoid these nocturnal predators and, in the process, lose some of their protective scales. As a result lesions (infections due to loss of scales) would develop and then the death of large numbers of valuable fish would result a couple of weeks later due to these horrible lesions. After a hard word from my boss I had to spend long lonely nights out on the sea-cages, quiet, still nights being the best to catch the culprits.

The process was all very quite simple. During an attack the water surface would literally boil and on a quiet, still night the resulting sound of disturbed water would give away the location of where on the farm the underwater attack was underway. You proceeded to that area and waited patiently and quietly in the dark, standing on the pontoon (a steel pontoon structure supporting the sea cage) beside the specific cage under attack. The seal would at some stage come up for air, normally between the net and the pontoon and, if you judged the next surfacing location just right, you would lightly touch the rifle barrel to the surfacing head ensuring a very quick and unexpected death for the seal but also a corresponding eruption of sea water as the physics of a large calibre rifle discharging inches above water is quite impressive. Immediately you secured the dead seal with a sharpened boat hook, fit for the process, before it sunk out of reach. What followed was a major exercise to get the animal clear of the cages with its nets, ropes, pontoons and into or beside a boat. Some of these seals were huge and lifting a dead weight from water into any vessel is a battle. Then it was a short boat trip out into the open deep water of Paterson Inlet, away from Big Glory Bay, where I would slice open the belly and wire fish plates (steel weights) into the rib cage of the animal so the evidence would stay sunk. The opposition didn't follow the weighting process and as a result the decomposing gases inside would make a dead seal float around for a long time for all to see.

The whole process was done by myself and sometimes a trusty assistant and within a month I had shot and quietly disposed of twelve seals, all caught in the process of gorging themselves on shareholder's salmon. I did end up sending a memo on the topic to my boss as I felt a very unfair burden was being placed on my shoulders but that resulted in very angry correction, not for shooting the seals but for formally documenting it as I had clearly been told not to do. Most of my staff had no idea of the extent of what was going on but were no fools and probably guessed what I was up to at night. Sadly, one staff member took matters into his own hands one day (without direction) and tried shooting a seal during the day, horribly misjudging his aim and blowing off the bottom jaw of the poor animal which could still swim actively but not dive. It was several hours before I could finish him off, a very unpleasant affair.

We had yet more growth in production which meant extra workloads and then the farm was hit with another algae bloom which, in the right conditions, can wipe out stock and a farm overnight. All of this resulted in a lot of other associated headaches and stress. Basically my life became very unpleasant. I had absolutely no social life nor women or a wife to help me travel through such dark vales in life. I was no longer out in the open, fresh sea air doing physical work but stuck in an office in Tay St, Invercargill away from the fun. I went to bed thinking about work, dreamt about work and woke up thinking about work. I was giving 110% to my employer as well as breaking the law for them. I could easily go on and on about this stage in life but I won't because it's unproductive to this story. Basically my life with Royalty was the classic skyrocket theory of modern work stress. I went from just a boy to the boss of a multi-million dollar operation in something like three years, I had reached the top of my trajectory. I started to become very inefficient as a manager. Everything got too big, simple little challenges that I once resolved in five minutes became big problems that didn't seem to have a solution. I was over-worked, stressed and my rocket was about to explode in a big way and I knew it. I needed an outside interest that was beneficial to me only and not Royalty Salmon to whom I had given too much dedication and loyalty.

During one of my weekly visits to the farms, I spent the night on the Royalty South Barge and was engaged in a conversation about investment – what to invest in, etc. My line of thought was simple enough, 'Basic Natural Resources'. We are living in a degrading world, both socially and environmentally. One only has to digest facts presented to us daily by the media to formulate this opinion. As a result basic natural resources which we now take for granted will become commodities in the future. Simply put, our forefathers took natural resources such as crayfish, paua, etc. for granted as always being plentiful and cheap, now such items are over-fished and have become commodities which as a result are now very expensive. By basic natural resources I meant a whole spectrum from clean drinking water to the good old Kiwi bach on the coast, from river gravel for making concrete to basic foods, etc.

I made mention that private blocks of untouched bush would someday have a value beyond the milling value of the trees. I made the very silly comment, "imagine selling blocks of forest inside the Park to wealthy people for escape retreats, etc." as I had heard that there were such pieces of land. This last comment resulted in a bit of ridicule. One of the main things male ego has challenges with is dealing with ridicule, especially when sarcasm is used to hammer one's point home, sarcasm being the lowest form of humour which tends to be the knife of intelligent people.

As a result of my silly male ego and the green giant greed, I started my research. A hobby of sorts, an interest for my brain away from the all-consuming Royalty.

It was surprisingly easy to research. A look at a topographical map showing forested areas in Southland, a visit to the Lands & Deeds Registry, the local council offices and the valuation department and I soon had a file. This file contained a copy of each freehold title in the Fiordland National Park, its valuation and each owner's rate address.

The titles in the Fiordland National Park are distributed between Preservation Inlet way down south and Martins Bay at the opposite end of the Park, way up North, involving 25 or 26 titles in three million acres of World Heritage Park. I had previously had a reasonably severe misadventure down in Preservation Inlet having walked there via Port Craig spending fourteen days in the bush, seven days of which I only had venison to eat and ended up having to be rescued of sorts from Lake Kiwi by Trevor Green and his trusty helicopter. All a bit of a story in itself involving gold, deer and fern roots but it's not part of this one. So my opinion of this southern-most location wasn't the best. Of the three areas in the Park where freehold titles are found, Jamestown Bay in my line of thinking was the cream of the crop. I based this opinion on a) its location to Milford Sound, being only fifteen minutes over the mountains from this tourist Mecca, b) its climate, being on a similar latitude as Timura and of course, c) that beautiful and scenic and sheltered little bay.

The next step was a hand-written letter to each of the five owners of Jamestown expressing an interest in purchase should they ever decide to sell.

The valuation of the titles at this stage was around $5000 which to me was unbelievable. Anywhere else in the western world a title inside a park and a World Heritage Park to boot would be worth a fortune but not in New Zealand at the time. Most Kiwis having such a wonderful country that isn't overpopulated cannot comprehend that fact and take it for granted that such land doesn't have a great deal of value. Comments like "too remote," "no access," I've heard more than once over the years to justify such low prices whereas I was constantly thinking the opposite –"limited commodity which is exclusive because of no access and remoteness, etc." Completely different mind-sets like chalk and cheese. Playgrounds for the rich as the poor kids can't afford the access etc. This thinking resulted in some ridicule towards my thinking. However, when I proved this concept with a sale, those comments and laughter were conveniently forgotten by those who made them, it being natural to preserve their large egos I suppose. That's a story for later.

Another factor keeping the valuation low was the introduction of the Resource Management Act (RMA). The general consensus at the time was that the Department of Conservation (DOC) would use this new government act to stop the development of freehold land in the Park, which is exactly what they tried to do with me – again another story for a later chapter. This new act meant two things to me: 1) – that the land value was in doubt, not only to me but to the present owners of these titles and, 2) – I was taking a gamble in buying such land. If I could not get permission to develop under the RMA then the land was worthless, however, if I did then the opposite was true so it was all a bit of a risk.

The first acquisition was from an industrial chemist. There's not much of a tale with the purchase, just a simple transaction of money for land.

The second, however, is a lot more interesting. The title's legal definition was Section 11, Block 3, Township of Jamestown. My address for the owner was sourced from a helpful clerk in the rates department of the Southland District Council. I duly wrote a letter to the owner expressing my interest to buy which, after several weeks, was mailed back to me unopened with "Return to Sender" on it. There was also a small written comment on the outside of the envelope, stating that the owner had not lived at this address for x number of years. Well, that is the way the cookie crumbles. I attached the envelope to the title in the file and forgot about it.

It was a while later, when reviewing the file that my brain finally clicked to the significance of the hand-scribbled comment on the returned envelope. That is, if my letter didn't get to the owner, neither would his rate demands from the council, the source of where I got the owner's address in the first place. It was worth a follow up. A visit to the council revealed that the rates had not been paid for several years, to the seeming surprise of the rates clerk across the counter. X number of years is a long time not to pay rates. Further investigation revealed that the Council was going to place the title up for a rate sale, that is offer the title for public tender. I for one was very keen and promptly wrote a letter of interest to the Council.

However, a bombshell was dropped when the rates department informed me that the Department of Conservation had been told about the unpaid rates and was going to enforce the 1952 lands act to have this title taken into the surrounding Fiordland National Park without giving the public an opportunity to purchase. A closed door – or was it?

If I could track down the owner or his descendants, purchase the title, then pay the unpaid rates, all prior to DOC enforcing the Act, then the title would be mine. It was a gamble but worth a shot. I knew neither DOC nor the council would go to any great length to find the legal owner, to all appearances he had 'abandoned' the land.

So begins a little detective story. The last name on the title was Mackenzie of

Walter Peak Station. Research showed that the Mackenzies had sold the Station. People who own or had owned high country stations tend to be fortunate in our society when it comes to wealth. My assumption was the Mackenzies would have retired to Kelvin Heights, an upmarket area of Queenstown so I wrote to all the Mackenzies listed in the phone book for Kelvin Heights, resulting in a call from an elderly lady who put me onto another elderly lady in Arrowtown and, bingo, the title belonged to her brother, now living in Christchurch and very much alive.

I hopped onto the bus, travelled to Christchurch and knocked on this man's door but no answer, so went away, coming back later to try again. Still no response. After the third attempt I happened to meet a neighbour who told me that the man didn't have much to do with the world, kept very much to himself, etc. I went back a fourth time and this time after much knocking he finally answered the door, only opening the door a couple of inches for me to explain the reason for the long bus ride. I was open and honest, telling him that he had three options. 1) pay the outstanding rates to retain the title, 2) do not pay them and lose the land to DOC and the Park or, 3) sell the title to me at Government Valuation being $5000 and I then would pay the unpaid rates for him. It was a gamble for me because I didn't know how far DOC had proceeded with enforcing the Land Act. I went back the next day. He had decided to sell. We signed the necessary documents, I paid him in full, hopped back onto the bus back down to Invercargill, then went straight around to the council offices, paid the outstanding rates, got a receipt of payment then got my solicitor to arrange a.s.a.p. the legal transfer of the title. This was all achieved prior to DOC taking any action to acquire the title due to unpaid rates. I was now the proud owner of Section 11, Block 3, Town of Jamestown, my second title inside the Park.

An interesting side-line to this story is the original title document given to me by the vendor in Christchurch. It was beautifully hand-written in an old, free-flowing style, an art long lost. The deed being witnessed by Sir ?, Knight of the Grand Cross, etc. but the really interesting part was the material it appeared to be written on. It looked like old greying wax paper, however, when I showed this beautiful old document to a collector I was told it was in fact written on 'velum', being either pig or goat skin, important legal documents of the day being prepared on skin because it had better longevity than the fragile parchment of the time. It would have made a beautiful and interesting framed wall piece but it was still a viable legal document so when I later sold this title it had to be transferred to the new owner.

I acquired a third title part way through my Resource Consent Application to the Council, a story as well but of no real interest.

Having the land is one thing, getting the permission to do anything with it was another. The Department of Conservation was to balance the scales by giving me a very challenging time with the considerable bureaucracy involved in gaining that special permission. I'm sure the saga of Section 11 didn't endear me to some of the staff in this conservation authority. "What goes around, comes around" as the saying goes.

THE PRESENT: Tea Time. Very dark, still and quiet outside in the peaceful little Bay I share with the Moreporks. Inside it's still the same Timora Merlot bottle of green glass sitting on the table but supporting a different melting, flickering wax candle. No guests staying, nor have there been for some time. There is venison stew, bones and all, made from a sinewy forequarter of a hind shot awhile back simmering away on the Wagner wood range. It is several days old, with meat chucks boiled away into a rich stringy brown mess of deer stew. Even the hunks of once tough, white sinew are now easily chewed and digested with the similar consistency of tasteless, white wine gums. It has plenty of brown barley, white rice and green, dried peas as filler. I'm also using up some very old spuds and carrots in it, which I'm sure most people would have thrown out due to their age and wrinkled appearance but, in here, you get the best use of any nutrients at your disposal. I have disguised the flavour of this simmering brown mess of stew with dried Maggi beef stock because five years of venison as my stable diet means that the taste has become a little tedious for me. I shouldn't complain, I should be grateful to my Maker because this low fat red meat, shot in the surrounding rainforest, is free except for the cost of the bullet and my time. There have been times in the first couple of years here in the Park when deer meat and rolled oats have been the only food that has filled the belly.

To help the stew go down is some home-made bread and even some butter (a luxury) from the pantry. To store butter when you don't have a fridge, simply bury it in flour, it lasts for quite a while. It's time to eat tea.

BUREAUCRACY

Chapter Three

THE PRESENT: Another rainy day, the third in a row. Thick persistent rain, typical Fiordland rain with oversized and bulbous raindrops. Rain which makes a very audible racket as it pummels heavily onto my green roof and the attached clear polycarbonate covered veranda to then cascade off in literal sheets of water.

The lake is overfed by the massive catchment areas of the Pyke and the Hollyford valleys and is in flood. The sandy beach in the Bay is covered in tea-coloured (tannin rich) water which is not quite invading the bush edge but getting there. Lake McKerrow's waters are rough with a strong northerly pushing white crested waves reluctantly up the lake. Waves that will crash and die on the gravel beach at the south end of the lake depositing in the process a new load of rainforest drift wood. Not a day for boating but for writing inside in the warmth.

Last evening I went out for a shot across the lake as there was no meat in the house and there is still none. The forest today the same as yesterday, a dark, damp place with a primeval prehistoric feel not willing to reveal my elusive food source. The return dinghy ride back home was just as depressing as the unsuccessful hunt, a cold wet affair, getting completely soaked as the dinghy broached each individual wave, contesting its right of passage home across those white-topped waves. The sky above filled with a ceiling of dark clouds hanging very low and angry in the valley. Probably a little silly of me trying to head home on such a contentious lake but it was either that or spend a cold, wet and unpleasant night in the bush. Having had more than my share of those, I opted to take a little calculated risk.

My accompanying mood on the wet ride home matching the nature of the sky above, dark, angry and very lonely. There was no bloody water awash in the bowels of my little boat as it wasn't carrying home a freshly gutted deer carcass like it should have done. There was no aroma of freshly baked bread to greet my return, the house being lonely, cold, dark and depressing, my fire out. Welcome to the flip side of living in a Fiordland rainforest where nature still dictates the rules.

Today has been better, although I have re-discovered an unwelcome leak in my roof. A leak which I thought I had solved on several occasions, a persistent, cunning sort of leak, whose source has not been easy to find but keeps coming back to laugh at my previous attempts to fix it. No feeling of contentment to start this chapter. My dark mood seeming appropriate to the chosen topic of this chapter, bureaucracy.

THE STORY: Things at Royalty Salmon deteriorated markedly, the company had a couple of major set-backs. The fish markets in Japan had a considerable drop leaving Royalty to record an unexpected loss to the shareholders. It was time for everybody to get a shake-up, starting with me at the top way down south at Stewart Island. The Managing Director, the henchman in charge of cut-backs, flew down from his head office in sunny Blenheim to a not so sunny Invercargill and gave me three options. 1) Retain my present role as Stewart Island Manager but start living in Oban on Stewart Island. The NZ Salmon takeover saga meant I was not well liked in the Island's very small and tight community and for good reason. Being asked to live in it would have been very unpleasant. 2) Take on a Farm Manager's role in the Marlborough Sounds, a step down the management ladder, or 3) leave Royalty all together. I chose the third option which, I sensed, pleased the managing director as I had become a burnt out, inefficient manager and we both knew it.

With no more commitment to my old employer, I put all my energies into negotiating the bureaucratic maze, necessary to develop my land in the Park.

The original intention was to sit on the land as a long term investment. But plans change. The value of my new acquisitions was still in considerable doubt because of the recently introduced Resource Management Act therefore I thought it would be wise to seek resource consent or permission to develop now as opposed to waiting ten or fifteen years when more controls would completely prohibit development to everyone except the very rich, the problem was just what to develop on my special bit of dirt.

Like most young blokes with an inclination towards the outdoors, the concept of owning and operating my own wilderness lodge appealed to the inner boy, I could make it into a dream lifestyle business where one could live and work in the great outdoors while pursuing manly recreation pursuits like hunting and fishing as just standard day to day fair and make money while doing it, kind of a perfect outcome for a boy of my ilk. So was born the idea of building my own little wilderness lodge on my recently acquired land inside the Fiordland National Park. I soon learnt that the size and shape of any little wilderness lodge I dreamt up would be dictated by the many rules and regulations that govern building on such unique land. So started my introduction to the nightmare of New Zealand's bureaucracy

Bureaucracy has its place, society needs laws and rules to function. Without these controls our basic human natures, being completely self-centred and, some would argue, by nature "evil" would cause complete chaos, eventually leading to our own destruction, hence the need for rules, boundaries, morals, governance, etc. Deep down I know this to be true, but my experiences with the NZ bureaucracy have left me very bitter and negative. I entered the arena with the conception that the rules were both consistent and fair. That people's greed and jealousy had no place on the playing field. That the referees were not influenced by such dark, human vices. Boy, was I in for a shock.

There are many Rules, Regulations and Acts involved in this wilderness drama but the main two players are the Resource Management Act, 1992 (RMA) and the Scenic Protection Order (SPO).

The purpose and principles of the RMA are very well intentioned being the preservation of the environment but, at the end of the day, its noble purpose has been somewhat polluted by human vice – jealousy/greed. The Act has become somewhat of an expensive joke, forming a toxic by-product of bureaucrats and consultants to feed off the limited resources of small business with very debatable benefits to the environment and some huge benefits for big business with monopoly mind sets.

A 'Resource Consent' application under the RMA can either be a 'Notified' or 'Non-Notified' application. A Non-Notified application means only your direct neighbours are informed of your proposed development and given the opportunity to have a say. A Notified application means advertising in local newspapers to notify the public thus giving anybody and everybody a say on your application. That process of giving people who may be biased a say in your plans, instead of having an unbiased consultant/judge, is where the Act falls down flat. Opening the door for the jealousy of the 'have nots' and the greed of the 'haves' to pollute the bureaucratic process and the general intention of the Act.

The Notified application is the more challenging and expensive of the two processes and obviously the Department of Conservation as my only direct neighbour made sure my application was going to be Notified. As a result I had to advertise at my own cost in Southland, Otago and West Coast newspapers, opening up a can of worms in the process.

Comments from the public are called either 'Submissions of Support' or 'Submissions of Comment' or 'Submissions of Opposition'.

The second player is the SPO which is a local set of ordinances that govern freehold land in the Park and is administrated by the Southland District Council. A quick over-view of the SPO is as follows. Only one dwelling per title, that dwelling not to exceed 150 square metres in floor area, the building not to exceed 4.5 metres in height, the bush clearance not to exceed 300 square metres, no subdivision, etc.

All the above legislation is kind of okay if DOC and the other authorities administered them equally for everybody but of course it doesn't as you will see later in my story of woe.

Now to give the reader a very quick and simple description of what I was actually applying to all the bureaucracy to do. My desire was to build and operate a little wilderness lodge on my land, with it being built to both the maximums of floor area and height restrictions allowed under the Scenic Protection Order, in a new forest clearing also cleared to the maximums of the same order. The dwelling plan I developed was a simple kit-set thermopanel log home, basically being the size of an average three bedroom home, which was all I was allowed to build under the rules. To make all that work as a commercial operation I had to call it a home-stay style operation, servicing a potential wilderness overnight experience from Milford Sound, 14 minutes away by helicopter, all of which needed the appropriate resource consents, building permits and concession licenses etc. Because I now had three seperate sections in the park, I thought it prudent to simply replicate the plans to build on one of my other sections as well. I was already going through all the costs and hassles, so why not times the paper work by two for the price of one, it gave me options for a later date, whether I built the second dwelling or not. Having the consents in place, or the right to build on the land, meant a much increased value on my other section, maybe to sell later to raise funds, it seemed a wise line of thought. That is if I could get all the necessary consents and permits in the first place.

This little kit-set log home in which I now sit very warm and dry, writing my tale industriously while outside Fiordland rain cascades down onto her green zincalume roof, has gone through a full Notified resource consent application with the Southland District Council (SDC) for 'Land Use', that is the permission to build. It has gone through another fully Notified Resource Consent process with the Southland Regional Council (SRC), being a separate authority to the District Council, for a 'Discharge Permit', that is the right to have a septic tank. It had to obtain a 'Building Permit', an 'Engineers Report' and a 'Fire Report'. During the building process it had to have a couple of 'Building Inspections', when finished it required a 'Compliance Certificate'. The HF radio in my pantry has a 'Radio Licence', etc. Even the firewood drying slowly under my veranda decking has a 'Salvage Permit' from the 'Indigenous Forest Unit' in Christchurch. All this bureaucracy separate to 'Concession License' required from the Department of Conservation.

All necessary in some shape or form for some reason or theory to give some bureaucrat, councillor or politician a meaningful job to justify his or her existence and excessive salary. But, at the end of the day, all very prohibitive to any small business trying desperately to get off the ground with much needed money and energies going into areas not directly associated to physically starting the business while the larger more fortunate entities can use such Government Acts to full advantage to take out the smaller opposition and establish monopolies.

To assist in navigating this unpleasant and inconsistent storm-tossed ocean of bureaucracy I needed a good solicitor, a good engineer, a good surveyor and a variety of other consultants and helpful people. I found a great solicitor in the form of Rex Chapman of Cruickshank & Pryde. I asked for a quote to achieve my aims, warning him that I was going to be the first to try developing freehold land in the Park under the new Resource Management Act. A test case of sorts. The figure Rex gave me was $5000. His final bill was under that figure which was a credit to his professionalism.

THE PRESENT: The West Coast sun has finally made an appearance. The forest has had a cleansing from the Fiordland downpour and now has a very clean, fresh smell and air about it, a kind of purification to the senses and the soul. My mood is no longer dark nor does it seem appropriate to be inside anymore so I'll leave further writing for another rainy day. Off to try my luck again at getting some meat for tea. The deer like to come out of the damp forest into the open ground after a period of prolonged West Coast rain to find some succulent grass to nibble on.

THE PRESENT: Another rainy day, but don't be fooled into thinking it rains all the time here, it doesn't. It has been some time since I last put pen to paper because the weather has been so good. The area has, at times, great spells of brilliant weather being on the same latitude as Timaru, with mid-to-late summer getting almost tropical. Spring is the time to avoid this area with what the locals call the 'Spring Floods'. It is the time of the whitebait and the white-baiters that invade the Martins Bay area for a couple of wet months to fish these little native fish or inanga. The white-baiters' moods chop and change to match the weather and their wriggling white catches. They at times engage in a style of Kentucky mountain inter-family feuding but are, in general, salt of the earth individuals who love the rustic, almost frontier, lifestyle. Good people who would bend over backwards and go the extra country mile to help you if things get a little tough, as they tend to do at times in remote wild locations like this. I'm not a white-baiter as the politics that develop at times would drive me nuts.

Mid-winter has the most stable weather patterns with a sort of little micro climate in north Fiordland being quite mild and pleasant with only a little rain, a climate that would surprise those hard working farmers battling that cold, damp mud of Southland across on the south-east side of those snow topped Southern Alps.

THE STORY: Going back into the drama and trauma of the Resource Management Act. As a pre-emptive move I decided to visit DOC, it being my main neighbour. The theory being to be open and honest about my plans, to establish a positive rapport with my neighbour, etc. It seemed wise at the time, thinking this open, honest approach would aid my course. I immediately walked straight into a green, brick wall in a bureaucrat I'll call Mr X. Mr X wasn't a bad sort of person, just doing his job in a very efficient manner, however, at the time I developed a strong dislike to him. Not his fault but completely mine. There was no scope for negotiation, it being made crystal clear that they (DOC) were going to try to stop or block my application. I was going to be a test case for them under the recently introduced RMA. Stop my application and they had a good chance of stopping all future development of freehold land in the Park, a very noble goal on their part but a real kick in the guts for all the ratepayers who happen to own land inside conservation estates (National Parks) throughout New Zealand.

I learnt my first lesson of bureaucracy. "Never be open about your plans with anybody who may oppose you." Common sense really. Animal cunning is the order of the day, especially when you are a small business mammal avoiding the far larger, carnivorous predator, whether he is a bureaucrat or a big greedy competitor. A good tactician would never consider such an approach. Giving information freely to an adversary was pure stupidity on my part. It was a mistake I was going to repeat a couple more times until it was clear who my opponents really were. As a result I have become very guarded about my plans and intentions even with friends and neighbours here in the rainforest of Jamestown Bay. A poor state of mind in which to live, but one that has helped me to survive up to this point.

My next stop was at the Southland District Council (SDC), the main authority handling my application and into the picture steps Bruce Halligan. Bruce is what you call a 'Utopia Bureaucrat', not influenced by anybody, doing everything by the book and not taking sides, administrating his role in a fair and honest way. I came to respect him for that. Bruce basically told me that I needed to revise some aspects of my application to fit within the guidelines of the SPO which I did.

To go into all the ins and outs of this period would bore the reader silly, if it hasn't done so already. Needless to say Mr X of DOC did a brilliant job as I had submissions of opposition from the likes of Federation Mountain Clubs who sent in two separate submissions, Southern Health who sent two as well and Forest & Bird, which is a pretty strong lobby group in New Zealand, of which I was a member at one stage. And, of course, DOC itself. The level of opposition to this little green roofed house in this beautiful and special Bay was as if I was building a ten-storey hotel, painting it bright pink and discharging raw sewage into the pure waters of Lake McKerrow – which I was not. The proposal was a building within the design guidelines of the Scenic Protection Order, a building on my own land, basically being a three bedroom home. This organised little campaign of opposition, however, knocked me down a peg or two and was a real credit to Mr X's abilities.

There were submissions of opposition from other parties but, counter to them, there were those of support. Welcome little rays of sunshine on dark, black days.

Two submissions of opposition are worth describing for the interest value of the story. Southern Health flew a gentleman down from Christchurch to attend a SDC pre-hearing. He was to oppose me twice, each time with the two authorities SDC and the SRC. Bear in mind Southern Health is responsible for the administration of our over-stressed and under-funded hospitals and such like. This gentleman from Southern Health opposed me on several grounds, one of which was 'Noise Pollution during the construction of the home!' Hard to believe, but true. I figure it cost the poor tax payer several thousand dollars to fly this guy down from Christchurch, accommodate him, feed him, pay him then fly him back again. The sort of money that would go a long way to covering the cost of a hip replacement and he was opposing a person building a three bedroom home on his own land, a home permissible under the District Plan. I suppose Southern Health felt it more important to oppose me than giving some old lady, who had faithfully paid taxes over a long life time and who had been on our famous hospital waiting lists a long time, a new hip. Excuse the sarcasm, I know it is the lowest form of humour but I can't quite help myself. I very much doubt if Southern Health opposed any of the big kids playing monopoly in the Fiordland National Park. One wonders whether the tourist ventures that operate in Milford Sound with their cattle truck style boats and buses had to endure the same degree of scrutiny and opposition from Southern Health around the levels of noise and air pollution as I did. I was left with the distinct feeling that smaller players make easier targets to bully for such petty bureaucrats.

The next submission of opposition that may be of interest was from an individual who is very fortunate to own land in the park, his land having been developed prior to the introduction of the RMA. I got wind that he was researching the issue of my veranda and floor area as not complying to the guidelines of the Scenic Protection Order. To counter this unwelcome threat to my very small project I got the definition of 'Floor Area' from the Building Authority in Wellington, the definition of which read 'from external wall to external wall'. The maximum floor area under the SPO was 150 square metres, mine though was 149 from external wall to external wall so I felt quite safe and confident. After all who could argue against the legal definition of 'Floor Area' given by the appropriate authority; it seemed to me very black and white. I got a big fright, however, at the Southland District Council hearing when my very intelligent opponent had come up with the definition of 'Wall' and successfully argued to the Council that the balusters on my veranda constituted a wall (!) which meant that my floor area was no longer within the guidelines as set out in the SPO. This caught me completely off guard. My intelligent solicitor Rex, however, earned his keep, lent over and whispered quietly in my ear, "Charlie, take the balusters off the plan." So simple when you think about it and this is what we did. The Council accepted the change quite happily, placing the only condition on my approved resource consent that the veranda had no balusters.

If you visit you will notice that I do indeed have balusters on my veranda. They are not there because of some cunning planning or deception on my part. I never changed the house profile as submitted to the council, nor did it occur to me to do so at the time. The house was built over the edge of an old lake terrace in the forest on purpose to give me plenty of ventilation and dry storage area underneath, both being very important factors when living in a damp, rainforest environment. This meant most of the veranda is more than 1.5 metres off the ground. Because it was so high off the ground it meant I had to have approved balusters to comply with the building code. This was a safety issue which was to override the council's condition not to have them on the building in the first place under the resource consent.

There were of course other submissions of opposition from people I did not know at the time but whose names are very familiar now, being associated in some way to the area or, more notably, a business in here. Their submissions were full of flowery reasons why my three bedroom house could not be built but hiding the true reason of their effort, being their own greed. Such is the RMA.

The Southland Regional Council was the next authority to deal with, it being completely separate to the District Council. The two should really be combined but that involves good common sense, a commodity lacking in the general, bureaucratic mind set, probably because it would do some of their colleagues out of a job. This separate council dealt with my resource consent to have a 'discharge permit' for my septic tank. This application was also Fully Notified thanks to DOC.

My friendly tax wasting Southern Health representative was back in the picture having another go at making life difficult for small enterprises, mind you there's not much noise pollution associated to septic tanks, although some may argue that!

Mr X from DOC had another interesting card to play in the form of a submission of opposition using an expert from the Department of Scientific and Industrial Research commonly known simply as the DSIR. They argued that my engineer had not designed a good enough system, that instead I needed a fancy four-stage system with an electric pump pressurising the septic tank discharge into 50 metres of perforated pipe dug into the forest floor to handle the sewage output of a six-person homestay? My own very reputable engineer disagreed strongly with this, his professional pride on the line, having designed a system with a simple soakage hole system which was very practical considering the location and the delicate rainforest environment, involving very little damage to the forest floor and maze of ancient root systems, a specific request I had asked for. Anyway, to cut a long story short, we had a pre-hearing at the council offices in which I bluntly asked Mr X if I accepted the DSIR system would he still oppose the application. The answer was a very unsure, "No." He had put all his eggs into one basket with the DSIR scheme and I think he had not expected me to accept such an excessive and expensive system with me having to battle it out in a full council hearing with all its associated costs and challenges. If I did accept the DSIR designed system, Mr X no longer had a valid reason to oppose my application. This put him on the spot in front of everybody at the council meeting, his uncertain "No" thus committed DOC to withdrawing the submission of opposition. I played my only card and accepted the DSIR system, thus avoiding an expensive full council hearing and was granted the all-important resource consent for a 'Discharge Permit'.

This whole chapter is dedicated to the unfairness and hypocrisy of bureaucracy so the reader needs to know that DOC, around the same time, had put in a twenty bed hut at Long Reef, Martins Bay about four hours walk north of here. Accompanying that hut is a simple pit toilet with no septic tank. They did this without any Notified resource consents for discharge or land-use nor, I suspect, any building inspections. So, all their arguments against my plans lacked any genuine environmental integrity as they were unwilling to place such expensive systems in their own huts, not that I wanted them to be burdened with costly bureaucratic procedure. However, what really rubbed salt into the raw wound happened just a short time later when a much larger, private, commercial operator in the park who opposed me during the RMA installed a standard factory septic tank system without the complicated multi-stage and electric pumps system that I had to put in, the system having to cater for 500 to 600% more people than mine, doing so in two separate locations in the Park and, what really hurt, it achieved all this without going through the expensive and challenging 'Notified' resource consent process I was required to go through as a much smaller operator. To me this was showing commercial favouritism, especially when the Head Conservator in Southland and the Mayor of the District Council were involved in the openings of these lodges. Yet another kick in the guts for a small enterprise struggling to do everything by the book, expecting fair rules for all but not getting them.

Is it the 'easy target' bureaucratic philosophy towards small business, or is it the authorities bending the rules to those with the most financial clout? Or both?

There is more to this story when you look into the concession license process managed by DOC. This is where money talks and the C in DOC stands for Commerce and not Conservation. In short, when you operate a business in the Conservation estate (National Park) you require a 'Concession Licence', DOC taking a percentage of your take (like a tax) which is fair enough. After all, if you are making money out of the National Park, you should be putting money back into preserving it. I'm all very happy about that, it makes very good environmental sense, it's a concept which appeals to me and probably to most people but what makes me really spit the dummy, is that the smaller you are the higher your concession licence fee percentage is and the bigger you are the smaller the fee percentage. Now how unfair can you get? My concession licence fee was 7.5% which was okay by me but one large and prominent tourist company operating in the Park, for example, pays only 2.5%. Bear in mind that DOC is a Government Department just like the Inland Revenue Department (IRD) which administers the taxes in New Zealand, yet IRD makes people on a higher wage/salary pay a higher percentage in tax than those who earn less down the economic ladder.

If you look into business in the Fiordland National Park you will see a market controlled by only a couple of very big operators mining tourist gold out of the likes of Milford and Doubtful Sounds into mainly private pockets which is no wonder when you consider the commercial bias/edge DOC gives them. Something is very amiss here. The loser here is not only small business in the Park but conservation in general. Imagine the money flowing into DOC to fight introduced pests, the biggest problem by far in the Park and a battle that DOC is losing, if the likes of these large tourist companies had to pay 7.5% of their take to DOC instead of 2.5%. With Milford Sound getting up to 4000 people a day this lost revenue from the big operators would amount to a considerable sum of money.

So you can see why I'm a little bit negative towards bureaucracy in general and its treatment of small business. It has not been that kind, fair, nor just to me here in the New Zealand wild.

THE PRESENT: The Fiordland sun has made yet another appearance to halt my negative, angry mood. Maybe it's God gently reminding me that there are better things to think about than past unfair treatments, hurts and grievances. That, at the end of the day, all this industrious, candle-lit writing is about salvaging my silly, male pride as opposed to exposing injustices done. As wise, old King Solomon of 4000 years ago said when talking about the actions of men to build themselves up, whether its wealth, power or prestige, "It's all vanity." It has a ring of truth about it.

With the arrival of the sun has come the friendly blowflies who have taken a keen interest in the delicious aroma of sweet, decaying meat carried to them on the breeze. I shot a stag last evening in the Hokuri flats. He is now hanging under my veranda and, no doubt, is the centre of great attention for the hungry flies. He will need to be dealt with before the maggots take control.

It is interesting to note that meat can be fly-blown but still be perfectly okay to eat. The true test of whether meat is edible or not is in that bitter pungent smell of decomposition that assaults the senses when you give it a good old, close up sniff. For hunters in the wilderness it can be literally impossible to keep flies from laying eggs on your kill, especially in summer. When that happens the trick is to simply scrape off the eggs which are laid in wee clusters and look like very minute grains of white rice. Once the eggs hatch then it's also the same process of scraping away with a sharp knife, but now you also have to separate the muscle groups to remove the wriggling maggots that have borrowed deep between the folds.

The very best meat is the well hung meat that develops a dark, hard leathery coat on the outside which, when you shave it off and discard, leaves behind a very soft tender meat inside. When this is cooked very quickly on a super-hot pan it melts like butter in your mouth. The trick is having dry, cold air to hang your meat in for up to a week, which isn't always possible in humid forest conditions, especially in summer. It's not the sort of meat one can get in the supermarket as its history would give the health inspectors kittens but it's the sort of meat our forefathers ate regularly prior to the advent of electricity and the advent of the over-officious, nanny state with its bureaucratic health inspectors. Not having a fridge or freezer, dealing with fly-blown meat and well hung meat is a reasonably common occurrence but, I can also say that in all the years of living in this quiet piece of wilderness and hanging and storing my kills in the old traditional ways, I nor any of my guests have never had any food poisoning under my roof. In fact I have even had the odd guest remark that it's the "best tasting meat that they have ever eaten." The thing to remember when it comes to food safety of your kills in the wilderness is always to trust your nose and not to let your guests see you scraping off the maggots from the bush meat they are about to eat.

| Chapter Four | # RAINFOREST GRAVES |

DESCRIPTIVE NOTE: Atop an old lake terrace, not twenty minutes' walk north of here is a grave. A grave hidden from the wandering eye of passing trampers on the Hollyford Track by thick Fiordland rainforest, trampers who have absolutely no idea it even exists, nor whom it embraces in the ancient lake gravels of Lake McKerrow.

This grave which has no marble tomb stone to explain who lies beneath the Kamahe entangled tree roots. It has only remnants of a lovingly made picket fence. The pickets have long gone, rotten to nothing by moss, mould, fungi and time leaving only the support beams which have partly collapsed to the forest floor. Two corner posts are still erect, but only just, being held upright by the partly fallen timbers. These two posts have neat holes through them to cater for those rotting support timbers. Holes chiseled by hand, love and tremendous sadness.

This very lonely grave appears to be solitary, but it is not because there are other graves along in the unknown Jamestown Cemetery, a burial ground of lost hopes and dreams, but their location is now no longer visible, lost to time, eternally hidden by the living, breathing rainforest.

This sad, old, lonely grave, atop an ancient lake terrace in Fiordland, surrounded by ferns and aged podocarps, in a remote section of New Zealand wilderness, contains five bodies, five siblings, children dead before their time, all from the same sad mother and father, the Webbs. The story of this little hidden grave is a real pioneer tragedy. It makes my little challenges quite pitiful in comparison.

The Webbs came to Jamestown in 1870 with hopes and dreams of being in on the ground floor of a new and soon to be thriving town and port. Reality must have struck home shortly after arriving in this very beautiful little Bay. The location is a tough one in which to exist, surrounded by the wilds of remote Fiordland. A tough one for a women and mother to try and raise a family with no school, hospital, or grocery store. A tough one for a father to support a family's basic needs of food and shelter. There was no community hall to shelter his family while he built a home. No sawmill down the road to buy timber to build that home. No paddock in which to graze a cow or plant a crop.

The tragic story of the Webbs is best told in Hall-Jones' book 'Martins Bay' so I will only tell the story to the reader in brief.

Two children died at around the same time, it was thought to be from eating poisonous berries. Dad buried one child on a dark stormy evening to return home to find another of his precious children had died and, because of the fear of an unknown disease, returned back through the damp dark rainforest to bury the second child. Heart-breaking stuff. The third child was lost shortly after childbirth, the fourth was a miscarriage and the fifth was a teenage son who died of influenza. Tough location, tough times and tough people.

The location of this grave is a poorly kept secret amongst the locals. Not marked off the main Hollyford Track as its ground is best untrodden by the masses, these fragile historic remains would not last long with regular visits.

In my forest wanders I have found another old grave in a separate location, who it holds is a mystery to me. But, more mysterious still is an apparent Maori burial chamber with intact skeletal remains in the Sarah Hills, south of Big Bay, similar in type to the one found on Mary Island, down south in Fiordland. A whispered disclosure by an old ex-government deer culler who trod the area for years but I have never come across it in my forest rambles.

THE STORY: Having been given all the necessary approvals, consents, permits and concessions to proceed, I found myself in a position where I did not have the resources to proceed. The RMA and its loving bureaucracies of DOC, SRC, SDC, SHB, SPO, DSIR having greedily drained my financial, physical and mental resources like a tropical leech depriving a victim of its life forces.

I won the battle but had lost the war. Some tough decisions to make, wisdom dictated that I couldn't proceed with the dream. The next best thing was to recoup by placing the land on the market. Land which I believed to be very marketable because we had overcome the considerable bureaucratic obstacles to prove that freehold land inside the National Park could be developed under the new Resource Management Act and hence would become valuable as a result. That was my theory but of course it took me a while before I was to actually prove this. A lot longer than I had envisaged, such is the way of greedy and arrogant dreamers like myself.

I put together a comprehensive selling document, showing photos and a map, as well as covering all the points associated to the land, such as survey, percolation tests, house profiles, legal descriptions, copies of the title documents, requirements of the SPO, RMA, as well as copies of the consents themselves. I felt it was pretty professional.

I headed to Queenstown, a place where the spoilt, rich kids play monopoly with inherited wealth in Unit Titles and Spec Houses, Vineyards and Bars. My plan was of making a quick fortune but that was not to be, as only a few real estate agents took me or my land seriously. There was even a little mockery by the ever-present Kiwi knocker, "Too remote," "Too many sandflies," "Too much rain," etc. They seemed blind to the fact that Milford Sound, my closest port of call, has the same amount of sandflies and rain, if not a great deal more than this special little forest Bay, but Milford in peak season still attracts thousands of people a day to gaze on its wonders. The laughter in their eyes didn't see the uniqueness of land ownership in a National Park, nor the commodity value of there being only twenty five or twenty six such titles in three million acres of World Heritage Park. However, my theory of a quick sale for my hard won effort was not to be, much to my bewilderment. Not to worry, things change if you stick to your guns.

So it was back to earning a living by stoking coal on the twin screw steamer, the *Earnslaw*, which operated on the waters of Lake Wakatipu. A job I had done on several occasions beforehand. A hot, dirty job with long hours; a good wintertime job to be stoking fires but a rotten summertime one. The *Earnslaw* was my financial safety net, I always knew I had a job working in her steel riveted bowels when I needed one. In my spare time I would visit the real estate agents around town to push my land. After a while I started to meet agents that were genuinely interested in my unique properties inside the National Park.

There was the odd tyre kicker at first, by the romantic dreamers, a little bit like myself, then I got my first real interest. A group of Malaysian Chinese expressed a desire to meet so we had a get-together in their newly acquired Queenstown restaurant. Three Malaysian Chinese, their Kiwi advisor, my female real estate agent and I sat down to tea served by an attractive Asian maid. At the beginning I felt very positive, all my work and effort had paid off and I was going to make a dollar, these guys sounded very keen. However, it soon became apparent that they could not read English and hence had not read my comprehensive selling document. They relied totally on their Kiwi advisor, an ex-fisherman from Fiordland, who was leading them somewhat astray. They told me that their intention was to build a hotel at Jamestown to service Milford Sound with their own boat to cater for their own tour groups? After hearing this, I thought it wise to explain the restrictions on the land because of the Scenic Protection Order which, after all, was designed to avoid such developments like a hotel. I wonder what Mr X in DOC would have thought of this situation, of me, his arch enemy, the big, bad developer of a three bedroom kit-set log home explaining and upholding the Scenic Protection Order to rich Asian businessmen wanting to build a hotel? Their Kiwi advisor in a very casual manner tended to sweep these issues away as not being much of a concern, "easy to resolve"! I sensed this wasn't going to go the way I liked. Next, a poster came out, the sort you find on fish and chip shop walls in New Zealand showing all the edible fish types found in our clean coastal waters. I was then asked to point out the fish species available off the Fiordland coast. This seemed to be a comical situation to be in but they were quite serious. The next question asked was about the photo showing a white sandy beach in Jamestown Bay. In broken English I was asked if the beach was "suitable for bad fish," followed with a boyish, knowing sort of smile. I had absolutely no idea what he was talking about, I looked at the agent and she shrugged too. "What was meant by bad fish?" I asked. The response was, "Beach suitable for women to sunbath." I clicked that he was referring to women in general by the musky aroma of their nether regions. I felt embarrassed for my women agent who took the comment in her stride. She didn't even react but just kept on smiling, waiting patiently for me to explain, that, "No, the beach was not suitable because of sandflies." The next question was asked about regular sea access for the boating of their tour groups around from Milford. I explained that you couldn't rely on a regular service using the sea. Their advisor, the ex-Fiordland fisherman, then blew me out of the water with the comment that you could "cross the Hollyford Bar over 90% of the time"! This was not good business and outright deceptive on his part. The little rugged West Coast Bar is dangerous and is only suitable for crossing when you get the right combination of tides and swell and, even then, crossing it needs knowledge of where the nasty rocks lie in the bar entrance. You need the right vessel, normally something small with heaps of horse power to get you out of trouble of the incoming wave surge greeting the outgoing swift river current. This Bar is not something you want to cross with paying passengers on a set timescale and I'll bet if he had worked the Fiordland water he knew it. I think he was probably after a brand new vessel to ply the Fiordland waters paid for by his rich Asian buddies. I lost this sale because I had to be honest. If I had not been I know it would have caught up with me in the end. Total and utter frustration.

The next lot of fun and games was equally as frustrating, involving three consecutive offers all in a row, all from the same source, all silly stuff. I took them with a certain amount of contempt as just testing the waters of my resolve. The agent who tabled the offer said he was representing another agent in his own firm who was part of a consortium, the other member of which did not wish to be identified? All very murky, almost underhand stuff, one has to ask why the need for secrecy? Their third and final offer was almost double their first and was $80,000 for all three titles in this pretty Bay, while my asking price was $277,000, a bit of a difference. In trying desperately to get me to accept this offer, the agent made some hard sell comments. The first rocked my confidence as it was probably designed to do. "Charlie, the principals of this firm think this is an excessive offer and you wouldn't get any higher and would be silly not to accept," or words to that effect. Boy, this put a real crack in my resolve, was I fooling myself, doubt flooded my whole being? But the next comment made me dig my toes right back in. It was real greasy, car salesman stuff. "Charlie, $80,000 dollars would make a pile of cash this high," using his hand to indicate the height above the floor of his little, well decorated Queenstown office with its schist rock exterior. Hard to believe what I was hearing, that the description of a pile of money "this high" would influence me into signing on the dotted line. Queenstown is full of such people, expertly cultivating people's decisions by manipulating their basic greed. Its foundations are not of sand, schist and mortar but money, jealously and greed. The poor little rich kids can keep it for their playground for all I care.

THE PRESENT: Outside a storm is raging. Blowing forcibly through the area with loud thunder and sudden lightning, gusty strong wind and heavy rain. Coming straight off the Tasman Sea with forceful determination and up the long narrow waters of McKerrow. It is a mean, miserable one, even making the trees outside my windows sway back and forth with the strong wind. An oddity in this normally sheltered little Bay of mine. The thunder and lightning is working its way overhead, each clap of thunder being very sharp, clear and loud as it rumbles over this wee Bay. The noise from this awesome abrupt power causes a small vibration in my little log home that makes my stainless steel flue guard on the kitchen wood range rattle with each sudden clap. It makes me feel very, very small in the scheme of things. Storms straight off the Tasman are very spectacular to witness as they assault the mountainous land mass of Fiordland rising out of the Tasman Sea in their determined path. On some of my first stormy nights in this wilderness Bay, I had even got up in the middle of the night, stripped off the cotton boxers (as there is no point getting dry clothes wet in a rainforest when you can help it, it being far easier to just dry off a body) and then headed down my little twisting path through the dark flashing forest to the beach to watch the tremendous light show as the storm moves angrily up my little lake. The novelty has long worn off and not something I do when I have guests, as a naked skinny body exposed in the flashes of storm lightning would possibly be a very disconcerting image for a sleepy guest to view through his or her bedroom windows at 2am in the morning.

This evening it is great to be inside and beside the cosy warmth of my wood range. The romance of watching, listening and feeling a storm in the middle of the night, in the middle of nowhere in my birthday suit has long gone. I am now very reluctant to go down to the beach to check my little yellow plastic boat in the flooding lake. I am much too comfortable here in the warmth and dry, but I must do what I must do as my little yellow plastic boat has a great tendency to sink in such conditions. Its far bigger green cousin was also subject to this unwanted scenario, which is a story for later. It has long since been sold.

I wonder if poor Mr Webb had to battle through a storm such as this to bury his little loved ones. It makes me realise that five minutes out in a storm is nothing compared to his hardship.

THE STORY: Back to the yarn. Nothing happened for a long time or it seemed that way to me. I got sick of stoking the old fire tube boilers of the TSS *Earnslaw* with her long hours and fine, black soot clogging my lungs. Even more, sick of Queenstown, a tourist town, a plastic, false sort of place with people addicted to a plastic lifestyle which for a lot of them will eat them up and spit them out.

Then all in one day, straight out of the blue I got two phone calls from two separate interested parties. One, from a Hamilton man, accepted my price on behalf of a company called Wolverines Investments, based in the States. The other from a Queenstown agent who told me he had an "interested party." Yep I've heard that before. "Who?" "Tim Wallis," came the agent's response, "Sir Tim Wallis." This name made me sit up and take note, like a naughty boy caught daydreaming in the maths class by his teacher. Tim is a well-known helicopter pilot and businessman, being famous in his own lifetime having made his name and fortune in deer recovery out of the Fiordland wilds by using helicopters, a novelty at the time and making this introduced pest that was killing our precious native forests into a multi-million dollar export commodity, hence a Knighthood. An amazing bloke. He is also very fortunate when it comes to wealth, the Southland Times publishing the annual 'Rich List' had his name at the top of the list in the South Island. Tim, however, was interested in one title only and wanted first option before going to the expense of a visit.

Obviously Wolverine Investments sounded the best bet as $277,000, plus GST, was not to be sneezed at, however, something was very amiss with the deal. I asked for a written confirmation of his verbal acceptance in the way of a faxed and standard "Agreement of sale & purchase" document but this was not forth coming. Meanwhile, the Queenstown agent was laying on the heat, as commission driven agents do when they sense a sale, "Sir Tim's not someone you muck around," indicating I could lose the deal. Boy, the pressure was on; phone calls were flying back and forth. I asked the Hamilton contact for the Wolverines accountant or solicitor here in New Zealand to clarify the offer in some way, there was none. I began to get very uncomfortable about all this. Why give a verbal acceptance when you couldn't back it up with a documented one! Something was very amiss.

One bird in the hand is better than two in the bush as the saying goes. I succumbed to the Queenstown agent's pressure but I wasn't going to make it easy for him. I told him that I would only give Tim first option as he desired, if he accepted the same conditions as Wolverine had already accepted (be it only verbally). This I gathered from the agent went down like a ton of bricks. The agent told me Sir Tim "reluctantly" accepted this condition on getting first option for all three titles but only if I could "prove the interest by Wolverines," that is table the Wolverines offer! Which of course I didn't have. Now, I was in a real fix having dug myself a nice deep hole. However, after some hectic toll calls north, I finally got a fax. It was not a standard contract, nor was it on any official company letterhead, just a plain hand-written document stating the offer, this was accompanied with a copy of a supposed company certificate. It would have to do and it did.

The visit was arranged, Sir Tim and wife Lady Wallis (Prue) would fly by helicopter from their base in Wanaka and would pick the agent and myself up in Queenstown then helicopter over the Southern Alps into Fiordland and my little Bay.

Out at the Queenstown airport, Sir Tim and Lady Wallis arrived in their Alpine Deer Group helicopter with Sir Tim at the controls. No greeting or introductions taking place, nothing asked on the trip in. Maybe Sir Tim wasn't used to people dictating such terms as I had done, I was a little out of my depth.

On the ground Sir Tim asked me to show him the borders of the three titles. Being uncertain on how to address him, I call him "Sir," he corrected me and told me everybody just calls him "Tim." Things were looking up. Now Tim's mobility has been severely hampered by several helicopter crashes over his very interesting life and he walked with difficulty on flat ground. So, taking him around the titles boundaries in thick Fiordland rainforest was an act. He used my shoulder as a support to navigate the vines, fallen logs and general fern covered undergrowth and with this simple physical contact the questions begin to fly and the ice was smashed. Tim is a devotee of applied psychology, just like all other successful businessman and in no time I was soft putty in his experienced hands. It became clear that he was still only interested in buying just one title and not all three. Food for thought during the flight back over the Southern Alps.

Watching the fantastic Fiordland scenery of forest, lake, river and snow-capped mountains through the Perspex bubble of Tim's helicopter passing underneath, I formed the silly notion that if I sold just one title to Sir Tim, I might have enough money to develop the other title myself. A silly notion as I was very much out of my depth. Developing remote, wilderness locations is only a game the very fortunate play at with their abundances. You don't enter into a champagne lifestyle on a beer income. It just doesn't work but I was caught up in a dream, being young, silly and arrogant.

I theorised about the present facilities in the Hollyford Valley, the Pyke and Martins Bay Lodges which were getting pretty run down, marketed as lodges but they were just basic, Kiwi-style baches with communal bunk-rooms, etc. I theorised that there was scope for a small, upmarket homestay to serve a growing visitor market to Milford Sound, fourteen minutes by helicopter over the mountains. A wilderness, overnight experience for visitors to Milford Sound, etc.

One should never theorise in business without first getting all the facts. The reader will probably gather that I made some big errors. Namely, that the growing Milford tourist market is controlled by big business who greedily maintain their patch. Most visitors to Milford Sound have been caught in the sticky marketing web of 'inbound tour operators', their tickets for boat, bus, etc. in Milford having been bought and paid for even before they set foot on New Zealand soil. All this tied up neatly by a couple of big operators. Most small businesses just don't have the money to gain entry.

Also, of course, those rundown Kiwi baches with their communal bunk-rooms were not to stay that way because there was a change of ownership in the Valley to those more fortunate than most who had the money to play at such games when I did not. Their wisdom versus my foolishness, but in my defense, I was not to know that at the time. The possibility did not even occur to me as I watched the famous Fiordland scenery drift swiftly by under me in Tim's helicopter.

These new names floating around the Hollyford breeze had a ring of familiarity to me. They were names of people who had opposed me during my challenges with the RMA, things began to make sense. This wasn't about conservation, it was all about money though obviously their submissions said everything but. Such is the way of the mis-mothered, human vice driven RMA and the bureaucrats who think everything is black and white. Poor things being monopoly pawns in rich men's games.

We arrived back in Queenstown and, after a little light negotiation inside the Helicopter Line hanger at the airport, a sale of just one title was made which included several conditions to my benefit. One of which was the supply and use of one of Tim's barges for getting building materials around from Milford Sound. I had just committed myself to a project that was way out of my financial league and that was to almost destroy me, the story of which all comes later.

A successful sale of one quarter acre title inside the Fiordland National Park for $80,000. It was the vindication I needed. So much for the mockery of the knockers. Boy was I glad I did not fall victim to the real estate agents pressure to accept $80,000 for all three, I got that just for one.

My male ego kicked back in, it was due for a come-back. I became a little bit proud and arrogant with my achievement, after all I had worked very hard to achieve it, however, pride comes before a fall and boy was I to come a gutser when it came to developing this very special little place of mine in the wilderness.

Yet another interesting side story concerns the Wolverine Investments. At different stages over the coming years when things got pretty bleak and I was scraping the bottom of the barrel, I explored the possibility of selling my venture here in the rainforest. During one of these down times when I was inside the barrel licking out all the small crevices at the bottom for financial nutrition to keep afloat and not doing at all well, I decided to approach the Wolverines New Zealand contact again to test the water and see if they were still keen at buying. "Yes," there was still interest but my concerns were rekindled as things didn't quite seem kosher. So, to alleviate those worries I rang Dunn & Brad Street Services, an international audit company that does financial audits on companies, etc. worldwide, giving the name and the location stated on the company certificate faxed to me first time round. Less than five minutes later the very helpful man at Dunn & Brad St rang back, "Wolverines Investments does not exist!" This for some reason didn't really surprise me. That was not to say the money didn't exist otherwise why enter into negotiations with me in the first place. One explanation could be that the money was probably a little shady or even outright dirty but issuing a false company certificate seemed to me to be fraudulent, so I went along to the Gore Police just to make them aware of the situation. However, because no actual transaction had taken place they were not interested in the antics of wealthy Americans and their Kiwi counterparts.

Not long afterwards, I was sitting in my accountant's waiting room and happened to pick up a Time magazine. It was published just after the Oklahoma bombing and there was an article on all the different vigilante groups in the States such as the KKK, etc. Some of these organisations are huge with paid up memberships in the thousands. Near the top of the list was a group called the "Wolverines"!

THE PRESENT: It is evening time and the raging storm has passed leaving behind a calm, dark water lake and a very still, quiet forest, even the few birds that have escaped the introduced rats, stoats and possums are deathly silent. There is a contrast of emotions in my being. Sometimes such immense stillness and

accompanying silence brings an incredible peace found nowhere else other than in the wilderness where man's background interfering sound is never found and the stresses of the modern rat race are hidden for a while. However, this is an evening silence that I find a little sad tonight. A remote piece of rainforest on dusk shouldn't be deathly silent but alive with the melody of natural sounds. I know that this special temperate rainforest was once renowned for the vibrant noise of many different and beautiful birds now mostly extinct because of the foolishness of man.

Sadness leads to resentment because I know DOC is losing the battle against introduced pests. Like all large government departments of its ilk, it is too top heavy, full to overflowing with over-paid, career driven bureaucrats and eccentric, long haired academics wearing the latest expensive outdoors gear and drinking fluffy lattes in some trendy, inner city, air conditioned cafe, wasting with the wanton disregard the limited DOC budget on new office furniture and the latest roll out of PR, HR and OSH courses for staff, all of which have absolutely nothing to do with coal face conservation. All the time while the poor staff on the ground, fighting the good fight, doing the hard yards, are under-staffed and under-resourced in their battle against the introduced animals that are causing this deathly silence in my large, green back yard. Boy! I'd better stop there before I go right off the rails.

What birds that are still around are few in numbers but are a wonderful thing to see and hear when you do.

To lighten my morbid mood a sole Bellbird has just started up, probably his last departing notes for the evening. Shortly, once darkness descends on my little Bay, a Morepork or two may start up as they tend to do on such quiet still nights.

It's time to stoke my kitchen wood fired range as it's nearly out and think about cooking tea.

Chapter Five	# ERRORS OF JUDGEMENT

THE PRESENT: There is mischief in the evening air, the sound of distant rotors beating the Fiordland stillness and the dull reports of fired shots, muffled high up in the Hokuri Valley just south-east of here. It's probably Jeff over from Milford Sound out for a bit of commercial deer recovery, although of late there has been a dark little R22 I haven't recognised buzzing the hills and killing my deer.

Silly, I know, but I feel certain ownership to these animals in my backyard. When you are the only person living in a remote area you tend to get a false sense of ownership to your wilderness surrounds. So my emotions are mixed at these evening sounds. However, Jeff has as much right to these introduced walking food sources as I do but I still wish he'd leave the Hokuri deer alone.

My ears have become very attuned to mechanical noises in here because they are rare and normally herald the arrival of potential visitors. Mostly the noises are natural and low key being peaceful melodies in my remote wilderness. The distinctive songs of Bellbirds and Tuis in their dawn and evening choruses or a lone sad male kaka searching for an elusive female or possums playing on my covered verandas in the middle of the night with their distinct thump, thump, thump of half hop, half walk, half play on my wooden veranda decks. Or it is Moreporks communicating to each other through the dark forest or heavy Fiordland rain on the tin roof (a lullaby) or the dull ramblings of distant thunder in the hill and vale surrounds or that eerie sound of wind in the trees or the comforting crackle of my fire on a still cold night or, better still, the throaty groans of amorous stags in the frosty autumn air. Such sounds make the New Zealand wilderness special.

Man-made mechanical noises means something is afoot in the Valley. Whether it's a noisy jet-boat coming down the lake, or a fixed-wing or copter, it tends to mean visitors could be arriving to invade my peace and tranquility. Visitors are good, especially if they wish to stay the night, as my empty coffers badly need their dollars, so I need to hide what needs to be hidden, cover what needs to be covered. Most of the time its people heading to Martins Bay and not to me but the noise still livens the system.

Sometimes the noises are super interesting. Recently, with jet boaters at the Hokuri Hut there were distinctive submerged thuds in the darkness of detonating charges underwater (and I know that sound), transmitted clearly to my tranquil Bay and my attuned ears on the still night air. Probably drunk gentleman farmers, playing as opposed to serious fishing. Falsely thinking that no-one knows of their

Lester eating lunch in our wet rainforest camp kitchen with Punga fireplace –
seven weeks living under plastic.

My lounge a few years later.

mischievous antics in the wilderness. It's amazing how well noise travels over still water on cold nights.

One evening I even heard an accordion echoing up my little forest track. Unexpected visitors up for a drink and an equally unexpected party thanks to the visiting of Bill Smith and his attached crew of mates.

THE STORY: Whereas staff management was my curse with Royalty, planning and logistics was my forte and I was good at it (at least I thought I was). Building in a place as remote as Jamestown, Fiordland requires a lot of thought and planning therefore it was going to be something I would enjoy. I'll side step the general wheeling and dealing which I did a lot of, just like most with Scottish blood flowing in their tight little veins do when it comes to spending hard earned money and I'll get straight into the basics of the tale.

I struck a deal with Thermopanel Kit-set Log Homes for the internal and external walls only. I would arrange everything else from windows to flooring, from roofing to veranda timber, to plumbing and electrical, etc. etc. and got some major savings by doing so. Mind you I had to, to make things work.

Now came the interesting part, the 'transport' of material into the wilderness. Read carefully because this explains my downfall and why I have found myself with all my life savings in the form of building materials dumped in the middle of nowhere onto a flood prone, river delta in Fiordland, a land famous for its huge rainfalls. This is like leaving your keys in a new, unlocked car in downtown Auckland, not a good idea. Building materials sitting miles away from where they should have been, being forced into the position of floating all these materials seventeen kilometres down a remote, wilderness lake on 44-gallon drums, a process that took three months to complete. And why I had to battle away in the rainforest for five years with virtually no capital. Surviving and developing a business with earnings less than a single unemployed male gets given by the welfare state. All of which is not an easy thing to do. It's been a tough mountain pass to traverse carrying a heavy burden. But then if that didn't happen I probably wouldn't have a story to write about.

As part of a standard stratagem of getting the best deal, I wrote to five different helicopter operators. A standard letter to each asking for costings of either a) transporting materials off a truck at the end of the Hollyford Road, an offshoot of the longest one way road in New Zealand, and b) off the deck of a barge or boat out from Martins Bay sailed around from Milford Sound, it being the nearest port. All responded, all a little different in their approach to my queries but, in general, I got a feel for the lifting capacity of their machines and their hourly flying rates. After some calculations I worked out a dollar to kilogram transport rate based on their quotes, for example it was cheaper to use a smaller machine and do more trips transporting per kilo onto site than using a bigger machine and doing fewer trips.

One quote though stood out from all the rest. It was very simple mathematics. His machine, a 500F would lift a 700 kilogram load and do it at the same flying rate as a 500D. A similar machine but which only lifts a 500 kilogram load. A wonderful saving of approx. 40% for each kilogram flown into Jamestown Bay. Savings like that are my cup of tea, they go well with my Scottish blood. So this operator was the one to visit and do business with, or so I thought with the information he gave me.

I prepared a list of questions, hopped into the car and gave this operator a visit to discuss his quote. He seemed a nice enough guy, inviting me into his home for a cuppa with his wife. Top of my list was, "Turn around flying time from off the truck at the Hollyford Airstrip into Jamestown Bay and back again?" A very clean, simple question with a very clean, simple response, "25 to 30 minutes." I took this as gospel having no reason to doubt it. This now gave me all the information necessary to prepare a 'Transport budget'. I had his lifting capacity at 700 kg, his hourly flying rate as shown on his written quote and the turn-around time of 25 to 30 minutes being his verbal quote.

Mistake number one. If someone offers you a great deal that beats all his competitors hands down, be very suspicious. I was not and it was to cost me dearly. For some reason, probably based on a youthful and foolish hero worship, I put helicopter pilots on a pedestal. To me, doubting a helicopter pilot was not part of how I thought at the time.

You may recall from the previous chapter that Sir Tim was contractually obliged to supply me with a barge to transport materials around from Milford Sound to Jamestown, however, I felt uncomfortable with this option of transport for several reasons. One being that materials could sit in Milford Sound for weeks waiting for the right weather conditions to transport around that exposed and rocky West Coast and over that unforgiving Hollyford Bar. The second was insurance, there was the possibility I could lose everything. I rang Sir Tim and asked if he would cover the insurance of the materials on his barge, knowing I was trying my luck a little and of course he said, "No," (very understandable). So the option of transporting by helicopter from the road end sounded better. Even though it was more cost, I could plan and organise the logistics for such things as builder, labourers, electricians, plumbers, SDC inspections, etc. instead of waiting for weather and sea conditions to transport materials around from Milford and hence save time and money. The big plus was I thought I had quite a saving using this 500F helicopter.

That was my line of thinking at the time. Boy, was I wrong, I could not have got it more wrong. Transporting around the coast by boat or barge then by helicopter off the deck is the only way to go and that is the stark reality of hindsight of a fool (me) who has been there and done that. I learnt the hard way.

Having made the decision to transport my hard won life savings in the form of building materials via the Hollyford road end direct to Jamestown Bay, I decided to write a letter to Sir Tim informing him I no longer needed the use of his barge (to break the contractual burden on him). I presumed he would be quite happy about this as the cost of getting one of his large barges from inland Wanaka on the eastern side of the Southern Alps to remote coastal Milford Sound on the western side of the Alps would have cost him a sizeable packet of money. In the letter I also explained why I decided not to use his barge, sighting the reason by giving him the helicopter details, 'turn-around time', etc. In his response was my first warning call, that I was being led astray by this helicopter operator. Tim's exact words were he thought, "....... quote was very keen," referring to the 25 to 30 minute turn-around time for each load from road end to Jamestown and back. Sir Tim is the guru of the New Zealand helicopter industry and I foolishly did not pick up on the clear warning he was giving me.

The next warning happened a lot later on, closer to D-day with a conversation with Jeff Shanks of Milford Helicopters who said he couldn't see how ...... could achieve that turn-around time. I did not really know Jeff that well at the time. Jeff, is a pilot of few words, he is well known as a very reliable, efficient and honest operator serving the helicopter needs of Milford Sound and surrounding Fiordland wilderness (you will hear more of him later in the tale). I thought at the time that Jeff's comment was just a jealous dig at a competitor who had won a successful tender over his own. I was very wrong yet again. Like Sir Tim, Jeff was warning me that this 25 to 30 minute turn-around time was a little bit off the mark.

By this stage I was far too committed to the project of truck and helicopter from the Hollyford airstrip. Even if I digested the warnings given by these two very renowned helicopter pilots, it was too late. I was about to stumble blindly into a nightmare of budget blow outs, when adherence to a tight budget was essential to business survival. To time blow-outs, which led on to lost earnings and lost opportunities, to destroyed dreams and eventually poor health, which I am just battling out of now.

I organised a daily planner sheet which showed dates and time frames for everything from forest clearance to the date of pile inspections, to the arrival of plumbers and electricians, etc. I organised a load sheet, the numbering, weighing and itemising of each 700 kilogram load. Both planner and load sheets I copied and laminated to protect them from the Fiordland moist environment, then sent them to all necessary parties; trucking firm, copter operator, builder, plumber, electrician, council inspectors, etc. even to friends who were going to be on site to help break down each individual load as it was lowered into the forest clearing and stored in the surrounding rainforest, leaving a cleared space for the arrival of the next load in thirty minutes time. That was the plan. Of course it didn't happen that way, it should have, but it didn't.

Trusting a verbal quote of a 25 to 30 minute turn-around time wasn't my only error of judgement. I was making them by the score, compounding each on top of the other, like an undertaker nailing the lid of a coffin closed. Digging myself a nice deep hole that would take years to climb back out of.

Mistake number two. My budget or total lack of finance to begin with. Developing wilderness lodges as I already stated is the sort of game only the very fortunate in our society play at, who have the fat on their budgets to weather unforeseen challenges. I did not have any such luxury, in fact my budget was so lean there was absolutely no fat. I was carving away good healthy flesh right down to the bare bone to make my goals achievable. Just outright bad business on my part. I was completely seduced by my own project. But then, after all has been said and done, I eventually did achieve what I set out to do. It just took a lot more time and effort than I ever thought possible. And involved sacrifices other than financial to achieve.

Mistake number three. Time of year! I planned my endeavours for September which is during the Fiordland spring, being in a hurry to just get on and do it. But talk to any local and you will be told spring in Fiordland is the worst time of year for weather and madcap ventures such as mine. It's the time of unpredictable and wet weather patterns and the 'Spring Floods' associated with them. Flooding here can be dramatic because of the huge mountain catchment areas of the Pyke and Hollyford Valleys, both combine to cause McKerrow's lake level to raise at an incredible rate, rising a couple of metres overnight to flood and invade the forest. Not a good time of year for me to be transporting materials over mountains, down a lake and through a rainforest. Not a good time of year to try to stick to a strict timetable.

Mistake number four. Communication. HF radios are the only communication that is practical for this part of the New Zealand wilderness. The Fiordland mountain mass of the Southern Alps presents too much of a barrier for the standard and far cheaper VHF radio waves to jump over to civilisation. HF radios, however, operate on a far bigger radio wave that bounces off the stratosphere over those scenic Fiordland mountains and back to land. The problem is that to buy and set up an HF radio is approx. $6 grand. My meatless budget just couldn't handle that expense so I was undertaking a huge logistic exercise without good communications, relying on pre-planning, yet another huge error, because of lack of capital. It would be a couple of years before the helpful Murray Paterson of Dunedin helped me set up with communication out of this special little hideaway in the Park.

A good chainsaw is several thousands to buy, but again my budget couldn't afford it so I bought a McCulloch for $299, another mistake. I thought I had a workable budget; that is if anything didn't go wrong.

Mistake on top of mistake on top of mistake and I'm only telling the main ones. I made heaps of them in my youthful arrogance. If I had made the same number of expensive mistakes when managing Royalty Salmon's affairs at Stewart Island I would have been down the road on my ear in a very short time. But I was dream struck and too narrowly focused on my goal. Plus I had my many doubters around telling me I couldn't do it, so male ego dug his angry toes in yet again and I blindly focused on the goal, forgetting to stand back and study the whole picture, which is good wisdom to do from time to time. Probably if I did I would have seen reality.

Soon I would be boating around the Wild West Coast from Milford Sound in a green plastic 5.7 metre boat with a mate called Mark Campbell to spend a week clearing a hole in the rainforest in which to build my little kit-set log home. This boat was also another of my many mistakes. A boat that did help drag some of my house down the lake and a boat that was within the scope of my limited budget, but a boat I aptly named the *Plantanic*, short for Plastic Titanic, because it had that tendency of wanting to rest on the bottom of Lake McKerrow under the waves, doing so on three occasions.

I have rambled quite a bit in this chapter but, by giving the reader the back ground about the helicopter mis-quoting, the reasons for not taking the main bulk of materials around by sea and some of the many mistakes I made, it tends to explain and shape the reasons to the disasters written about in the up and coming chapter. Where everything goes wrong. I have tended to put the main blame for my failure on the helicopter mis-quote of the turn-around time given to me and it had a massive bearing on what followed. Even if the pilot hadn't mis-quoted, I still would have had some huge unplanned stuff ups. Just not the same scale of time and expense.

THE PRESENT: Night time and there is a rodent in my ceiling which, in the stillness and darkness of this peaceful Jamestown night, is industriously and nosily rolling away the green poison rat eggs I have kindly placed up there in the attic for its diet. The noise he creates is magnified because he is rolling the mis-shaped egg directly on top of the fire line GIB material of the ceiling above. Down below I listen to this new unwanted sound at the candle-lit kitchen table, my messy book notes strewn out in front of me. The noise makes him sound like a beast of a rat but, in all probability, it is just a small little mouse, battling away with a discovered treasure. A find that probably equals him in both body size and weight. This little furry animal will be dead within the week as the anticoagulant he digests tonight will thin his blood and cause him to die of internal haemorrhaging. I'm just a little miffed that this process isn't taking place inside each and every rat, possum and stoat in New Zealand tonight. These three introduced species have played their horrid part in destroying a very special rainforest eco-system once full of many noisy birds but now sadly silent partly due to introduced pests like my unwelcome visitor in my attic.

It is his noise that annoys me at the moment because it tells me I have unwanted rodents in my attic, which is a rarity. His cunning method of entry into my little hideaway in the Fiordland forest is a mystery.

Chapter Six | DISASTER

A MEMORY: The barge on which I float is awash with cold water. Each individual wave that is pushed down this narrow Fiordland lake rides up through the many gaps in the makeshift deck. 44-gallon drums and the timber pre-framed floor joists form the main flotation and construction of this wet barge. On top is a deck made up of the house veranda decking. All held and bound together with three braided polypro ropes and four inch nails. Each wave works its way up through the cracks between the planks, beginning at the front and then moving down to the back as the wave motion passes underneath and down the length of this rocking, makeshift barge. A process that is a continuous movement of water, white spray and creaking timber.

I am not happy. This isn't the first barge load floated down the lake nor will it be the last as there are still several tons of building materials perched on top and behind a huge mass of drift wood at the south end of Lake McKerrow, nearly 18 kms away from where it should be. It is not a healthy place for my life savings to be sitting. An ever constant worry in the back of my over-burdened mind, however, it is there now and I cannot turn back the clock to change this unpleasant, unwanted situation, I just have to go forward and work it all out. However, it is not the reason for my present unease.

The reason I'm unhappy is the change in the weather. We started in the early morning with a flat glassy lake but now there is a strong northerly wind blowing across McKerrow's surface, causing in the process a deep sharp chop or wave motion that is typical for this remote narrow lake. A wave motion that is not only soaking my house materials, some of which were never designed for full immersion baptism, but also causing me grave concern that the barge will break up due to the ever constant, conflicting motion transmitted through this very makeshift structure. I am not concerned about my own personal survival, very much a side issue, but having a barge break up mid-lake and having a hundred bits and pieces of my house floating around, being damaged as they smash back ashore with the waves or worse still being completely lost! Not a good situation to be in when building a kit-set home and not having all the pieces, especially away in a remote place like this. The present situation is made more challenging because I am no longer in control as the barge on which I am being unhappily towed gives me no form of control. I am being towed by a small, very dented, alloy fishing boat called the Orgasm which is skippered by a very helpful and weathered fisherman called Dale Hunter of Big Bay fame. A captain who appears to be asleep at his wheel. I

Above:
Dismantling one of my many makeshift barges in Jamestown Bay.

Right & below:
Floating building materials into Jamestown Bay.

know he is not, he is just dozing in the constant up and down motion of these close knit waves. Towing an unshapely and burdened barge such as mine is a very slow process, not something that can be rushed. I'm just a spectator to the unravelling events, afloat in a lake of uncertainty.

That was almost five years ago. Dale delivered me and the barge to quiet Jamestown Bay intact without losing anything. In fact, of all the tons of building materials helicoptered from the Hollyford airstrip to the south end of Lake McKerrow before being floated down this wilderness lake on 44-gallon drums, then carried by hand onto site, each and every piece being man handled five or six times, I lost only two lengths of PVC down pipe to the lake bottom. Incredibly there were no broken windows, there was no water damaged GIB board, etc. When all the money was gone and I had to float materials down the Hollyford River from the road end, then down the lake, a process which took three unpleasant days, I still didn't lose any building materials. I did lose a lot of other stuff on that disastrous winter trip, such as my father's seagull outboard motor, my rifles and almost my life but no building materials. That tale, however, is for later.

THE STORY: Mark and I started the chainsaw a couple of days behind schedule, the Fiordland weather had not been good. We had tried coming around the coast from Milford Sound earlier but had to turn back to its welcome shelter, having got an unpleasant hammering out in the open sea of the Tasman – which is not a nice place for a small and overladen plastic boat when she gets angry. Overnighting in the Milford Lodge, we got an early start and after a couple of small challenges, made our way out through the sheltered grandeur of Milford Sound with her very impressive sea cliffs and those scenic misty peaks dominating the early morning light. Leaving this majestic fiord we entered into the open sea and swell yet again to follow the rocky, exposed coast line north to Martins Bay and the infamous Hollyford Bar. This time the open ocean was not storm-tossed like the preceding day, instead it offered us a gentle open swell on a lovely oily glassy sea, without a breath of wind to cause concern or discomfort. Successfully crossing the bar at Martins Bay we then made our way up the Lower Hollyford River with her long, wide, gentle curves into Lake McKerrow and on to Jamestown Bay.

We set up a very practical bush camp which consisted of a punga fireplace with a black plastic shelter overhead supported by a framework of bush poles, becoming our pioneer forest camp. Kitchen, dining and living room all rolled into one complete with a mud floor when it rained. Then started the battle.

The schedule allowed seven days to clear a bush clearing, large enough in which to land our loads of building materials. We now had five days to achieve that aim, which at first glance looked a very achievable goal, but we only just made it. Nothing, however, was ever lowered into this clearing by helicopter!

Now the error of buying a very cheap 14-inch chainsaw made itself extremely evident. This is virgin rainforest with big, old trees, several centuries old with girths to match, all smothered in a massed array of attached vegetation in the form of vines, mosses, ferns and any other plants that can establish a foot-hold in the nooks and crannies of these ancient podocarps. Attacking one of these giant granddads of the rainforest with only a 14-inch blade powered by a mass-produced cheap engine was like scrubbing a parade ground with a tooth brush. In military terms an achievable goal but a lot of hard work and you wear out the tooth brush in the process, exactly what we did to that cheap McCulloch chainsaw. Plus, when you chop down a tree in a man planted forestry, you can normally avoid hung up trees, taking advantage of the straight lines in the plantation for good felling management practice, but nature, and especially a Fiordland rainforest, does not allow for this and we had several hung up trees to contend with. Their vines and branches interlocking in unpleasant marriages high above our heads, created the necessity to undercut large tilted logs with dangerous and unpredictable pendulum results as the interlocking branches above twisted and tore away to let the log finally crash to the ferny, forest floor.

It rained all the time which is very normal for that time of year in Fiordland. Working in wet conditions with wet clothes and gear during the day, to cook under dripping black plastic over a smoky fire in the evenings before retiring to sleep in semi-damp sleeping bags at night. It was tough going, I was glad to have had someone like Mark around to help. We had worked together on the sea cages in Big Glory Bay, hunted, fished and dived together. Both of us knew the pluses and minuses of the outdoor life, knowing that such conditions sometimes come with the hunter/gatherer lifestyle. On several stages the electrics on the chainsaw played up because of the excessive moisture, our solution was to remove the bar and chain and place the main body into a small portable gas oven designed to go over a gas ring and roast chickens and the likes, not cheap McCulloch chainsaws. It worked, however, but only for a while until something else went wrong with it, which was always when you needed it the most. Small engines and I just don't get on too well as I'm not the mechanically minded type. We got the clearing finished within the time scale I had set, however. But only just.

Goodbye to Mark and hello to Lester, the kit-set builder, Kurt his teenage son and Barry and Sugar, two helpful mates. All four arrived by helicopter with Mark utilising the backload back to Milford Sound. After one night in a wet, partially flooded tent both Barry and Sugar rebelled, opting to grab the boat each evening after work and head down to the DOC hut at Hokuri to reside. Common sense really as neither of them were young chickens, their days of sleeping on uneven, wet ground in a small tent were in the past about thirty years earlier. Barry is a skipper on the TSS *Earnslaw*, a big abrupt sort in both frame and character who had fished the Chatham Islands and 'called a spade a spade' and Sugar his mate retired in Queenstown from managing ski fields and the such like. Both very generous, practical men who could turn their hand to almost anything and did so. Both were hard working individuals who loved the unusual endeavour I was attempting and enjoyed helping out. Ideal blokes to have around.

That fateful day dawned. The transport truck and trailer arrived at the Hollyford airstrip as planned after being driven up from Gore to Te Anau, then up the Milford Road, the longest 'No Exit' road in New Zealand, to cross over the 'Divide' in the Southern Alps, which is aptly named because the water catchments are divided and fall in separate east-west directions. Truck and trailer descended down the steep mountainous gradient into the turbulent headwaters of the Upper Hollyford Valley, branching north-west off the busy Milford Sound road. Down this beautiful, peaceful Fiordland valley, past Gunn's Camp to the bush airstrip of the Upper Hollyford near to the end of this quiet 'no exit' gravel road. The helicopter made a noisy entrance as all helicopters have a tendency to do and the process of flying my house down the Hollyford Valley and down the length of Lake McKerrow to Jamestown to the waiting arms of Lester, Kurt, Barry and Sugar began.

However, things did not go as I had so arrogantly planned, just as the reader has already probably guessed. The first helicopter load arrived at Jamestown Bay but was not lowered into the forest clearing as planned but onto the beach in the Bay about 100 metres away through the forest from the building site. The pilot indicating that he would 'long strop' the loads into the site later on. This was a new development to me as it would involve an extra cost to each load to lift them into the clearing later. I had to accept this unexpected change, mainly because I had no other option but to do so. He was the pilot, it was his helicopter so I left him to do the job. He did around three or four loads direct to the beach at Jamestown Bay but did not average anywhere near the 25 minute turn around as he had quoted, more like 35 minutes or over. Yet another unwanted cost to each load taken from a very lean budget. The theory of transporting all my materials in one day became unrealistic as other issues became involved, like the day-wind blowing down the length of the lake adding yet again to the turn-around time of each load, plus the shape and stropping of my loads was not adequate nor safe for the pilot to fly. This was especially annoying to me as Lester, Kurt and I had compiled the building materials into 700 kilogram loads using the truck scales at Gore Services, a process that took a couple of days to complete. I then had called the pilot with the intention of asking him to pop down to Gore and check out the loads and stropping . It seemed the wise thing to do considering the large endeavour and expenditure I was undertaking. However, he was away working his helicopter in another location and his brother took the call. He was also a helicopter pilot and was looking after his brother's affairs. He told me in a very casual way that a trip to Gore "wasn't necessary to check the loads and it would be okay on the day," or words to that effect. Of course, it was not.

I had calculated my 'copter budget on his upper quote of thirty minutes and added 10% on just in case things went wrong, standard budget wisdom in any building project but these four new developments of a) long stropping each and every load onto the site, b) misquoted flying time, c) extra flying time due to the day-wind on the lake and d) the unstable, poorly stropped loads were turning my poor budget into a joke.

Anyway, it was dawning on me that things were not working out as I had hoped, there was no money to cover this extra flying time but I had no choice but to keep the ball rolling forward, its contours no longer rounded and smooth but rough and unshapely. After a conversation with the pilot I made the huge mistake of telling him to take the materials as far as he could within the scope of my budget I had allocated him – which, as it turns out, was to the head of Lake McKerrow. On the map this is approximately only two thirds of the original distance to Jamestown Bay. This was to be the biggest mistake of the project, other than the fact I was embarking on a rich man's project with a poor man's budget. I should have got the pilot to stick to the original plan and flown all the materials direct to Jamestown, then long stropped all the loads into the forest clearing before only paying him the sum as calculated by the number of loads multiplied by 25 minutes per load (his verbal quote), then multiplying this figure with his hourly flying rate as supplied by his written quote, letting the court sort it all out at a later date. That is if he was unhappy about it, which I'm sure he would have been but that's the wisdom of hindsight. I was probably too stressed at the time to even consider this logical and simple option. I had quite a bit on my plate at the time.

Even with the shortened flying distance, approximately cut by a third, the process was to take several days, with typical Fiordland weather upsetting the applecart along with poor communication.

By the time the pilot had used up my entire allocated transport budget the situation had become a right mess of huge logistical proportions with my life savings in valuable building materials sitting in three places in the Fiordland National Park. I did not have materials landed in the forest clearing where they should be but sitting on a beach about 100m away through the rainforest. Most of the building materials were sitting on a flood prone delta at the head of Lake McKerrow, miles away from where they should be and, worse still, I had a sizeable amount of material still sitting at the Hollyford Airstrip. The pilot had left the more difficult loads like roofing iron and windows whose flat surfaces caused challenging, aerodynamic issues until last. By this stage the budgeted money was all gone for this pilot and so was he, leaving me with a very challenging situation to resolve.

With my materials sitting at the top of Lake McKerrow, my fancy laminated planner and time schedule on it was now an unhappy joke, a bygone memory of when I had good logistical skills managing two sea-cage salmon farms. Now it had all turned to custard because of a misquote and my own stupidity. It suffered from the domino effect because everything revolved around materials landing directly onto the site. With this not taking place time schedules for the arrival of plumbers, electricians, council inspectors, etc. was all affected by the preceding event or domino. A far more serious matter was money. I became very conscious that there was no money to cope with this sort of stuff up. There was absolutely none, not a penny, to weather a disaster of this magnitude and I still had to keep writing cheques or lose everything I had worked very hard to achieve. It was very difficult and stressful while all the time living in a damp tent with no phone, fax or regular communication to seek help, assistance or guidance. I just had to battle on with the resources I had.

I started by bringing materials down the lake with my boat, beginning with cement and piles to keep Lester and Kurt busy. I had been up and down the lake a couple of times when Dale Hunter puttered his little fishing boat into Lake McKerrow from out of the Tasman Sea and arrived on the scene. He very quietly took stock of my messy situation, offered his welcome assistance and started putting my nose in the right direction, showing me the way to go.

To describe Dale Hunter and his very interesting life is a book in itself, if not several of them. Not a book you could publish while he still lives and breathes as it would trouble many feminine waters. This very interesting individual could be aptly described as New Zealand's 'Crocodile Dundee' but without the big mouth, big ego and good looks. His countenance is pretty rugged to look at, weathered, strong and without an ounce of fat. His natural ability with women, however, is contrary to my conception of what women see as appropriate characteristics in a man but he never fails to find and obtain those wonderful female comforts; I won't go there as his many female exploits would also fill pages. A very short description of the man. He started working and living in the bush at the age of 17, trapping possums and shooting deer for a living, ending up in the Pyke Valley in the 60s as a deer culler, initially using pack horses to get his meat out of this remote and mountainous, beautiful valley, progressing from land to water transport using jet-boats in the turbulent Pyke and Hollyford rivers then to air transport via fixed wing planes to get his feral carcasses to market. He had to learn to fly in the dangerous, turbulent air currents of the Fiordland mountains and to build his own airstrips in the wilderness. Then came the heyday of the helicopter deer recovery which changed the lives and methods of the New Zealand deer cullers from humble ground hunters to romantic predators in blood-stained flight overalls, many of which never survived this exciting and dangerous period. In 1968 Dale moved the short distance to Big Bay and started crayfishing and live deer recovery and spent the next 35 years living a very simple but interesting life in this very remote area. In both the crayfishing and deer recovery Dale became a wealthy man, self-made, but to look at him in his old worn clothes and how he lives a very subsistence, almost hippy lifestyle you could easily be fooled into thinking he is very poor as he doesn't live his wealth. His digs are simple, basic and rustic with driftwood door handles, outside bath and an open stone fireplace. There is no arrogance of inherited wealth about his character as his wealth is self-made through hard work, sometimes dangerous, over many years. Fishing the remote west coast by yourself in a small boat is not for the faint hearted, nor is flying semi-drugged feral deer over the mountainous Southern Alps in a small plane. Dale isn't one for talking or blowing his own whistle either, you could easily describe him as quiet and his conversation simple but I have learnt to listen and respect his comments. That in short is a very brief introduction to Dale Hunter, a very interesting bloke. He is my closest permanent neighbour, about five or six hours walk from Jamestown Bay through the rainforest to Martins Bay and then along the rocky West Coast to his interesting digs at Big Bay.

With the unexpected arrival of Dale on the scene I stopped trying to use my little boat to transport the house materials down the lake and adopted Dale's barge theory. Collecting old 44-gallon drums out of the bush, residue leftovers from recent copter deer recovery, I started making barges using these old drums for the flotation and the house possi-strats (manufactured bearing timbers) to hold the old fuel drums together. This worked extremely well, considering the unwanted situation I found myself in.

Dale got me started and then left to do his own thing, but he left me in a far better shape than before he arrived.

Now, instead of five men speed-building my wilderness lodge, we had only two, with three blokes transporting materials to them. Soon Barry and Sugar were gone, their planned week in the Fiordland wilds over and I was left to battle up and down the lake by myself.

Another disaster that may be of interest during this depressing period which was now stretching from days into weeks then into months, was the sinking of my 5.7m plastic boat at the Demon Trail Hut.

There were still house materials at the Hollyford airstrip made up of roofing and windows, both hard items to transport because of their large flat surface which do not fly well under a helicopter. These difficult loads had been left until last by the pilot, however, by this stage I had changed helicopter operator and engaged Jeff Shanks of Milford Helicopters to finish off. Several years later while flying me into home he described my endeavours at this early stage as "madness," which in truth is an apt and honest thing to say considering the unwanted situation I found myself in. Jeff doesn't mince words. Anyway, I had arranged to meet Jeff at the head of the lake to un-strop the loads as they arrived. Unlike my first copter pilot, Jeff was using the still, early morning air to work which meant that I needed to be at the head of the lake at the crack of dawn. I decided to take the boat full of 44-gallon drums up the lake and stay overnight at the Demon Trail Hut. To accompany me was Dale's son, Craig, who was going to help me for a couple of days by making a barge and towing it down the lake with my boat, the *Plantanic*. The lake was blowing a mild northerly so I moored the *Plantanic* in a little sheltered cove just south of the Demon Trail hut and settled down to a worrying night of lost hopes and unsettled sleep.

Early morning, just before first light, an unusual sound broke slowly into my semi-conscious dream. A hollow, metallic sound like empty tin containers banging together in the waves. I knew what caused such a sound but half hoped that I was just having a very bad dream, but as I become more awake I realised I wasn't. That sound echoing up to the hut through the forest was very real. Out of the sleeping bag and down to the little cove to be greeted with the miserable dawn sight of several empty 44-gallon drums at the water's edge, banging together in the wave motion splashing onto the gravel beach in the once sheltered cove. 44-gallon drums that the night before were safely and squarely sitting on the deck of my boat, *Plantanic*. As for this plastic mistake of a boat, all I could see was about ten inches of green plastic cabin sticking out of the cold water, the rest was under McKerrow's disturbed surface, sitting unhappily on the gravel bottom. A very, very depressing sight to see first thing in the morning out in the Fiordland wild. What happened was very simple. Overnight the wind had swung around 180 degrees to blow in the opposite direction from the previous southerly direction, now straight into the little cove in which I had safely moored *Plantanic*. The wave motion swamping my boat caused her to settle on the bottom. Over the next couple of years *Plantanic* was to sink a couple more times in Jamestown Bay, before I was forced to sell her as I was in need of the money to keep the project going.

With it sitting on the bottom, what was I to do? I still had to get to the flood prone delta where Jeff was landing the windows and roofing, this was about four or five minutes by boat from the hut but about an hour's walk away through the rainforest. I started running down the track, hoping to arrive before Jeff to unstrop those valuable loads of mine and hopefully gain some sort of assistance to salvage my sunken vessel. After my arrival I waited for the expected sounds of an approaching helicopter to echo off the mountain sides and down the Hollyford Valley to me. Those eagerly anticipated rotor noises, however, never reached me as Jeff was not able to fly that day. A fact I was totally unaware of because I was un-contactable in the wilderness. After a couple of anxious hours of waiting, wondering and worrying as to where Jeff was, I headed back through the lonely forest to the Demon Trail Hut not sure what to do.

Things were getting on top of me, compiling and taking their toll on my reserves. Everything that could go wrong was going wrong, physically, mentally and financially. I was stuffed and very close to completely losing the plot altogether. Half way back to the hut the enormity of my whole situation struck me. A sunken boat with no means to retrieve it, stuck in the middle of nowhere. My life savings sitting in three different places in Fiordland, everywhere but on the building site. The bulk of which was on a flood prone, river delta in a land famous for its rainfall and flooding and now in a situation with no boat to retrieve them. On top of that I had a builder on the going award rate with no materials to work with, now forced into an unplanned situation of writing out unexpected large cheques for money I did not have and the overall prospect of losing absolutely everything I had worked so hard to achieve. Years of disciplined lifestyle and saving gone! It all got too much and I stopped dead on the Hollyford Track, completely overwhelmed and fell on my knees and tried to cry. All male ego, pride and vanity aside, I just wanted to cry but it wouldn't work, tears just wouldn't manufacture, I just couldn't cry. My life was getting close to rock bottom and I was unable to rid myself of pent up sadness through a good cry. There were no witnesses to what I considered to be a shameful event so it should have been easy. I was alone in the wilderness on a steep rocky track surrounded by thick, damp Fiordland podocarp forest with just the birds and they had better things to worry about than a weak male on his knees unable to cry. So I prayed to God, for assistance. It seemed a last resort. Natural human desire to have someone to talk to, someone to listen to one's problems. This helped, getting things off my chest and getting me back onto my feet and pounding my way resolutely back to the Demon Trail hut in a slightly healthier state of mind. Trying desperately to formulate a plan in my mind to save the situation. For starters, this meant walking five or six hours back down the Demon Trail which navigates the rugged side of Lake McKerrow to Jamestown Bay and then another hour out to Martin's Bay to the white-baiters who I hoped were in residence, to seek assistance to my plight. Bear in mind that I had already done quite a bit of walking that day and I had been through days of stress, worry, sleepless nights and hard physical work already, thrown in with a poor diet (as eating hadn't been a priority of late). Now this walk and day was going to be a real toughie, a marathon on mind and body. I was getting my mind psyched up for it as I headed back through the rainforest to the Demon Trail hut.

Tramping down the Demon Trail was not necessary because, as I arrived back at the hut, I also arrived to the very pleasant sound of an approaching boat. Dale arrived un-expectedly on the scene, a very unique answer to my prayer. Dale was supposed to be back at Big Bay, fishing in the Tasman, not sailing around in Lake McKerrow. I had not expected to see him for some while. To those who know Dale and his antics, the suggestion that he and his dented alloy boat named the Orgasm was heaven sent is laughable as it would be very difficult to describe the bloke as a saintly character. But that is what happened. God's presence was to make Himself more and more evident to me here in the wilderness the longer I spent in amongst his beautiful creation of forest, lake and mountain. A concept that took me awhile (years) to digest and adjust to. Even longer to admit it. But it all seems so very obvious now.

Dale took in the situation in his quiet, unhurried way, looked me directly in the eye and simply and quietly said with no change to his normal tone, "Charlie, you cannot afford to make such mistakes in here," meaning Fiordland in general. Probably the worst telling off in my life and I have had a few such as sergeant majors, for example, screaming profanities in the early morning on a hard, frosty parade ground in Waiouru because I was out of step with the rest of the squad (sergeant majors being the loudest and most anatomically descriptive people on the planet). Dale's quietly spoken correction however was right, such mistakes in remote Fiordland with no one around to help could easily result in a loss of property, if not loss of life.

We salvaged my sorry excuse for a boat and towed the rotten thing back down the lake and down the Lower Hollyford river to the white-baiting camp of the Drysdale family who were in for the whitebait season. The two brothers, Charlie and Neil, took to my two water-logged outboard motors as if they were their own soaked children and in no time had them stripped down, cleaned, re-assembled and operating. I was back in business. Good people, the Drysdales.

The process from when the first materials were landed at the head of Lake

McKerrow, to the last of the building materials, a kit-set kitchen complete with a young family of mice, arriving on site in my little remote Jamestown Bay were three long, hard, worrying months. My original schedule allowed only one or two days!

The planned schedule for the main house construction had been one month. The theory being to get the house built as quickly as possible so as to get a business going and money coming in. In the end it took almost two very tough years to get the Compliance Certificate before I could take paying guests. Two very tough years without hardly any income. All in all a complete and utter disaster but one I can take a little pride in battling out of, to ultimately succeed.

THE PRESENT: It's been a while since I started this book project. Gone are the candles and so are my messy hand-written notes, replaced with a cheap word processor from Cash Converters bringing much needed order and discipline to my rough hand-written scribbles. A distant thumping from an old hand start Lister generator supplying the electric power echoes through the dark, familiar rainforest from its simple punga covered shed out in my backyard. Also a new acquisition, this heavy little generator was brought around the coast by yet another helpful fisherman, Dale Coker of Milford Sound. Another interesting character, huge in frame and heart who has rendered me assistance over the years.

I try not to use this old Lister too much because the economics of my meagre existence here does not justify the simple luxury of constant electricity due to the cost of flying in precious diesel. So, when I do run it, I make sure I utilise it to the absolute fullest, pumping water into my header tank, vacuuming or washing or using the word processor, trying to do as many things concurrently as possible. Only running the generator about three or four hours a week. For the rest of the time I revert back to the simple life with soft candle light in the evenings. The distant night thumping of the ancient but reliable Lister being replaced with the repetitive call of those small nocturnal owls, the Moreporks, who share this beautiful little Bay with me.

BUILDING AMONGST THE PODOCARPS

Chapter Seven

A RECENT HUNT: A clean, crisp morning, a light blue, dawning sky showing promise of a good day to come. A typical end of summer morning in this part of North Fiordland. I'm a little weary, having been up for a couple of hours, tramping around the gravel lake shore from home. Doing so under fading stars to approach the Hokuri River flat just on first light. Straining my vision to pick up any dark shaped movement out on the open river flat, feeding on the early morning succulent dew covered grass. I've shot a few deer on this first lake side clearing which is fifteen minutes' walk from home. It is several acres in size, a typical river delta roughly triangular in shape, two sides boarding the lush rainforest, the third boundary the gravel lake shore of McKerrow. The Hokuri River dissects the delta as her tannin waters tumble over polished granite boulders to empty into the tranquil surface of the Lake. But as hard as I look and hope I see absolutely nothing that resembles a silly, easy deer. Not surprising to me as over the years I've probably knocked over all the less intelligent animals in this clearing. The wiser deer, especially those cunning old hinds, probably treat this area with a little bit of hard-earned respect, only feeding on its nourishing grasses in the dead of night while I'm tucked up in my lonely bed, dreaming about unavailable comforts, best not described here.

There are several clearings along the course of this remote Fiordland river. Formed in this rainforest valley floor by the destructive force of many bygone floods. Very familiar forest glades to me which I stalk slowly and unsuccessfully through in the new budding day without seeing a thing. It is now fully light, getting well past that optimum stage of first light when the deer head away from the dangerous, open ground for the security of the thick, lush rainforest where they will laze away yet another quiet Fiordland day undercover. I shoot about three quarters of my animals in the forest around the backdrop of the home Bay but classify these deer as hard won whereas, to get an easy deer out in the open river flat at this time now approaching mid-morning would be unusual and a blessing.

Being weary of my unsuccessful hunt, I have lost the necessary concentration. Having focused my mind totally to the goal for the last couple of hours, I now let the small thing wander onto other fields of interest, completely unprepared for the sight that greets me as I climb up over an old river bank in the Upper Hokuri River flats.

Three Red stags, majestic in bearing with the Skipper Range as a picture perfect backdrop behind them. Right out in the open ground, obviously crossing the river and her peaceful clearings, slowly ambling their way back towards the forest and doing so in no particular hurry. They are less than forty yards away, two are looking elsewhere, blissfully unaware of my presence but the third middle stag is suddenly tense in body, looking directly at me. Probably as surprised at my sudden appearance into his field of vision as I am of his. I shatter his backbone, destroying his prime back steak in the process with my horribly hurried and misplaced shot. Very poor shooting but I have learnt from many frustrating experiences that when these well-educated Martins Bay deer become aware of a human presence they don't hang around for you to always make a clean, accurate, killing shot. But this shot is particularly bad in its execution.

He drops his hindquarters instantly, leaving him staggering but standing on his strong forequarters, like a dog sitting on his backside. His mates bolt in completely opposite directions, in fright at the sudden loud report of the .308 in the still, peaceful morning air. Both stop after very short sprints, however, in utter confusion, not knowing what made the frightening sound in their tranquil domain, nor aware from where it came, looking for the companionship they had only seconds before. Because I am standing still their attention is not on me but on their poor, distressed mate, the main movement centre stage between them, dragging his hindquarters around in pitiful small circles on the grassy river flat.

I let off another rushed shot in the direction of another animal, in the knowledge the first one was not going anywhere and watch in complete disgust as the stag bolts for the river where I give him the third and final round in my rifle and still he flees right up the opposite bank into the secure forest, giving no indication that any round had hit home. I am absolutely gutted with my apparent misses and poor marksmanship. I look in the opposite direction, expecting to see the disappearing hindquarters of the third stag as it reaches the dense forest cover across the glade and am further shocked to find him, not fleeing into the green, safe foliage as would be healthy, natural and normal for a deer in this situation but standing side on presenting the perfect chest shot for me to hit, only now I have an empty rifle. His tense, worried attention alternating between me and his wounded mate, shocked by the sudden turn of events, in this unfolding drama. In a slow exercise of pure frustration, I place the crosshairs of my scope on his very stationary front shoulder and pull the trigger, listening to the dry click as the firing pin hits an empty chamber. This very silly but lucky stag only wakes up to the danger and takes his leave to the forest when I start to move towards his wounded mate. His education on carnivorous humans now complete.

I engage in an unhappy, unpleasant dance with this wounded stag because he still has the agility and ability to face his opponent, half standing on resilient fore legs. As the now useless antlers he tries to present in his defense become a handicap they become handy handles to grab, enabling me to twist him off balance and bear his thick, hairy neck to my cheap but sharp knife. After the bloody chore was complete, I set off for the river in the direction of the second animal I had shot at and very quickly come onto bright, frothy blood splatter on the white Hokuri

River gravel, indicating that my shooting wasn't that bad after all. Frothy, aerated blood comes only from a lung shot, leaving a very easy trail to follow in almost any terrain unless of course it is raining or getting dark or both. I find him dead only a few yards into the forest, his once safe haven.

Now comes the mission of carting all this mass of meat home, requiring two sweaty round trips and most of that day. A nice hot, sunny day with annoying blue body blowflies to accompany me in my efforts, attracted by the sweet aroma of my heavy burden.

It would be a lie to say none was wasted, it being a regrettable fact that I have no way to store such kills so I only take the prime cuts. The back steaks for my guests, the two sets of hindquarters are for a barter arrangement with the Hollyford Valley Walks Ltd. supplying their lodges at Martins Bay and at the Pyke/Hollyford confluence, a forequarter to feed myself and any passing tramper off the Demon Trail. The rest is left to rot where it fell.

The barter arrangement is a hindquarter for either a 9kg gas bottle refill or for 20 litres of fuel. Four hindquarters gets me twelve bottles of their guest wine. Wine that helps digest the back steaks served up to my few guests. Guests that have taken the time and trouble to discover my little, secret forest haven on the Hollyford Track. Secret because there is no money to advertise. This arrangement of barter no longer exists but at the time it helped to keep me operational with absolutely no money to fly in such simple commodities as gas and fuel.

Each season I shoot twenty to thirty animals, the stainless Ruger rifle perched beside the kitchen wood stove is well past its century. Killing not in bloody male ego induced sport nor because of my strong environmental views of purging the Fiordland rainforest of this destructive introduced mammal which are seriously affecting this sensitive and special ecosystem. Very simply it is because it is a handy and cheap food source for a bloke surviving on the smell of an oily rug. A basic food that will only store seven to ten days without a freezer, depending on the humidity, temperature at the time and how effectively I have been able to keep it protected and hidden from the ever- present and persistent blowflies and their multitude of maggoty eggs before I need to get another. Most of the animal being wasted. Not a situation I like but just part of life here in the wild of quiet Fiordland.

THE STORY: My disastrous tale continues. Getting the building materials to Jamestown Bay was extremely stressful and time consuming for me, getting them from the beach through the forest onto my building site was nothing but pure hard, physical work. No truck or forklift here, all done by human back, hand and muscle. Mostly mine.

In my tight and silly budgeting I bought a very cheap, kit-set wheelbarrow from the Warehouse. Dad in his wisdom suggested that I take it out of its boxing, assemble it, and check that everything was okay, before going to the expense of flying the thing into this remote site. Good advice, common sense stuff. As the biblical proverb says, "There is wisdom in grey hairs," but his son chose to ignore this sage and wise direction because it required unnecessary time. After all, I arrogantly presumed that nothing could possibly go wrong with a simple, cheap wheelbarrow bought at the Warehouse. I had more important things to be doing with my time! But it was like the error of buying the cheap chainsaw because, when I unpacked the thing at Jamestown, I discovered that the tyre was flat.

A small, simple thing, very easy to resolve in town, becomes a big thing out in the bush. There is no way to inflate tyres here in the rainforest of Fiordland, no BP service station just down the road. So, much to the disgust of everybody concerned, materials had to be carried through the forest. In desperation I tried using the wheelbarrow, flat tyre and all, for some of the more challenging heavier loads which soon completely stuffed the deflated rubber tyre and wrecked the cheap Taiwan manufactured rim in the process. Next stop was trying to fill the empty tyre with a concrete type of mix with the expected dismal results, finally adopting, after some period, a wooden tyre which was semi successful and served a purpose. This wooden tyre is now the subject of humour years later when nosey trampers notice it on a well-battered wheelbarrow stored under the house. The sort of thing you see in Third World countries where they have no other option but to make do with what they have. About three years later I deemed I had enough money accumulated to splash out and spoil myself and get a real tyre with an inflated tube filled with wonderful compressed air. Boy it's handy to have a wheelbarrow, a real luxury especially for carting things like firewood or gravel and such like. Living in here makes you appreciate such simple little things that most just take for granted.

Piles, cement, bearers, timber, bath, kitchen sink, etc., etc.; everything was lugged up my little twisting forest track. Not far in distance, only about seventy yards up onto the old lake terrace but enough to be an unnecessary pain. Especially things like my large, fragile floor to ceiling windows which became a real act to navigate through the forest. A job that required four careful men, one in each corner, scrambling over wet moss-covered logs and fighting undergrowth to reach the final resting place in my walls. In all, there many risky adventures of being trucked over the Southern Alps, helicoptered down a beautiful remote valley then barged down a long, unforgiving lake before finally being manhandled through thick Fiordland podocarp rainforest. None were broken, cracked or damaged in any way. Quite amazing considering how fragile a large sheet of glass is. The only danger they face now is when the large native wood pigeons try to fly through them which happens periodically.

The weather continued to be unkind to us. Spring in north Fiordland is a time best spent elsewhere, not getting depressed in this wild remote rainforest with the continuous heavy Fiordland rain soaking everything you wear and own for days on end. Unless of course you're a mad white-baiter then it's the only place for you to be catching the little transparent native fish that spawn up these quiet, peaceful and remote West Coast rivers during the wet months of spring. Sometimes these quiet, peaceful rivers are not so quiet and peaceful, the white-baiter can be a very territorial sort of person, defending his patch of river with incredible dexterity of verbal abuse, threatening to overflow into physical violence, directed at anybody that may be perceived to be catching his whitebait prior to them swimming into his or her set net. These domestics that arise sometimes require the local copper at Te Anau to be flown over the mountains into Martins Bay to sort out the disputes. It is illegal to fish for the whitebait in Lake McKerrow, it being a pastime for the Lower Hollyford river only, which pleases me as it keeps my nose clean and out of the trouble that arises at this time of year.

Barry and Sugar stayed their planned week while watching my disaster unfold, chapter by depressing chapter, then both these helpful mates were gone, back to Queenstown, dry beds and warm accommodating wives leaving the three of us to battle on. Lester and son Kurt building while I carted materials down the lake and onto site. Young Kurt found his new work environment both foreign and challenging, constantly needing to apply sandfly lotion and change into dry clothes until he had none left. Spend any time in the New Zealand bush, either working or playing, you soon learn to always keep one set of clothes dry for evenings indoors or under canvas and just re-use your wet clothes, boots, etc. for the day activities. At times this line of thinking increases your survival when the going gets a bit tough in the temperate rainforest of Fiordland.

Soon both Lester and Kurt were gone as well, gone for a much needed break from the forest, the weather, the sandflies and me. They left me to continue the never-ending chore of building material cartage. A depressing, worrying time for me, not because I was alone in a wild remote place, but because the future of my project was looking so very, very bleak with visions of a half-complete home rotting in the rainforest.

In one of the few helicopter loads that did manage to reach my little Bay was a Wagner wood stove, bought at a good price directly from the factory up in the North Island. This grey, cast-iron stove was too heavy to carry up my little forest track to the house site so it was just left on the beach in its wooden packing box. The theory was that an opportunity would present itself at some stage when several visiting men would be available and willing to help get it up onto the building site. At this early stage of life here on the shores of McKerrow I did not have any idea how regular the spring floods were, nor how quickly her waters could rise in flood, nor anticipate the height she can achieve. This Wagner was to survive three spring floods being completely submerged once and partially submerged twice. It now sits in my kitchen, heating my water, baking my bread and roasting my legs of venison, none the worse the wear for its several freshwater dunkings. To get this handy little wood stove off the gravel beach I had to take it apart and cart the pieces separately up my track before reassembling it in the kitchen. Even then I had to grab the helpful hand of a passing tramper to get the main heavy casting off the beach and on to the site, a struggle for two men with many rest stops and discussions along the short way. It was heavy.

Not only was the Wagner subject to the flooding in the bay but other essential

Foundation work in new forest clearing.

The hard work of carting building materials off the beach up into the forest clearning
– not a small chore.

bits and pieces associated to my wild and disastrous building project also shared the experience. There was a large 2000 litre black, plastic water tank and an even bigger grey, plastic sewage tank, in shape similar to those small, deep-diving subs as seen in the National Geographic minus the small round port hole windows, both floated well when affected by these typical Fiordland floods. There was a great deal of timber and pre-framed rafters on the beach as well which also floated well with the rise and fall of McKerrow's changeable lake levels. It was necessary to tie and secure all these floatable items to trees and bushes around the Bay as these spring floods easily invade the forest at their height. It is an incredible sight to wander down to the sheltered Jamestown Bay in the early morning light after a night of very heavy Fiordland rain and gaze on a flooded Jamestown Bay, the lake level right up into the rainforest covering the beach in dirty tea-coloured water. A still, calm bay partially filled with floating building materials, all very secure but in a real mess of twisted ropes and additional lake drift wood ranging from straw-like twigs to larger water-worn logs to complicate the salvage. As for the materials such as GIB board that could not handle such baptism in water, these were high and dry, safely elevated up on the old lake terrace in the forest, stored well off the ground under several layers of thick, silage plastic.

During this stage of development I lived on site in a constantly damp tent and did so for seven miserable, wet weeks. My first wonderful night under this tin roof in a far from completed house with only framing for walls was true and indescribable bliss. The constant loud noise of heavy rain cascading down onto a tin roof is sweet music to the ears of anybody that has spent just one cold, wet, sleepless night curled up under some old fallen rotten log in the forest, let alone having lived in a tent for seven weeks in a rainforest. Rain on a tin roof is a sound that transmits a secure knowledge to your brain that you will sleep dry tonight. I love that very special sound, it is a lullaby that puts me out like a light. As long as I know that the *Plantanic* down in the Bay is secure from the flooding, I will sleep like a baby.

Lester and Kurt returned, their batteries recharged and the three of us attacked the construction. My bygone joke of a planner had allowed a month to get the main shell of the house completed. Being a kit-set log home, I had budgeted on five men to help achieve this goal. I still believe this was a very achievable one, that is if I had the materials landed directly on site as planned. The three of us, Barry, Sugar and I, had to spend considerable un-budgeted and frustrating time, floating and carrying materials onto site with only Lester and son Kurt to construct the dwelling with what I could get to them in the way of building materials. In my planning I had decided to help motivate the builder, Lester, to construct the main house shell within the planned month by paying him a good award rate. Now, as a result of not having the planned labour around to assist, his allocated time for the project went right through the roof. This meant I had to fly him and son in and out for breaks from this building nightmare. The cost of his extra building time and his additional helicopter transport to and from Milford Sound added to my skyrocketing expenses.

Money I did not have at the time, nor had any hope of getting considering my financially risky situation. The worry and stress of this whole miserable mess was too incredible for me to describe properly, I had absolutely no option but to battle away the best I could and work it all out.

Yet another disastrous domino effect of the dead planning sheet was the arrival of my electricians who were faithfully following the stuffed up schedule. They arrived by helicopter as they were supposed to, on the day they were supposed to, but --- there was no house to wire up. Being a good bunch of blokes they spent a couple of days helping Lester, Kurt and me cart materials onto site and building. At a later date I had to fly them in yet again to wire the house.

THE PRESENT: Bill Smith has just made a noisy arrival in my Bay, as is his way. Beginning with a buzzing of my house with a low level fly-over in his blue and white Cessna which he pilots extremely well. (Bill Smith isn't his real name but to preserve his privacy I'll use this name.) He is now arriving back in the Bay on the water with his equally noisy jet boat after leaving his plane at the Martins Bay airstrip. The Smith family have a holiday retreat here, about 300 metres away through the forest which is the only other building in the Bay. Bill is a man of tremendous energy who attacks any project or endeavour with the full force of a Force-10 hurricane. My peace and tranquility in this little haven of mine is now completely shattered with the arrival of this storm front from the farmlands of the muddy south and will remain so while he is in residence in the now disturbed rainforest. I will have to relearn very quickly the art of sharing my little Bay and will resent his abrupt appearing for all of five minutes. When he leaves though I'll likely feel lonely for all of five days. He is a man that thrives on social interaction and communication being very blessed in those abilities. He is one of those persons that needs people around him constantly so he would have flown in with a group of his mates. Normally salt of the earth, farmer sort of people, good healthy minded, hard-working people, talked into flying over the mountainous Southern Alps probably at short notice with their friends Mr and Mrs Smith, to spend a couple of days R&R and mischief in their little holiday bach at Jamestown which is empty most of the year.

Any yarn about my existence here in the Bay would be incomplete without mention of the Smith family. They have been of tremendous assistance to my survival here. Their hospitality is legendary, they have filled my shrunken belly more than once and that is not me given to over-exaggeration, having been a little under nourished in my first couple of years here. A story of hunger for later. They have supplied me with work out on their farm when I needed money. They have helped in many other constructive ways for which I am very grateful. Of course, it is a two way street in here and I try to balance the books when I can which I have to admit is hard at times.

Having said all that, Bill and I do not always see eye to eye and I have learnt, through damage to my fragile male ego, not to enter into any challenging conservation with this very intelligent gentleman farmer from Southland, especially when he has been pouring the whisky which he does in Niagara-style portions being the natural host he is because I know I will lose any verbal contest should I take his bait and smoulder for days at the failure to defend my position. He likes to bait me, like a cruel, confident cat playing with a poor, half-dead defenceless mouse, mainly over my insistence that the freehold titles in here are worth good money. He argues the complete opposite with passion, trying to convince me of the foolishness of my thinking. The real, unspoken issue is Bill would like to keep this special secluded Bay in the Park very in-house, a private remote playground which is understandable from his perspective, whereas I am the young upstart from the working classes who has made these unique titles in the Park common knowledge to the masses and am greedy trying to make money from them as my life's passion. So it's a natural clash for us. It's not pistols at dawn stuff, more like rotten eggs and flour bombs thrown at opposing teams in some festival raft race, his very articulate tongue being his throwing arm which he uses with painful accuracy, normally in the form of biting sarcasm. On this thorny issue my solo raft will win the race, be it covered in rotten eggs and flour, I will raise the winner's trophy. Anyway, it's best to leave his juicy silken worms on his dangling hooks untouched, if I can. My discipline to this has improved greatly over the years with silence being my best defence for my frail ego when I sense he is baiting me.

I better go over and say, "Hi." In all probability I will have a very content stomach filled with fancy cheeses, yummy crackers and Wilsons Scotch Whisky by the time I stagger back along the beach and up my twisted forest trail in the dark. Finding my way back to my rainforest home in the dark is a skill born out of necessity living in this very simple place with no convenient shop to sell torch batteries nor any street lighting to guide my feet. I've become quite good at it, even when Bill has been doing the pouring.

TRAGEDY IN THE PYKE

Chapter Eight

A SAD MEMORY: On entering the Upper Hollyford in Brian's borrowed jet-boat, the first thing we notice is fruit floating down the current. An oddity in these swift blue waters with an apple here, an orange there, objects very conspicuous in a turbulent wilderness river in Fiordland. After entering the Pyke River from the Confluence we spotted a pack on the water's edge then shortly after, I saw Jem, one of ....'s employees, his jet-boat driver. He was in a sitting position amongst the large boulders on the north-west side of the river, the area overhung by moist, dark Fiordland forest that is clinging tightly to steep terrain on the valley side. He made no response to our noisy arrival, his position being very still, very quiet, very sombre, this did not look good at all.

.... nosed Brian's boat into the rocks, having to hold the boat's bow onto the dark rocks at right angles with the jet unit still engaged due to the swift river current of the Pyke. As I scrambled over the alloy bow to Jem, reality struck home in an ugly way. He was cold, lifeless and blue, skin deprived of oxidised blood. His front was covered in vomit, his mouth and nostrils had excreted a fine white froth, flecked with a little blood. I lifted his head from its resting position on his chest and felt his neck for a pulse, which I never found, but his neck was surprisingly warm to touch, the only part that was. Jem in fact had been dead quite a while but I didn't know this. The facts as I saw them at the time were a warm neck and the possibility life could still exist (which it didn't). You naturally give 110% to preserve life and that's what I did. I coached ....'s friend into giving CPR, a process she was initially very reluctant to do but braved through feminine emotions of sobs and tears to give a good effort while I gave mouth to mouth. In my time I've done a couple of St Johns' courses, a Padi Rescue Diver course, etc. but they can never prepare you properly for the real thing. The rubber dummy you work on is on a flat, raised sterile surface in some warm lecture room which makes it easy to tilt the rubber head back to keep the airways open. In the situation that Jem was in, however, it was far from straight-forward. I had to cradle him like a child, bracing my knees under his spine, to act like the legs of a table as we were wedged in between the huge, dark granite river boulders of the Pyke while my upper body lent over his chest to administer mouth to mouth. This being done so as to keep his head back and his airways straight, lungs open so that ....'s friend could do heart massage on his chest, all this wasn't as easy as it sounds. There is no horrible acid taste of stomach bile with a lecture room dummy after having to be a little sick over the rocks while working on him. Nor is there the unpleasant sound of air and water competing for lung space and airways in the rubber dummy. A rubber dummy is a lifeless object, not somebody you know. We worked on him for about twenty minutes. I gave my absolute best. Jeff Shanks arrived but could only land his machine on the opposite side of the river because of the rugged steep terrain on our side and the forest overhanging the river.

At some stage you realise that your actions are not having any productive effect. Jem was dead and had already been dead a considerable time. We were very much 'Johnny come latelies' in this unhappy, riverside drama.

The only place we could take him was the Pyke Lodge. The only way we could practically do this was to drape Jem's body over the bow of the jet-boat so we could negotiate the swift currents, rocks and logs of the Pyke. My emotions were blank and cold as I'm sure they were for the others. I remember thinking that Jem's body could easily have been a deer carcass draped over the bow as this was the most practical place to put them in a small boat in such wild country with swift, dangerous waters. Reality had come and gone to be replaced with a sad scene, the whole situation had an unreal motion picture feel to it, as if I was not part of events, just the audience to an unfolding sad drama.

At Pyke Lodge I hunted up a teaspoon of jam to mask the unpleasant acid taste still residing in my month. The place was understandably very sombre. There was no point hanging around, the police were on their way in via copter from Te Anau. Jeff offered me a ride back to Jamestown in his copter, flying low in the mountain valley hunting deer on the way, life goes on and he has a living to make as copters aren't cheap things to run.

A major regret of mine was making some very incorrect assumptions about the events that I was not there to witness. These assumptions were based on Jem's body position in the rocks and the vomit and froth on his chest, looking as if he had been pulled from the water but then left to choke on his own vomit. However, this was not the case as explained later by a doctor friend. I should have kept my silly mouth shut. Another of life's learning curves.

The hero of the day was a bloke called L.P. who was with Jem at the time of this jet-boat tragedy and who did his utmost to save Jem before going to seek help via the Pyke Lodge radio upstream. This was when we arrived on the unpleasant scene, finding Jem perched between the large grey boulders of the Pyke. L.P.'s actions to retrieve Jem's body from the river must have been a courageous act and he did his very best in very tough and challenging circumstances in attempting to revive him.

I wasn't given any opportunity to attend a funeral service which made me a little sad at the time. Two or three years after this tragic event I met Jem's father, a sad man who was visiting the area of his son's untimely death. He came in for a cup of tea with friends. I got the impression that he was unaware of my involvement, talking about the events as if I hadn't been party to them or had any knowledge of them. I did not change that impression.

THE STORY: A step back in time and my story continues. Lester and Kurt were now long gone, leaving me with a 'closed in' home with walls, windows and roof as per our arrangement. However, there was still GIB stopping, painting, tiling and fireplaces to be done inside and verandas outside before I could get a final building inspection and take guests. So I was left to battle on, alone in this special wilderness of tall trees, heavy rain and hungry, persistent sandflies.

There was heaps to do and lots to worry about, plus a new burden was thrown into my stewing cauldron of concerns. Those rundown lodges at the Pyke and Martins Bay with their communal bunk-rooms have changed hands, to people who have plans for the scenic Hollyford Valley and money to action them. Money that most of us cannot comprehend. Old money that has class and breeding to send sons to Christ's College with their old boys networking in New Zealand business. My plans of an upmarket, overnight experience for Milford Sound had trodden on the toes of some very fortunate and powerful people and I was blissfully unaware of the fact at the time as I was doing battle with the vice driven RMA. The Southland Angling Association had sent in a submission of opposition. Fair enough I supposed at the time but my aim was 'Wilderness overnighting from Milford Sound'. As for a fishing lodge! Well that was probably down the list a little in my project goals. Nor would a small three bedroom lodge have any major effect on the local fishing but I accepted that maybe this was one of the few genuine submissions not based on any human vice. It was not until I became aware of the new names floating on the Hollyford breeze that I recognised one as the only signatory in that submission of opposition from the Southland Angling Association. The name was one of the new owners! Boy, I realised in a hurry I couldn't compete with these guys. I was very much the poor kid playing in the rich kids' sand pit and I hadn't even known until I started building my little sandcastle in the Park.

The Fiordland National Park is the commercial playground of only a fortunate few, DOC being the unwitting booking agent, marketing arm and maintenance department for privately owned companies like "..... ....". But, I was in this mess up to my neck, I had no choice but to battle on all the same. There was opportunity to balance the scales (more than once) but I didn't. Not because I was practicing the Christian 'turn the other cheek' philosophy but because I was burnt out physically, mentally, financially and running scared of these guys, their contacts, their money and their greed. Doing my best to keep a low profile but still keeping going forward all the same.

I soon met this new driving force in the Valley and find the main man, a real nice, down to earth sort of bloke. But we both suffer from opposites in human vices. For me it was pure and utter jealousy of these rich kids and their play money rolling over all my hard work. For them, on the opposite end of the vice scale, was that green giant, wanting the Hollyford Valley to themselves, not wanting a poor kid having a commercial play in their sandpit. However, in the principal of good neighbourhood relationships, a very important commodity in the wilderness, we maintained a cordial, almost friendly contact, even helping each other out when things got tough out in the sticks when the situation required. Things in the Valley were about to change as the money poured in.

The work and battles continued in this solitary lifestyle of mine. I had to tidy up the dead mess of vegetation outside, just basic landscaping with the removal of tree stumps, logs, etc. There was a need to establish good drainage so water wouldn't pond around this rainforest home and yard. There was a need to stock up on firewood to cook the food and heat my water, house and me. There was a need to hunt for food to fill the belly. Everything seemed to involve some small battle. Nothing was easy here in the wilderness as it is out where you have easy access to such handy, wonderful things like diggers and bulldozers, electricity and hardware stores, food, freezers, regular income and helping hands. Life was nothing but several ongoing challenges, small, medium and large, doing my best to resolve them alone.

Tree stumps had to be removed. Not just baby tree stumps like those found in your domestic gardens, but rainforest granddaddies spreading a network of roots far and wide, grown slow and strong over the quiet centuries, cemented into and at one with the forest soils, binding, entwining, at one with neighbours of all shapes, sizes and kinds into an interwoven carpet of subterranean roots. One old man stump took me three days of frustrating effort just to get movement in its thick, age old, butt stump, doing so with a wee 1.5 tonne winch I was working with at the time to be followed by another day to finally break him free from his embrace with the earth.

The first process in all the tree stumps I removed was to dig to expose then cut the roots in a circle around the stump which meant clearing each individual root of soil and rock so I could swing the axe into clear wood and not blunt it on stone. This involved some work, time and persistence. As the trench got deeper, the axe became useless and was replaced with a small tomahawk then finally a blunt handsaw to get the tap roots under the tree butt. The second part of the process was winching the stump over, using all sorts of rope and tackle arrangements in the process, remembering all the double purchase techniques Dad had shown me, putting them to good use. Once its tight hold on the forest earth was finally broken, then it was winch and tumble the stump over in the rough direction you wanted it to go, then re-winch and tumble it again and again and again etc. etc. etc. until the stump was out of sight, hidden in the adjacent ferny forest floor. Such efforts left good size craters to be filled back in and levelled out.

Disturbing the dark humus forest floor created an irresistible message to the sandflies of blood with them being attracted to my movement, the dark colours and scent of newly exposed forest soil and, of course, my salty, sweaty scent. They would home in on these irresistible signals in their hundreds taking their fill of my blood, if they survived their dining experience which a lot didn't. So I would battle on with axe, shovel and winch making slow progress but progress all the same with these mighty tree stumps. At times, the ever present, ever persistent cloud of sandflies would win for a while and I would have to escape inside, to re-attack the job once I recovered my composure, energy and patience to their bite. A couple of stumps I tried burning out, but that was not very successful.

The fun of powergel to resolve such challenges was to come later, doing so on dark stormy nights to hide the noise.

Then there were a couple of old logs that had fallen years and years before, probably before I was born, to be cleaned up. All covered in an abundance of lush vegetation, drowning in moss, ferns and small shrubby plants, looking like small abrupt growing walls on the forest floor. We had built over one, it being under the front section of the house which is almost a storey above the forest floor. I wanted it out of the way so I could walk freely under the house and utilise the large storage area its removal would create. When cutting these old logs, I would first cut away the vegetation before digging away the moss and dark rich humus underneath, which would be several inches deep, to expose the rotten wood, then use the chainsaw to slice easily through the rotten, paper mache wood. This rotten, white sap wood was full of stagnate water like a sponge, making the chain on the saw spray tea-coloured water like a mini fountain until it hit the old heart timber deep inside, the blade then stopping abruptly. This heart wood was the complete opposite to the rotten sap wood. It was rock hard with a very deep, rich red colour, blunting your chainsaw chain in seconds and creating heat and steam in the process. It seemed to take a life time to cut just one ring section out of these old rotten logs, with several stops to re-sharpen the dull chain, before you could finally cart that section away. I worried away at those massive decomposing logs for months, an hour here, an hour there, until I finally got rid of them. It seemed to me I would spend more time working on getting that cheap chainsaw going than on productively cutting with it. Many a time I felt like taking the axe to the cheap, unreliable chainsaw with passion but didn't. The iron heart wood burnt like lumps of coal in the kitchen stove which was a plus.

Any camp of permanence in the rainforest needs good drainage to stop a mess of mud. An unwanted commodity in a rainforest camp so I dug trenches, deep trenches, breaking through the root layer to the soft easy digging of the ancient lake gravels. Each time it rained, which obviously happens quite a bit around here, I would duck outside and make a mental note of the areas of ponding water to resolve later. I sloped a large area of the backyard to drain freely down one side of the house and away down the terrace towards the lake. Once I got good drainage in the back yard, I laid down some drainage pipe then covered the ground in black plastic to stop the weeds and then a layer of coarse gravel to keep boots and feet clean even in the downpours. Bear in mind that at this stage I was working with a shovel, pick and a wheelbarrow with a wooden wheel. Over time the back yard tidied up really well. It could rain for days on end and I could go under the house, grab a handful of dirt and it would be dusty in feel, filtering easily down between the fingers. There are not many huts in wet Fiordland that you can say that about.

Firewood was another learning curve. Without money and any regular supply I had to be very frugal with my generator and the precious diesel it consumed. I

Firewood is a constant chore.

Firewood drying under verandas.

needed heaps of firewood to keep things warm and cosy inside. In the rainforest you need to keep any firewood off the ground, to stop moss, mould, fungi and rot. You need to get it under shelter as well and it needs ventilation through it to dry properly. You are wasting your time burning wet timber, it doesn't give off good heat and clogs your flues quickly. I learnt that once a tree is down in the forest it is best to ring and split it when it is wet and fresh before getting it under cover as soon as possible, otherwise a black mould would grow which over time would make the timber dozy. Ringing, chopping and stacking was work I sort of enjoyed. You could switch the brain off from the worries of life and work on automatic.

There was a challenge with communication. That is, I had none! In fact it would take almost two years before I got my own HF radio. In the short term the problem was solved by the generosity of the Smiths, Bill being quite happy, even insistent, that I use the HF radio in their bach to make calls out to their Southland homestead being the receiving station. This also became a sort of safety net for me, not that I felt the need for one, but it was to help put minds at rest out in the outside world. Touching base now and again, letting my parents know that Charlie hadn't got mis-mothered in the wilderness, broken a leg, got sick, etc., etc., etc.

Financially, I had a major ray of sunlight with loving parents stepping in and giving me a loan to service all the unplanned debt I found myself in. Not good on my silly male ego having gone from being responsible for a multi-million dollar venture at Stewart Island and establishing my own finances at a young age, to even being able to start such a project in the first place, to then falling flat on my face and having to go to my parents cap in hand asking for money for a failed venture that they had in good wisdom advised me against. No bank in their right mind would consider such a loan, but my concerned, loving parents did, saving my bacon in the process. I was still, though, operating in a fool's paradise financially. I had given so much to the project, and was still giving my all, so I could not walk away from it. This loan covered my unplanned and unwanted debt to other parties in this nightmare fiasco but that was about it. I still had a battle to complete the project.

The only other memories of that first winter were having to adjust to not having electricity. No electric lighting in the long winter nights, of having to go to bed early, to read a Wilbur Smith by a flickering candle perched on a wooden stool beside the bed. There was no TV, video, radio to chew up the long, dark hours on the winter evenings. Amazingly the body seemed to naturally adjust to this extra sleeping time. There was a frozen header tank in the ceiling at one stage which required having to run a tilly lamp under it for half a day to get the water flowing in my pipes again.

Spring came around again and so did the influx of the white-baiters to Martins Bay. Dale gave me good advice, telling me to keep out of the politics of these fishers of bait out at Martins Bay. This I was more than happy to do having had more than my share of vice-driven conflict. The baiting community and its politics is like the Tasman Sea, sometimes oily calm and flat with everybody getting on a treat. At other times it's suffering a wild storm, a tempest of angry emotions tossed back and forth between the three main family groups. The weather, sea and white-baiters are changeable overnight. Jamestown Bay is far enough away to be of no real concern to me. It helps that I'm not a white-baiter and I got to know all three groups without taking any sides.

Summer ticks by with hammer, shovel, axe, pick and rifle in hand. The Smiths came in and out at various times with friends, introducing new faces and names to me, adding a little fat into my diet and sometimes throwing entertainment into my life with their holiday antics. Dale visited from time to time, leaving me when he departed a little wiser about surviving in this remote place.

Autumn came and there were stags roaring in the forest and hills behind home. Time had flown. I had started in November in the spring of 1995, summer had fled passed along with the autumn and winter. The spring of 96 revolved around to summer and autumn of 97. I was now headed towards my second winter in the wilderness of North Fiordland.

CONCLUDING NOTE: Jem's sad demise was not the first in this mountainous wilderness, nor will it be the last.

I was kayaking home from an outing down at the south end of Martins Bay to get a feed of paua, a rich, green-fleshed shellfish which sometimes I collect to have a change from the lean venison diet of mine. On entering Lake McKerrow from the Lower Hollyford I noted, in the distance, a Squirrel helicopter leaving Jamestown Bay. When I arrived home there was a hand-written note on my dining room table from the local Te Anau bobby, asking if I could shed any light on a body found at Big Bay of an unknown male, the note giving a quick description. It rang bells for me. A couple of days earlier a mature solo male tramper off the Hollyford Track had popped in for a cuppa. A nice sort of bloke who indicated he was involved in the medical field and was from the Wellington area. He was well equipped and I could tell by the nature of his gear that he had done a bit of tramping in his time. His destination was Martins Bay and possibly Big Bay. All this I radioed back through to the police via the DOC radio at Te Anau office.

I later learnt that he was indeed my friendly visitor having come to grief in a creek called the McKenzie which is at the southern end of Big Bay, very close to where Dale lives. Like a lot of Fiordland creeks, when it's not raining you can cross it without getting your knees wet and sometimes even crossings without getting socks wet are possible. But, when it has been raining and in flood you need to be careful and very respectful of its mean currents. Graham Mitchell, a part-time local from the north end of Big Bay had been out for a wander along the beach, probably out for a hunt. He noticed a pack at the water's edge and went to investigate, sadly discovering that it was still attached to the poor owner. Modern tramping packs have fancy waist and chest belts to help take the load of the pack on the hips, etc. It is worth noting that when crossing any creek or river, it's always a good idea to undo such strapping so if things do go wrong you can still swim without the burden of a pack tied to your body.

Jamestown Bay's local Hokuri creek has also claimed lives. Like Dale Hunter's McKenzie creek, the Hokuri can be crossed most of the time without too much trouble and I have done so hundreds of times. However, back in the 1960s two girls were killed crossing this water course, the body of only one being found. As for the other, all they found was her pack. The relatives got together and funded the three-wire walkway that now crosses this river further upstream. It adds another twenty or so minutes to the walk so it is only used by trampers when the Hokuri is in flood. Even then some opt out as three-wire walkways aren't everyone's cup of tea.

THE PRESENT: Today there were porpoises in my wee Bay. Apparently Lake McKerrow is only one of a small few fresh water lakes around the globe that hosts these lovely sea-based mammals. These very playful creatures cross the Hollyford Bar from the Tasman every two to three weeks but have no real set timetable to their fresh water visits. They spend up to a day playing in the lower Hollyford River and Lake McKerrow before heading back over the bar to open sea. I'm told that they are the same pod that plays with the tourist boats in Milford Sound. The theory is that the fresh water visits help them deal with pesky marine parasites on their skin. Normally there is a big pod but once there was a slow moving, solitary animal in the lake for several days which was very odd. Due to its large size I'm guessing it was old and probably unwell.

I recently met a lovely group of adults and young girls tramping through the Valley, the young, energetic ladies doing the Hollyford trek to go towards points for their Duke of Edinburgh Award, all coming in for a cuppa. I offered them all a dinghy trip down the lake then down the lower Hollyford to Martins Bay, a scenic trip most don't see when tramping the Hollyford. On the way down the lower Hollyford River we met the visiting pod coming upstream the opposite way, much to the unabated delight and eye-popping awe of my young passengers. These huge creatures came right up beside my small boat and circled it, almost within touching distance, twisting on their sides so both parties could gaze at each other through the clear water, surfacing and playing around my boat and the very excited young ladies onboard. The day was beautiful, so still and quiet we could hear clearly the porpoises distinctive happy clicks echoing through the hollow hull of my vessel, communicating unknown comments to each other. That is once the adults got the excited teenage screams of delight to abate and listen carefully to that beautiful and very unique sound of nature. Excited teenage girls can make a lot of noise, very rare sounds to the ears of a self-imposed bush hermit.

Writing about these lovely, intelligent, playful mammals (the dolphins, not teenage girls) and their visits to the waters of my wilderness hideaway seems a nice way to finish what is otherwise a very sad chapter of loss.

| Chapter Nine | # ALONE IN THE WILDERNESS |

A MEMORY: I'm in my second winter here in the wilds of Fiordland, I haven't seen or spoken to a single soul for three months. By this winter of 1997 I had learnt that this is a very quiet time of year at the end of Hollyford's 'Demon Trail'. However, there are now human voices down in my little Bay, echoing clearly up through the quiet forest to my alert, attuned ears. This is suddenly a tremendous and scary novelty to me so I'm off and down to have a nosey at this noisy invasion of my peaceful wilderness solitude. Obviously it's trampers coming off the Demon Trail. There have been some passing through in winter, leaving their telltale signs of fresh footprints on the sandy beach of my little Bay, but they have been very few and far between as I haven't seen or heard them in their passing, my place being mostly obscured by the thick rainforest from the beach and Hollyford Track unless you are looking for it. Most trampers miss my hideaway in the forest, they are too busy observing their leather bound boots in their final league journey of the Hollyford Track concluding at Martins Bay. Too focused on pounding feet to notice my log home sitting up between the podocarps to their right. I hide and watch these invaders in their trespassing, secure behind thick protective ferns in the forest undergrowth. Hidden in the knowledge that most don't see the forest for the trees and that they are not on the lookout for some weird, skinny, bush hermit in holey, thread-bare clothes intensely watching their passing. They tramp noisily past like a herd of elephants on migration, completely unaware of their intrusion, nor of my presence and predatory gaze. They are soon passed, forever gone. I'm back to the comfort and security of my silence and solitude.

Suddenly I become very aware of the seriousness of what I have just done. Three months of not seeing or talking to anybody and I hide!? A shocking realisation that it's not healthy to be this way. When the house behind me in the vine-covered trees finally gets that long awaited Compliance Certificate to take paying guests I then can't operate very well if I hide from potential clientele. That is pure madness. Deep inside I know it is not good for me mentally to shun human contact in this way, no matter how comfortable it feels to do so. After all, we were designed to be social beings.

I have heard people talk of hermits in wild places and the 'bush sickness' that afflicts them, where you get so used to being alone that when someone does visit, you resent the invasion of your space, peace and security. The truly silly thing is that you are also tremendously lonely as a result and it's a horrible rotten contradiction to be in. To be very lonely but avoiding social interaction. We can be weird beings at times. I probably would make a good case study for some student's psychology thesis.

This situation gives me a real jolt so the next time someone passes my forest domain I force myself down onto the beach. This time I am visible to the approaching trampers, not hiding in the thick foliage of crown ferns. I ask them in for a cuppa which is a novelty for the passing trampers and a real effort for me with sweating palms and pounding heart but it works out really well. Over time it becomes very natural to do so and it has become known on the track via the DOC hut books and wagging tongues that you should pop in and have a cuppa with 'Charlie' at Jamestown Bay when passing. Now I really enjoy these visits and the social interaction they give me, meeting some really nice 'down to earth' people. It's also handy as some stay as paying guests while others talk about my place hidden in the rainforest of Fiordland. A mini form of backpacker networking without heaps of cost in expensive marketing. It makes the free cuppa and tooth rotting chocolate, raisin fudge a small price to pay. It works out well considering the situation.

Sometimes we have to break unhealthy moulds in our lives to grow. I have a lot more to break yet as I find I naturally slip back into the old comforts and false securities of human isolation if I allow myself to.

THE STORY: Food was becoming another challenge. Within two years I could draw my knuckles down my rib cage and feel the bones connect as my knuckles moved down and racked each rib in my boney cage, not that I ever had a Mr Atlas frame. Nor did I ever run right out of food, but my pantry became a little bare and my diet became very, very basic, revolving around the simple basics of rolled oats and venison. Both being cheap commodities out in the sticks but not necessarily supplying all the nutrients your body needs to stay healthy and keep starvation at bay. There was absolutely no money available for the luxury of getting a regular food supply flown in. What I had in the pantry was it and I had to make it last the distance. Basically I lived in here full-time for a year and a half before I started a six-monthly re-supply of my walk-in pantry. So those important nutrients and vitamins found in fruit and vegies weren't much in my diet during that eighteen months.

Now and again Dale Hunter would pop over the Hollyford Bar in his dented alloy fishing boat from his Big Bay home to spend the night, bringing with him a cabbage or even watercress which grows like a weed around his hut. Sometimes there was even a couple of crayfish or paua as well to dine on that evening. I enjoyed these visits from my coastal neighbour and the greens he introduced to my poor diet. At other times the Smiths would be in at their holiday retreat in the Bay, usually with a load of friends, and when they departed they would generously leave behind their perishable items for me such as butter, eggs, fruit and vegies as it is not worth the effort and expense to fly such things back out. On these occasions it was like Christmas, such simple things being new luxuries to my meagre existence out in the sticks. But most of the time it was surviving off the land. That meant hunting.

When I started in here I had a touch of male arrogance about my hunting abilities. "Yes," I had shot a few deer, probably more than most, but "No," never had to rely on my hunting abilities to feed myself. Like any male that does a bit of hunting or fishing there tends to be a hint of ego about his abilities. I was no different, although I probably wouldn't have said so back then. Before living in here the success or failure of a hunt wasn't really a big issue as there was always food back in the camp or on the barge. There was always money available to buy tucker and, of course, a shop to buy food from. The hunt was for the experience of being in the bush and mountains, for the adventure of the stalk, for the resulting adrenaline rush when you got onto an animal, for the ego and tale of success back at camp if you got it, for the freezer to fill at home and for the meat to give away to friends. It was very different in here and initially I found that I wasn't that great at it and the ego and tummy shrunk as a result.

After having quite a few learning curves which came with each passing experience and each passing year, I got a little bit wiser, a little bit better and the senses started to develop and that was the trick of bush hunting, developing the senses. In our modern, comfortable, sterile societies our basic senses of sight, smell and hearing have become somewhat lazy, adapting to the modern environment we are in, brought up with, schooled in, work in. Our sense of sight, for example, has become very used to just one dimension of depth, flat surface observation such as a TV screen, a newspaper, a computer, etc. We have lost a part of our multi-depth perception or vision. This is especially noticeable in city folk who 'can't see the trees for the forest. In thick rainforest, you learn to look through the vegetation to see shape and movement otherwise you miss the action and a lot of interesting stuff hiding in the forest. It's a skill and sense anybody can tune into over time, but first you have to have patience to train your vision. Most don't, finding the thick forest too impregnable to see through, too intimidating with its dense encompassing feel, too much like hard work, preferring those easy hunting experiences out in the open country.

Over the years I have taken people out for a wander in the rainforest and have seen deer, pointed them out to my company and they just don't see them until the animal takes off, even then some miss the moment. Any hunter worth his meat will tell you, it's way too late by that stage. You want to get your shot off before they take flight. I am reluctant to take people out for a bush stalk now as I find such experiences very frustrating. Some people tend to have a romantic notion of a hunt in the rainforest but the reality of Fiordland's wet rainforest normally means getting wet, cold and dirty as you move through, over and under the living and dead vegetation. Plus, the combination of having more than one person's scent and noise adds to the failure rate of getting onto anything of note. After a few hours the romantic novelty soon wears off for them and they tend to want to be back on the track or open river flat that doesn't have moisture-laden vegetation soaking through their clothes, doesn't have supplejack/kareao vines, bogs and fallen, decomposing logs obstructing their every move for hours on end.

River flats and open ground are a different story and can produce easy animals to knock over at the right times. Even then, some people still don't see the animals

Hunting, Lake Alabaster – Mount Tutoko in the background.

In the backyard with me holding a Stag head.

until its way too late. Their vision just isn't used to picking up the animal's shape and colour, their sight only really clicks into gear when triggered by the movement of the animal.

To a lesser degree it is a similar situation with the other senses of smell and hearing. The trick with those senses is not so much your own ability but to be totally aware that the deer's ability to hear and smell far out-performs yours. Be paranoid about it as 99 times out of a 100 it's your scent or noise in the forest that pre-warns the animal to the danger. The deer has a sense of smell over 200 times stronger than our own, so you are wasting your time hunting with the breeze on your back, you always hunt into it so that your predatory, meat eating scent isn't carried into those large, hairy, herbivore nostrils. You always go as quietly as you possibly can. In the forest the best way to do that is bare foot. Some may laugh but it works for me. With boots you can't feel those noisy dry twigs under foot and, being barefoot, your sensitive under-soles not only feel those dry twigs but force you to go a lot, lot slower as it is impatience through moving way too quickly in the forest which loses a lot of deer. Finally, intense concentration is a must. Throw in regular breaks to refocus the mind so you don't day dream. It is during those moments when you always spook and lose your animal because your mind drifted away to another place while your body is just going through the slow, careful and automatic motions of a stalk.

For a very lonely celibate bush hermit that wandering mind tends to go to an obvious destination of all celibate men. The torturous, unwanted thoughts of a flirtatious women with lovely long legs, welcoming silky warm thighs encompassing moist budding rose petal delights which for time in memorial has driven poor celibate males mad in want. It is a battle of huge proportions to keep a lonely male's mind away from such thoughts. I know it's very unhealthy on my mind, body and soul to torture myself with such unavailable female comforts in the wilds of Fiordland but I am human and sometimes I lose that age old male battle so I hope the reader forgives me for my short-comings and frankness.

Anyway, other helpful factors to a successful hunt or stalk is becoming familiar with the deer's natural habits, time of activity (these being dawning day and closing dusk) and rest periods (middle of the day). Knowledge of the terrain helps, the lie of the land and the watercourses, the density of forest whether it's open or closed, also important is time of day (and sometimes time of year) that you are stalking. Where the clearings are, the best route, method and times to approach those forest glades. And, if you are doing the noble and time-honoured profession of poaching the freehold blocks out at Martins Bay or across the lake, knowing when the part-time owners are not in residence is very important. Put all that together and you start to knock over the animals, to put meat on the table, to fill the belly.

All that though took a while for me to get down to an art. When I started I was only knocking over about one animal in every three or four that I actually spooked in the forest because I didn't see them in time or I was too noisy or I wasn't concentrating hard enough, etc. There would be hunts during which I never got onto any animals at all because they probably heard and smelt me miles away.

These learning curves were hard on the body because it was normally in need of the energy of the iron rich meat I was hunting. Now it's about one in two animals. That is for every two animals I actually see in the green mess of bush I will get one.

HISTORICAL NOTE: Hunger has played a part in my life in here but I was not the first to go without in this remote wee Bay. In September 1872, William Henry Homer made a notable entry into Queenstown being described on his arrival as "a moving bundle of rags, starches and bruises." He brought news of a famine at Jamestown.

Shipping had stopped coming over the evil Hollyford Bar with the result supplies in the fledgling settlement had become exhausted. Food had run out and it was brave William who was selected to cross the mountains to get help. This he did, battling first the dense rainforest and dangerous rivers of these deep green valleys, then the snow bound mountains to cross the Southern Alps before he descended down the other side, through open beech forest, finally making his way out to Queenstown with his dramatic news of starvation in this little Bay.

On the 27 October 1872 the Wallace made a successful crossing of the Hollyford Bar bringing with her 'five tons of flour, five tons of potatoes, one ton of sugar and fifteen boxes of tea,' which brought relief to those settlers here at Jamestown. With challenges like that, people started moving on from this pretty place. By 1879 this little, quiet Bay was reported as "deserted."

THE STORY: I was beginning to learn to fend for myself on the food front but mentally I was starting to get pretty down by this stage. The project had become one battle after another, after another, after another, there seemed to be no end to them. Sometimes in dark weather patterns I would stop work altogether for days and try to escaping the mind from life's worries with a novel. This gave short term releases from all the challenges in life but didn't solve them once the novel was finished. In my small library stacked up in the dining room corner are several books which have been re-read up to three times in the last seven years. At the time I was fighting dark thoughts of failure, dark thoughts of giving up, dark thoughts towards those who were wanting to destroy my project. Just plain old, dirty, nasty, dark thoughts. Dark thoughts feed and gain strength on dark thoughts, soon everything loses its taste, colour, passion, there is no vibrancy to life. Life doesn't seem worth the effort and the rifle beside the wood range promises a fool's release. Such thoughts would have brought me to destruction if it wasn't for the uncomfortable move towards a faith in God. Not just a vague childhood interest I had in the possibly of God's existence but a deep down certainty that God really does exist. This parabolic shift in my thinking towards genuinely believing in God's (Christ's) existence didn't come easily, nor was it like a bolt of lightning, it was a slow, dawning process that took a couple of years to solidify in my mind and soul. In the process reversing many of my past attitudes and dark thoughts which at a time would have seemed inconceivable, even laughable. It mainly came about because of science, the medium that normally is used to destroy God's existence. Becoming aware of some basic scientific facts, information which we don't learn about in schools because it really rocks the applecart of evolutional thinking and the concept that God was not necessary to create life in the beginning. These facts bring about way too many tough questions for the so-called wisdom of men and science to answer, so it's put in the 'too hard basket', sometimes even hidden and glossed over. Over time I applied these new understandings to what I saw in this very special, living, breathing and vibrant rainforest of Fiordland that surrounds me and it started to make real and logical sense. Seeing design and purpose in nature hit home.

But there still is some dark water to flow under my very unstable bridge yet, a couple of years to pass before I get onto that topic in this story. There is a bit of bleeding to be done yet and that is meant in a very literal sense!

DEER EXPERIENCES: Some hunting experiences from over the years to finish this chapter. Hunting can involve a lot of physical energy and great distance can be covered in your forest wanderings. One day I got up early before dawn of day and hunted from Jamestown Bay to Hokuri, then up to the Hokuri forks, then half way up the Sara Hills, contouring around them, then headed roughly west, back towards the lake. This movement took the whole day and I didn't see or hear a thing. Physically and mentally I was very drained.

I could just make out the calm, blue waters of McKerrow between the trees when I got onto a hind and her yearling, both completely unaware of my presence. However, I wasn't able to make a good chest shot because of the thick vegetation. They soon sensed that something wasn't quite right in their forest domain and I had to let fly at close quarters. One good shot is all you need to drop a deer, this time it required five hurried shots which meant a reload as I only hunt with three in the magazine. Two of these rounds hit home so I had meat to cart home. I was grateful for it but very tired and not looking forward to lugging the animal home, which was a few kilometres away. So I gutted the deer, made a pack out of her by locking her forequarter shanks through her hindquarter shanks, heaved her onto my back and with my bloody and dripping burden battled towards the lake which was about seventy yards away. When I broke through the forest onto the beach I was pleasantly shocked to find myself standing smack in the middle of Jamestown Bay! I had shot the deer no more than 300 metres from home after having spent the whole day and a lot of energy looking for one.

I have had many a frustrating experience of being incredibly close to a deer without even knowing it before the deer bolts, normally giving me a big fright in the process, leaving me very gutted at the lost opportunity especially when that's the only deer I have seen all day. They have an incredible knack of being able to blend into their environment, which I suppose is natural when you're a wild animal avoiding a predator. Over the years I started to switch on to them.

A close encounter came about when up the north-facing terraces of Mt Webb. During the day I had spooked a couple of young stags. The area showed a lot of good signs of deer droppings and fresh prints. The bush wasn't too thick and was reasonably open to hunt through, although there were a lot of dry twigs under my feet, slow going for soft under-soles. A large, fallen log was my target for a stop to listen and rest the brain, as you cannot keep up the necessary intense concentration without such breaks. I was about two yards away from the log, about to climb onto its moss covered surface, when I saw a branch move directly on the other side. "No way could that be a deer," it was just too close! My noise and scent would have given me away metres back, but the branch moved yet again, with some vigour and, sure enough, it was a stag, sitting there, scratching an itch, rubbing his neck on that dead branch. I duly shot him only a couple of yards away from the tip of my barrel.

A similar situation happened with a 'yearling' in thick forest. When I saw it I thought it was dead because I was so unnaturally close to it and it was lying on the ground but then I noticed its chest moving and an ear flicker.

The biggest fright from a deer came about one still, quiet Fiordland night. I awoke to a pesky possum playing on my veranda, a very distinctive noise. I grabbed the torch which I knew had nearly dead batteries and the wee .22 rifle. To avoid wasting the precious batteries (no shops in the wilds to buy more) I left the torch off, until I really needed it to spotlight this introduced mammal for the cross hairs of my scope. I moved carefully into the bush, barefoot and naked except for my undies, going very, very slowly, one felted footstep at a time, heading toward the noisy possum in the forest which had since vacated my veranda to the forest floor. It seemed to take forever but I sensed by the twigs he was breaking on the forest floor that I was close enough to illuminate the scene and deal with this little furry pest. I was not greeted with the expected small commotion as I treed a possum pest, instead it was a huge mass of frightening noise and red hide movement of more than one deer vacating the area. The bush seemed to come alive around me, I had no chance at a shot, I was just too shocked about the whole event to act, not that a wee .22 would have made any difference anyway. The possum got away.

My easiest deer was shot off the front veranda, but I'll leave that story for later.

THE PRESENT: Trampers have just left after a cup of tea and a feed on my sugary chocolate and raisin fudge. Over the years I have lived in here, the numbers tramping the Hollyford Valley have increased dramatically, mainly due to the money thrown at marketing by the new kids on the block down at Martins Bay. Some days I'll have several parties pop in for a cuppa and munch on my melted sugar, butter, raisins and cocoa, other days none visit. Like all things in here it's either a feast or famine. I either have plenty of fruit and vegies or none, plenty of ammo or none, heaps of hanging meat or none, heaps of fuel for the outboard or none, heaps of visitors on one day and not get any for days on end. Such is the way of life here on the Hollyford Track.

Chapter Ten

THE HOLLYFORD RIVER

DESCRIPTIVE NOTE: Fiordland is a vast, mountainous region that abruptly rises out of the sea, a barrier to interrupt a strong westerly airflow. An airflow abundantly rich with evaporated moisture stolen from the Tasman in its passing. As this cloud of Tasman hits the mountain barrier of the Southern Alps, it is forced upwards, cools and condenses back into water and it rains and, boy can it rain. Dusky Sound, mid-Fiordland has the second highest rainfall on the planet. Water is a commodity that Fiordland is famous for. There are hundreds of lakes and thousands of rivers and streams either cascading down steep, rocky mountain walls or tumbling through rocky gorges or just meandering quietly through lush, overhanging rainforest. Water in abundance in this wonderful moist region.

The mighty Hollyford River starts life as a small mountain stream, a new-born infant, its pure waters from the snow melt of the Darren Mountains. It becomes an active child in the rocky cleft of the Gertrude Valley, very close to where the Homer Tunnel has been driven through for access to Milford Sound. It grows into a restless, angry teenager cascading down the upper valley section, giving tourists on the Milford Road an example of a very scenic and turbulent mountain stream. Maturity takes hold as it becomes a young adult proceeding down the Hollyford Valley and away from the preying tourist eye where it grows into a river as hundreds of tributaries add their contribution. As the gradient of the valley lessons, it ages yet again, becoming a more sedate river that meanders through a very picturesque, forested, valley floor. All under the watchful eye of a snow capped and rocky Mount Madeline, a mother of a mountain that dominates this pretty valley.

A marriage takes place with another mature river, the Pyke, at a place called the Confluence where the Pyke loses her name in the binding partnership with the Hollyford. The river continues on its course down the valley until it empties into the long and narrow Lake McKerrow. My home lake. It leaves this lake and is now called by some the Lower Hollyford River, aged to a graceful, elderly lady with a wide body of water, long slow curves and a sedate moving current. The Hollyford ends its life after a long scenic journey from the snow bound mountains to the sea at the Hollyford Bar. Binding into the Tasman Sea, to be reborn anew in the never ending circle of evaporation and condensation.

THE STORY: Money was very tight, nothing new for my meagre existence in this wilderness outpost. Yet another belt tightening exercise meant selling my big

Winter wilderness river (Hollyford) in which I floated down the building materials.

plastic boat to release some much needed capital. A boat which by the time I sold it had rested on the bottom of Lake McKerrow three times, hence the name *Plantanic*. All sinkings involved battles of salvage, one of which I've already written about. The other two sinkings just similar depressing stuff, cold wet affairs with endless winches, posts and ropes. In its place I down-sized and purchased a yellow plastic dinghy 3.4 metres in length. The intention was to float this yellow tub down the Hollyford taking along the veranda timber, handrails, balustrades etc. I needed to finish the veranda to get the final inspection by the authority before I could legally accommodate anybody. Not a good option floating materials down the Hollyford River. In fact a very, very bad one but the only economic one available to me at the time. With no fat on the budget for the copter or boat charters to get the materials or little yellow boat onto site I had no other choice. If I wanted to keep the project moving forward I had to act. It was always my battle to keep this endeavour going forward in any way I could.

I packed my tramping gear into a big, black, plastic barrel, bought at Todd's, with a screw lid top, buoyant, strong and water tight. This same barrel now sits atop a Kamahe tree, an alternative water tank. Into this black barrel went my pack as well as my wet suit from Royalty Salmon diving days. I grabbed Dad's trusty old seagull outboard. It had given decades of reliable service being an early model of outboard, very simple in design with an old fashioned pull rope start to fire a single piston petrol engine. I was thinking it would act as a great auxiliary at Jamestown and be of assistance in getting me and materials down the nearly 18 kilometres of lake. I grabbed my old, fully wooden Lee Enfield rifle, a real collector's piece with trench sights and ammo lock. These trusty historic rifles weren't mass produced until the 1914 -18 War yet this was factory stamped as 1912 so I treasured its rare uniqueness. I grabbed my hammer action shotgun, yet another collector's piece, thinking both firearms would make great wall pieces in the lodge to be.

After a night at Murray Gunn's Camp, which is part way down the Hollyford Valley not far from the road end, I set off. It was wintertime with stable weather patterns and a low Hollyford River. Ideal conditions for boating for those who know what they are doing. I thought I did, male ego making its appearance yet again, but in reality I was just fooling myself. I did have plenty of experience rowing dinghies around sea cages full of King Salmon but absolutely none rowing a grossly overloaded dinghy down a fast flowing, wilderness river. They always seem to manage well in the Walt Disney wilderness adventure movies. For me I was in for yet another unpleasant learning curve which involved three very physically demanding and uncomfortably hard days.

Murray Gunn, a local identity and son of Davy Gunn who features prominently in the Hollyford and Martins Bay history, had given me a warning to watch out for the log jams. Very good advice. Now to describe what a log jam is, it is a build-up of logs, branches, twigs, etc., all residue remnants of bygone floods, of forest trees that once stood tall and proud on the banks of the Hollyford, now broken river flotsam. Such dead log jams tend to accumulate on the outside of the river bends, the current flowing through, under and over the mass of broken, rainforest vegetation. From a casual glance they look relatively harmless but in fact are not. They act as giant sieves, becoming river traps, the force of water and the unmovable mass of vegetation catching and sometimes holding the unwary under, depriving them of air and life. I knew all this but I didn't give them the respect they were due and paid for it.

No sooner had I got away from the quiet and deserted road end and into the fast flowing wilderness river than I soon realised that not only was I grossly overloaded but also very unbalanced in my boat packing. The result, the hull of my little yellow boat was not trim in the water, that is it did not sit evenly in the current making steerage with oars very difficult. I re-beached my vessel on the gravel bank and tried repacking again with not much joy. Twenty six lengths of 4x2 timber was the problem, it doesn't pack well in a small dinghy and never would.

Away I went once more, slowly getting the hang of things, managing to get about four kilometres down the river, when in a lapse of concentration I got caught starboard side on to a small log jam. The force of the current caused the port side and currently the up-current side of the boat to dip down. Once water went over the port edge it was all over. The sheer quantity and powerful force of the fast flowing Hollyford River caused a very abrupt flip. Motion seemed to slow down, my only conscience thought was grabbing the plastic barrel for floatation and getting my frail body out of the situation. Desperately trying to get away from the perils of this nasty and dangerous river obstacle as fast and with as much physical energy as I could muster.

This approach worked extremely well as I am still here to tell the tale. I safely reached the bank on the opposite side from the log jam and took stock of things. It wasn't a pleasant situation. It was a shady section of wilderness river, the towering mountain mass denying the depths of the valley any winter sun, winter's frost still lying in the shadows of the brushes and boulders on the river side. I was wet, very, very cold and a little shaken by the turn of events. My little yellow dinghy was now upside-down, having popped up from under the log jam downstream from it, held in the strong current by the bow rope which was entangled in the offending log jam. I could see my veranda timber floating away down the river in a disorganised, undisciplined array along with all the other bits and pieces of flotsam, my lost cargo. Dad's seagull outboard was history, my historic Lee Enfield rifle was history, etc. Items lost to the river's gravel bottom, a very sad tale.

It didn't take long before I realised I needed to react to my present predicament very quickly, to salvage not only my property but myself as well. Lean living in the bush meant a very lean body with little fat to insulate me from the winter cold and boy did I feel that cold. The combination of the shock of the situation and the cold winter water of the Hollyford meant I had the shakes badly, violent, uncontrollable shakes. A healthier person would probably have fared much better but for me the shakes possessed my whole body. I needed to act very quickly or lose the ability to work my body, especially much needed hands and fingers.

The first priority was to open that plastic barrel and put on my wetsuit then dive straight back into the cold river to salvage my boat before the cold made me incapable of such action. Although this was a very unpleasant thing to be doing, it wasn't too dangerous as the boat was now below the log jam, down current, a blessing. Once back ashore with my sorry, upside-down boat in tow, I then had to bush bash my way down the river side, to salvage what gear I could, namely the oars. I was a 'boat up the creek without a paddle' as the saying goes. I found an oar, but only ever the one, another blessing as I now at least had a paddle for steerage. No rollicks to be found, which wasn't surprising, considering that they were made of metal and foolishly not attached to my stricken vessel.

All this activity of physical exertion meant my wetsuit was soon working as designed with my blood circulation warming the water trapped between my skin and neoprene. Life was improving.

Getting back upstream to my beached boat, the next mission was to get to the Hidden Falls hut before night fall. Wetsuits are not designed for frosty nights on cold river banks in the winter wilderness. The process for boating was now completely different. It was to now paddle not row, making cross current movements to the inside of each and every bend of this meandering river until the water was shallow enough to hop into the water and pull my boat around the inside of the bends, thus avoiding those horrible log jams on the outside of the bends. This worked very well but chewed through the time. In the process I was also able to salvage all my precious timber from my river mishap, a piece here, a piece there, etc. Yet another blessing as I only had enough timber, neatly calculated, to finish the job at home. I got to the hut well after nightfall with no guiding light or torch which was quite a feat. No dry matches, no candle, no food, but I did have a dry sleeping bag filled with an old fashioned woollen singlet, long johns and socks. I hung the wetsuit in the hut so it wouldn't freeze overnight and hopped into bed feeling out-right sorry for myself. Wintertime, not a soul around, just me and the mice in the hut. The first company they had had for a while.

The next morning dawned with clean, crisp, frosty weather. I was soon involved putting on a very cold and wet wetsuit and heading back down to the Hollyford to reach my boat. Away I went again. The process of evading the outside bends and their attached log-jams was the same as the afternoon before, very time consuming.

There is a gorge called Little Homer opposite Little Homer Saddle on the Hollyford Track where there is a stretch of rapids. Angry, white wilderness waters tumbling violently through and over car-sized boulders. Not suitable for almost all boating, including my plastic yellow dinghy. Several years back a group of keen jet-boaters put in a forest track of approx. 300 metres to bypass these rapids. So I began my portage of boat and building materials around the rapids. Yet another time consuming exercise as I could only carry two to three lengths of timber at a time. Back and forth, back and forth, using this very convenient forest track. Finally, I dragged my boat through and then rolled my egg-shaped barrel through the forest. Eggs don't roll very well.

By the time I got to the Pyke/Hollyford confluence, it was late afternoon, early evening, the sun long gone from the Valley. The decision was made to try for the McKerrow Island Hut for the same reason as the night before, to avoid a cold, wet winter's night in the rainforest. This involved another portage around another set of rapids just downstream from Stick Up Creek, doing so in the dark. The process meant a lot of time in the chilly river shadows, sometimes just ankle deep, sometimes waist deep and sometimes even short swims. Senses fully engaged, going by feel of rocks underfoot, feeling the speed of the river flow against the back of my legs. Going by memory of what lay ahead, going by the sound of flowing water and rapids ahead. Going by very limited vision with the dark, shaped silhouette of the forest overhanging the river's edge in the night sky and barely being able to distinguish the white, disturbed water in its interrupted flow over rocks and logs on the black, river surface.

Now when I look at this section of the Hollyford River I still wonder how I did it. Sometimes I get the opportunity to jet-boat up this section of the river in the Hollyford Track Ltd's jet-boat and would love to tell the passenger sitting beside me of this night-time experience of floating building materials down this wilderness river. I don't because they would probably not believe me so I just sit there and look at the logs and rocks jutting out of the swift, wilderness current, remember the night and wonder how I did it.

I got to the McKerrow Island hut about three or four hours after nightfall in a very tired state. I felt around the window sills of the hut in the hope some helpful tramper would in thoughtful kindness have left a candle for the next person and was rewarded for the thought and effort. It was an amazing comfort when ignited. I had battled so long in the dark, straining my senses to their absolute limits, everything dark shadows and cold, swift currents. Something as small as a discovered candle lifted my spirits and morale considerably. Life was improving.

Looking back on my third day I can reflect that the Man Up Top must have been watching my endeavours. The weather was great, not a breath of wind and, more importantly, a flat, glassy Lake McKerrow. I could have easily been stuck at the Island hut for days until the weather was right for the massive paddle with just the one oar.

The long narrow Lake McKerrow is roughly 18 kilometres long and 2 kms wide. It is bordered on two sides by sizeable mountain chains which, like a lot of other Fiordland lakes, causes a funnelling effect for wind, creating in the process a very deep, dangerous chop or wave on the surface which tends to move down the lake caused by a southerly wind or up the lake by a northerly wind. On the wrong day it is very unwise and unhealthy to be in a small boat on this lake. A simple equation – if you get side on to the weather, you flip. If you are not close to shore you either die of drowning or exposure, neither a good option in anybody's book.

So away I went. Standing in my little yellow boat because you can't paddle with a rowing oar by sitting down. I kept very close to the shore with Jamestown my goal.

If you have ever paddled a rowing dinghy with a single oar you will find it is a challenging process, impossible to keep forward movement in a straight line. You tend to zig zag to your destination.

The whole day without a breath of wind and a very flat, considerate lake. I left the McKerrow Island hut at the south end of the lake at day break and got home to Jamestown Bay with about two hours of light to spare. The 16 kms probably was more like 32 kms of zig zag paddling which took virtually the whole winter's day to complete. Needless to say I was a very tired boy by the time I pulled my boat and cargo of timber ashore in Jamestown Bay.

I arrived home very tired after three days of battling the Hollyford River, very grateful to arrive home at all. And I didn't lose any valuable timber!

When asked about how I got the building materials onto the site, a very common question, I can say with all honesty that I floated my balustrade timber down the Hollyford River. There is, however, always a shade of doubt which crosses most people's faces with this statement, especially after they have just walked three days down the Hollyford Track beside which the wilderness Hollyford River runs.

This little epic is also a source of humour for some locals that know of my antics but it doesn't worry me. "Yes," it was a silly thing to have done but at the end of the day I had no other option as I had no money. It is very easy to solve challenges when you have money, it's a completely different story to solve them without.

However, despite this nightmare wilderness river run of cargo, I still did achieve my aim with the timbers of my veranda having quite a tale to tell. So all in all a happy ending.

HISTORIC NOTE: I'm not the first to have had such challenges getting bits and pieces into this little place of rugged wilderness. The McKenzies and their poor cow deserve a mention, if only to remind the reader and myself that our forefathers had it far, far tougher. Their pioneer hardships living in such places as this (and hundreds of others throughout early New Zealand) cannot be comprehended by the present couch-bound and processed food addicted generation. There was no welfare system or free lunches back in the 1800s. You made things happen in life, normally done through hard, physical work or you starved. It was a pretty simple equation.

The McKenzies arrived in Jamestown Bay in 1876, late comers to the dying settlement and set about making themselves at home as best they could in this little Bay with its sheltered sandy shores, beautiful scenery and hungry sandflies. The McKenzies had a young daughter called Alice who was later to write a book called Martins Bay about her early life in these parts, mainly out at Martins Bay, which is worth a read if you're a history buff. In due course, Mrs McKenzie became pregnant, that being pretty much the norm for pioneer women of the day, later giving birth to a son, Hugh. She did so during a flood, refusing to leave the cot with her newborn child until the flood waters had left the house! Which was fair enough.

Husband and wife decided it was wise to get a cow to supply milk for the new members of the clan and probably dreamt of the luxury by-products of milk such as butter to have on their camp-oven bread. By this stage there had already been two sinkings on the Hollyford Bar. Now supplies for this quickly dying township were being landed at the south end of Martins Bay or at Big Bay further up the coast. Landing cargo every three months or so, if the weather was right and sea conditions allowed. As a result the McKenzie's cattle had been landed at Big Bay which meant walking out to Martins Bay then around the rocky headland of Long Reef to Penguin Rock and on to the long sandy beach of Big Bay. Part of this small herd was a cow with a calf, now obviously producing milk, which Mrs McKenzie was practically keen to get. The cattle had been pushed over the side of the Government steamer Waipara to swim ashore through the surf onto the beach as there were, and still are, no wharves in any of these places. It is much the same today as it was hundred and thirty years ago, just wild, remote pieces of New Zealand coastline with no road access, town or people, except of course Dale Hunter hiding in the sheltered lee of Penguin Rock.

Today, Big Bay is only six-eight hours walk away. There is the Hollyford Track part of the way and the Big Bay coastal track the rest of the way. Back in the 1870s this was not the case. The McKenzies, husband and wife, set out to cut a track through the damp rainforest to the coast to retrieve the cattle, especially the cow. Bear in mind this was in the age of canvas, rolled oats and axes, not modern equipment like poly-props, freeze-dry food and chainsaws. No dry DOC huts along the way to shelter them from the elements nor a safety radio service available should things go wrong. This slow process took them three weeks to accomplish! Probably hard, physical days and cold, damp nights. When they finally arrived back home to Jamestown Bay with the poor cow in tow she was dry! She had stopped producing milk because she had been away from her calf for too long. Now wouldn't that put a run in your panty hose, but I bet they carried on with life all the same – tough times, tough people.

THE PRESENT: Dark forest outside my windows with flickering candle light reflecting off the glass. A barely audible rain on the roof, a slight aroma of a well-hung leg of venison in the dining room where it hangs off a hook beside my ranch slider. My dining table partly covered in roughly scribbled notes of this book. My wood range fire is almost out as I have been too focused on writing to notice but now there is a slight chill in the air so I know it badly needs my attention. If I stoke its little firebox tightly with wood tonight I will still have enough healthy embers in the morning to easily restart it anew. Time to sign off and I do so.

Chapter Eleven

SILENT FOREST

THERE ARE A couple of friendly feathered locals in my forest home to introduce, sadly their numbers aren't great.

Firstly there is a black coated Tomtit, sporting a proud, fair chest of creamy white feathers. A very small and elegant gentleman but in looks only. He regularly does the rounds of my veranda, hunting up the little insects confused by my dirty windows. Sometimes he is momentarily confused by sandflies that are inside the glass, but it doesn't take him very long to nut it out. My little rainforest home is his territory, a domain he aggressively defends against any other little male Tomtits that happen to stray into his piece of Fiordland rainforest. He will chase the intruder away with both speed and agility through the rainforest until he is satisfied that the intruder is outside his little domain. He has no real fear of me. Most of the time he completely ignores my presence, going about his day to day chore of survival. I have learnt the Tomtit call, a barely audible, intermittent whistle which, when I recite it, agitates him to hunt up the source of the impostor in his domain. From time to time I see a visiting female which has the exact same shape but which has a very drab grey coloured coat of feathers designed to camouflage herself on the nest. Some uneducated folk confuse the Tomtit with the Bush Robin which does have a similar shape but a larger body with different colouring and much longer legs. To see a Robin here is a rare thing.

Next on the small bird list of friendly locals is the Fantail. A wee darling of the forest. A close friend who accompanies you when you walk through their piece of forest on your wanderings. They have absolutely no fear of man, in fact they actively hunt you out in the forest, not because you offer good company like most would like to imagine, myself included, but because the warm blood pumping in your veins attracts the sandflies to feed off your red warm nectar, which in turn attracts the Fantail to feed on the sandflies. You are a walking fast food outlet to them, the KFC of the rainforest. They have a beautiful fan of feathers for a tail arrangement from which they get their simple name. A tail which they proudly show off, wee flirts of the forest, like a young women in her prime with a peach like backside wearing a pair of tight jeans one size too small knowing full well its visual effect on the boys. They bounce and strut around the forest branches with an aerobatic agility which simply amazes the eye to watch. The combination of tail, agility, friendliness makes all who see it fall in love with this small little bundle of feathers. But, like the seductive flirt, they are shallow in nature as the Fantail only stays when you have something to offer. Once the sandflies have gone, they leave without even a backward glance.

The Bellbird doesn't dress like the Tomtit gentleman of the forest, nor does she flirt her backside around the catwalk branches of Fiordland like the very friendly Fantail. The Bellbirds are the guardians of the rainforest, the policeman constantly on the beat. A bigger bird than the Fantail and Tomtit, about the size of the common blackbird. Initially they appear a very drab, green coated policeman in appearance. I don't know the difference between the male and female of the species but once you take the time to observe them a little, you do see beauty in both shape and movement. There are a couple of Bellbirds that call my freehold piece of National Park their home. Like the Tomtit they also regularly do the rounds of my veranda. Their target are the juicy spiders in the eaves and there are many plump spiders from their many meals of sandflies. Enough spiders for him or her to check out at least once a day. From time to time I watch them chase blowflies on a hot summer's day, which is a sight to see and can bring a smile to the face. The Bellbird has a strong alarm call that notifies the forest of any unwanted presence. They will follow a stoat, landing on branches above the stoat's path, constantly twisting and turning their bodies and head to get optimum view of the horrid, furry little beast below while constantly calling warnings for all the forest community to hear.

The singer of the forest is the Tui. He is also the school bully, an odd combination, but the world is full of odd combinations. He has a shiny black coat of feathers with a little tuft of pure white feathers on the front of his neck. He looks like an undertaker in a new black suit wearing a white bow tie. The Tui is about half a size bigger than the Bellbird, well suited to bully his cousin around the treetops, probably because they compete for the same food source, nectar and insects. The two also compete in the dawn chorus, mainly a sad memory of generations past. Both have beautiful songs but it's the Tui which can generally out-sing the Bellbird. However, the Bellbird can deceive the hearer because he can imitate his much bigger neighbour so I am not always sure if it's a Tui or Bellbird making the early morning wake up call. It's kind of special to think when a bird wakes up the first thing it does is sing! Grateful to be alive. Reckon we all could learn from that, especially me. Maybe it's a little design feature of God's planning that birds sing first thing in the morning, a sign of happiness or maybe even gratitude and thanks. An early morning chorus to remind us we have no right to be grumpy when we wake up. There are not many Tuis here and I rarely see them. Although, out at Martins Bay when the flax is in flower and literally dripping with nectar you will see them more often.

The fat, glutinous kid on the block is the wood pigeon. Most of the time his only interest is eating, eating and more eating. He is not the sharpest tool in the shed either, being a little slow in mind. He is a large bird, in fact I understand the New Zealand Wood Pigeon is one of the largest pigeons in the world. He loves Kowhai flowers in the spring. Apparently his flesh is reasonably good tucker when hungry and starving in the bush but I have never tried it myself. 'Tree Top Tegel' is an affectionate name for this large bird. The method of cooking, once described to me, is to take the complete whole bird, that's the feathers, guts and all, cover it in a thick mold of wet earth clay and place it in the embers of your fire. When ready, break off the fire-hardened, baked clay and the feathers will come away from the flesh with the clay. Slit the tummy and the innards will just fall out cleanly from the stomach lining. Then go and get your tin opener and open a tin of baked beans for tea.

From time to time a wood pigeon will try flying through my windows. It is amazing that none of the windows have broken to date as they hit with a real bang, leaving at times a little tuft of feathers sticking to the glass. These less than smart birds always seem to survive the impact as I have never yet found a dead one around after the noisy impact. Although large and stupid, they can be surprising graceful in flight, especially above the tree canopy. They seem to fly up and catch a little air thermal, gliding up and down a bit, like a roller coaster in the air, without flapping their wings.

The little chatterbox of the forest is the Kakariki although I rarely have the pleasure of either seeing or hearing them. Probably only once or twice a week I will hear their lovely little forest chatter, about once a month I will actually see them. Up close they are a pretty bird, a parakeet just a little bigger than a domesticated budgie. All green with the exception of the face which can be either yellow or red.

The Kaka is by far my favourite, a big forest parrot. He is similar in appearance to his mountain cousin the Kea but nowhere as mischievous, friendly nor as playful as his famous cousin, a bird the tourists love on our mountain pass roads but which the car insurance companies hate. The Kaka is very different, he is the sad local. He has two very distinct, very different calls and to the uneducated it is hard to imagine the calls coming from the same bird. One call is a sharp shriek, almost an unpleasant sound in the forest. The other call is a whistle which can be very mournful to the ear. Sometimes during the full moon when the Fiordland skies are clear and the moon lightens everything in a silvery glow, he will start up his mournful whistle in the very dead of the night. It's a sad call because I know the studies indicate that these large parrots we hear and see in our forests are mainly only males. It's a dying, lonely population, heading for extinction and most Kiwis have no idea of his plight. He is a bit like the main character in the 'Last of the Mohicans.' His call to attract a mate in life is falling on the deaf ears of long dead female Kakas. Females who have died on the nest, killed by the introduced stoat. I really relate to the loneliness I can hear in that mournful whistle on still, cold, lonely nights, when the full moon is up and my bed has only me in it. His midnight calls make me sad, a mixture of knowledge of the plight of his species and my own desperate male loneliness for the physical comforts only a women can offer.

The night is shared with the lonely Kaka by my little mates the Moreporks. Dinky, dwarf owls that regularly call out and hunt in my special Bay. Unlike the mournful whistle of the Kaka this little character can put a smile on the dial. His call sounds exactly like his name, 'More-Pork', 'More-Pork' echoing through the still, dark rainforest. Sometimes you see them in the daylight, mainly in the mornings and evenings, a special treat as they are an interesting little predator to look at. A small, compact body with big wise eyes and a head that seems to pivot in a 360 degree arc. Once, when hunting outback, I had one check me out, landing very close on a branch and looking me over with an intelligent gaze. That didn't seem to satisfy his curiosity, lurching off the branch and trying to land on my head, something I didn't allow because these little owls are predators and have sharp, wee talons to skewer their prey with. Why I fascinated him I have no idea as it was a very unnatural thing for any wild bird to want to do.

The true predator of the forest is the New Zealand Falcon. She is the evil politician of the forest, proud in her position to lord it over the other birds with utter ruthlessness, disguised under a cover of proud and arrogant beauty. She fools you with her noble appearance but it is a false coat that hides a rotten core of self-interest. Once she has you in her sights, she attacks and kills. The community of forest birds hate and fear her and like the bureaucrats in our concrete and glass jungles she doesn't really care as long as she gets her feed of blood and flesh. There is one in residency up the Hokuri Flats. Sometimes in spring she gets a little agro with me and my hunting wanderings through her territory, actively dive bombing me like a German Stuka, full of hate and anger. Coming very close to you and making you duck each of her angry attempts. Once I felt her connect with my hat, an unpleasant feeling so I let her territory be. Truth be known the New Zealand Falcon is a far more noble creature than the bureaucrat.

Waterfowl such as small Teal and large Paradise ducks are a common sight on the lake and the Lower Hollyford River and from time to time you see white Egrets around, a very elegant bird. On very rare occasions in my wanderings I have seen Blue Ducks, a very endangered bird which likes fast flowing waters.

It would be nice to describe the Weka and the Kiwi, the Riflemen and the Robin to you, but there are none here to describe, they are all sadly gone to the introduced rat, possum and stoat years ago.

SILENT FOREST: There is a deep sadness about New Zealand forests, a dark pit that has an unfathomable depth to it. Very few have a knowledge of, nor can truly comprehend, how bad things are in the forest ecosystems of New Zealand. It's New Zealand's dirty little secret. Our special forests in these islands were once literally alive with birds. Birds of unique shapes and bizarre sounds, found nowhere else in the world, now most are sadly gone.

Prior to humans coming to these South Pacific isles, there were no mammals except for two species of bats. There were no four-legged predators. The forest was literally alive and humming to the constant sound of birds.

Then we humans came along and everything went to custard. With man came the mammals which were to devastate our very special ecosystems. A visitor to New Zealand agriculture shores will see mammals left, right and centre. From sheep to pigs, cows to deer, cats to dogs. Every single furry, hairy, woolly mammal was introduced, some unintentionally, others intentional. On my kitchen table made of recycled timbers sits a Forest & Bird Magazine, inside there is an artist's poster depicting a forest edge scene. Through the forest it shows 43 different bird species that have gone, extinct since man has a settled here. Bear in mind that in the history of time man's presence is relatively new in New Zealand. That's right, 43, not a small number of species, never to be heard again echoing through the forest. Their colours, sound and antics never to be seen amongst our ancient forest trees, all because of man.

Over fifty percent of these extinctions were associated to the Maori, who firstly introduced the rat which decimated the small bird population and the forest invertebrates. Then the Maori went about burning the forest in their hunting practices to get the Moa, the largest known ground bird ever. The Moa was obviously a yummy bird to eat, in order for such huge tracts of New Zealand forest to be burnt. It is estimated that most of the deforestation of New Zealand was associated to this hunting practice, although it's not seen as PC to mention statistics such as the above, most happily presume it was the early European farmer that holds this dubious record.

But of course the European had an equally bad hand at destroying the ecosystem. When Captain Cook sailed around the coast of Fiordland he made mention in his ships log that he could hear the birds a mile off-shore. Another unusual situation noted by an explorer of early Fiordland was that he had to shout at his deck crew to be heard because the bird sound was so great. Yet another explorer by the name of Charles Douglas complained in his journal he could not sleep at night because the nocturnal birds such as the Kiwi and the Kakapo were keeping him awake. Now, almost all of the Fiordland mainland forest is deathly silent.

The European introduced the normal farming animals associated to his colonisation of foreign lands. Farm animals such as sheep, cattle, chickens, etc. but he made huge blunders trying to make New Zealand his little South Pacific England, with trout in the streams, rabbits in the grassy meadows and majestic stags roaming amongst the open oaks. The gentleman colonist introduced deer, rabbits etc. as sport and a memory of a far-away home land. Sounds good in theory but both the deer and the rabbit became big problems. The deer took to the huge expanses of New Zealand wilderness where they thrived and no one worried about the effect they were having until the middle of the 20th Century. The little cuddly bunny on the other hand soon reached plague proportions on the farmers' land, very quickly forcing farmers to walk off the land. Picturesque, green grass lands became ugly dust bowls with the huge numbers of rabbits. So, to counter this, the colonist farmer in his simple wisdom introduced the weasel, the ferret and the stoat, all natural predators of the rabbit. These little furry predators soon found that our native and unique ground bird populations were a far easier targets than the rabbits. The Australian brushtail possum was another unwise introduction. The theory behind their introduction was to start a fur trade in the fast growing colony, however, the possum also thrived far beyond expectations. The Australian brushtail possum is kind of monkey-like in body, almost cute in appearance, having no real similarity to the North American rat-like possum with its ugly long snout and rodent-like tail. It has a nice thick coat of fur with an equally fluffy tail and took to our New Zealand forest with a hungry vigour. There were no predators here for him and he had an abundant food source, ideal conditions for a population explosion. For a while numbers were semi under control, the possum trapper making a good dent in the population. But, with the advent of the anti-fur lobby offshore the market for possum fur literally dried up. It was not worthwhile for the hardy trapper to battle the elements to kill the introduced possum for its thick fur coat so its numbers are literally snowballing out of control. This cute looking bundle of fur is killing our forests at an incredible rate. Fly over many sections of New Zealand forest and you will see huge areas of white, dead trees, trees that took hundreds of years, if not a thousand years to grow, killed by this introduced mammal in a matter of a few short years of their nocturnal grazing. DOC now estimates that there are 80 million possums in New Zealand consuming about 17 tonnes of vegetation inside our conservation estates (National Parks) each night. The animal rights people in Europe with their anti-fur lobby is helping to cause the extinction of many New Zealand species of Flora and Fauna in their feel good ignorance. But it's not just the trees being killed by the possum, it's also the birds. Possums are not vegetarians like most think, they are in fact omnivorous and enjoy eggs; birds' eggs.

Wearing the warm fur of the New Zealand possum as a garment to be either fashionable, or practical or otherwise is literally an act of conservation. From my experience of mainly European backpackers on the Hollyford Track, I have learnt that they can't quite grasp, or even digest, the concept that killing and conservation go hand in hand. Spend a night in a DOC hut with a group of European trampers, take the opportunity to knock the visiting possum over the head with the hut axe and you will soon discover what I mean. You walk back into the hut, after your practical, hands on, act of conservation and you will probably find the hut silent and full of dirty, hateful looks. To them it was a cute looking, furry local which was great fun to feed and has every right to exist. The naive European trekkers are simply the product of their environment, uneducated to the realities of New Zealand conservation which is all about killing and more killing. A conservation concept which is very hard for them to grasp.

The rat, another introduced species, a small and some may say a reasonably inoffensive mammal. He is probably one of the worst introduced pests affecting our small bird populations. The best way to describe his horrible effect on my special surrounds is to recount a visit I had. A young bloke wandered up my trail for a cuppa. I soon discovered he has just finished a study on Fantails and told the shocking story of how he had twelve Fantail nests under surveillance and that only one of the twelve nests got fledglings reared and off the nest. The other eleven nests where lost to rats. Not only eating the eggs and the young chicks but, in some cases, actually killing the adult bird on the nest as well.

The rest is sad New Zealand history and it's still ongoing. The statistics are not looking good for most of the surviving native bird species. Our forests are silent, most don't notice because they don't know what it was like. The overseas tourist and the city dwelling Kiwi visits only for a fleeting hello to our natural wonders. They tend to be blown away with the visual delights of our parks in dense lush rainforests, still pure lakes, cascading rivers and majestic mountains, they don't notice the sad silence in the forest. They are missing a vital ingredient of the whole picture.

Above:
"Dead possums, good possums."
From left: nephew Jason, friend
Scott, me and nephew Craig.

Right:
From left: nephew Rob,
nephew Sam and brother John
with dinner.

Into the picture steps DOC, the knight in shining armour. DOC, our Government Department of Conservation rides to the rescue of the damsel in distress our precious environment, on a hungry war horse, a charger called 'Taxpayer Dollar'. A massive pot-bellied, unhealthy looking beast of an animal, that greedily consumes the green tax dollar, inefficiently digesting it to produce smelly belches of PR rhetoric from its mouth and foul health and safety farts from its anus. A government department with fancy, architecturally designed, visitor centres dotted around New Zealand, staffed with well-meaning and well-qualified zoologists and biologists who passionately study species extinction and lick stamps, to sell you nice glossy books on New Zealand nature and give tourists directions.

The public is being deceived, the morning and evening silence in my forest domain is testament to the sad reality that DOC is just another inefficient government department of mainly office-bound bureaucrats and academics, severely mismanaging conservation in New Zealand.

The DOC soldiers are in the main good, healthy-minded people who have a genuine passion for conservation but it's DOC's upper and middle management who simply don't see the trees because of the forest. They have lost the focus of 'on the ground' or 'rock face conservation' to their new demigods of Academia, of Bureaucracy, of Commerce and of Culture. Taking much needed money, resources and time away from their 'Bio-diversity Teams' which engage in genuine, on-the-ground conservation work of killing the introduced pests to conserve our natural environment.

Some examples of the new demigods that DOC chooses to worship. Commerce – The Southland Conservancy who manages the conserving of the three million acres of Fiordland National Park, my slowly dying backyard, prefers commerce over conservation. The 'Visitor Asset Team' which looks after visitors (tracks, huts, visitor centres) is a team or department that has absolutely nothing to do with the conservation of ecosystems, however, it has more staff and a bigger budget than the 'Biodiversity Team.' The 'Biodiversity Team' are the coal-face workers, the ones who are passionately trying to save our forests. In reality more money is spent on commerce than conservation, makes you wonder why they bother having the word 'Conservation' in their title when they spend more money on keeping the European backpacker happy than saving a dying ecosystem.

So why doesn't 'Joe Public' know such interesting things. Simply put, the DOC 'Public Relations Team' allows only positive media releases, never anything negative about the running of the department.

How do I know such things? Years of interacting with bio-diversity DOC staff, some of whom are friends, demoralised by this large mismanaged government department and the losing battle with introduced pests.

An example on how the tax hungry demigod of academia is polluting practical on the ground conservation work. I went into DOC Te Anau to ask for some Fenn traps. These are little kill traps for stoats. My theory was to kill the local stoat population to give the local bird population a small chance to repopulate a little in my wee piece of rainforest. I was directed to a small office to talk to the 'expert'. I stated my case. This confident academic responded that the studies show that such an action would create a vacuum in my area and thus make the problem worse, so therefore was a waste of time. Okay that kind of made sense. I left the office with that thought spinning around in my uneducated head, trying hard to digest the logic of this approach to conservation. But, as I hit the DOC car park, I clicked what he was saying was completely illogical. Being an intelligent and academic person does not always mean you are a practical or wise person. The logic is like saying you shouldn't feed a man dying of starvation because the studies show he will only want more food if he lives. One dead stoat must mean the extra survival of several bird species to breed, creating a breathing window for the species. Supplying more breeding stock for the following seasons, etc. What an attitude to take. Later DOC had a reversal of thinking and, guess what, another academic in DOC told me other studies had indicated completely opposite results. Both these academics came from the same office and probably both had excessive salaries to boot. Again, very simply put, it's not rocket science, in the New Zealand ecosystem a dead stoat is a good stoat, a dead possum is a good possum. End of story. A lovely, practical DOC gentleman by the name of Allan Man then supplied me with enough Finn traps to cover my area. And I did my bit.

DOC badly needs to get 'back to practical basics in conservation' but I know it won't, as there are way too many Academic, Commercial, Bureaucratic and Cultural empires within its ranks, all controlling their own personal and political dominions. Too many votes, power and money in those other budget areas to seriously consider such a rethink to get back to the basics of practical conservation.

The silent forest is a memorial to DOC's mismanagement and bureaucracy. A silent forest is DOC's legacy to pass onto our kids who will have no idea what a healthy forest should sound like. As a result, our forests will continue to die and our children will never hear that very unique Kaka whistle in the wild on a still moonlit night.

THIS CHAPTER started out well intentioned as I love my feathered neighbours who share my little Bay in the rainforest and want to share them with the reader. But I have unintentionally let the chapter descend into a horrible pit filled with my own self-opinion and anger when maybe I shouldn't have. The reader can probably guess from reading my tale of woe (there's more to come) that I have a personal 'barrow to push'. That I'm a bit like the wounded, angry animal forced into a corner and lashing out at its perceived tormentors (bureaucratic empires in general, not just DOC). However, they are just the product of a silly legislative environment and are human at the end of the day. So I shouldn't end this chapter on a bad note. It's not all doom and gloom, there is a little glimmer of hope on the horizon because what little DOC money does actually get through to the bio-diversity workers on the ground is being actively engaged in conservation work by some very lovely and passionate people on such projects like the 'Off Shore Islands Restorations.' With some very notable successes!

Chapter Twelve | # ANOTHER CHANCE

SPRING TIME IN FIORDLAND and it's yet another whitebait season. A time of unpredictable and unstable weather patterns. It is when my tranquil little spot suffers the most from seasonal flooding and the invasion of people. Although invasion implies armies of people, that is not really the case, far from it. When you spend so much time in solitude any visit, whether it is just one person or ten, does feel like an invasion of my special space and my hard won lifestyle. Such visits also break down the false security I have found in the solitude of this wilderness home. The sense of intrusion only lasts for a short while, at least until you adjust to the presence of people on your home turf.

The classic example is winter-time when you know that you are the only person in the area, having been so for a very long time. Then the faint sound of a fixed-wing away in the distance heralds the arrival of people to Martins Bay who I know will be based miles away with dense podocarp rainforest dividing them and me. These winter visitors are very unlikely to even wander anywhere near my little forest hideaway but for some strange reason, it still feels like an intrusion into my peaceful wilderness existence. Silly how the mind of a self-made introvert, bush hermit works.

Back to springtime and whitebaiting. The main base of whitebaiting activity is away in the Lower Hollyford River at Martins Bay. It's far enough to keep me well clear of their wee troubles that flare up. Me up here sitting quietly in the lush rainforest at Jamestown, while they bicker over whitebaiting down in the tidal estuaries of the Lower Hollyford. The white-baiting community there is made up of mainly three family groups so we are not talking large numbers of people. For their six to eight week stay, they may only visit me at Lake McKerrow once or twice, if the baiting is slow and tempers are quiet. The Smith family, however, are different. This whitebaiting family use their small tin-covered bach at Jamestown Bay periodically during spring. Commuting each day down the lake and then down the Lower Hollyford River to their whitebait stands. So for periods in spring I have to learn the art of sharing my special little Bay. When they first arrive it takes a while for me to adjust to their sudden presence in my quiet existence. Time to adjust to their noisy throbbing generator echoing though my still, dark rainforest at night. But their warm hospitality and yummy pre-drink nibbles (a treat for my meager diet) normally wins me over very quickly. And sometimes it's even sad to see them go.

When the Smiths are too busy out on their Southland farm to come in during the limited whitebait season, they have friends who help them manage and run their whitebait stand from time to time. The main one is a gentleman called Ian.

A MEMORY: Ian McCauley is in whitebaiting and residing at the Smith's crib in my little Bay. He's a nice sort of bloke, with a very mellow and honest character. Not one for rocking the boat or blowing his own trumpet, the type of bloke I like. This short term, lifestyle break in the Fiordland wilds, chasing small, semi-transparent native fish offers Ian an escape from the outside world to a more simple, sedate lifestyle. He tends to come in just by himself and when he's in residence I am normally over there for most evening meals. Enjoying his great company and especially his fresh stock of fruit and vegies which he happily shares with me. But not this particular evening as Ian has got company, a friend visiting from Te Anau. I will give them both some breathing space to socialise.

I was saying goodbye to another Fiordland day, wandering down my little bush track to the beach to see the closing day. Dusk in the Bay can be a nice time of still water and air, a hushed peaceful forest, the birds having roosted for the night and the little Morepork owls have yet to wake up to rule the night. A semi-peaceful experience with the exception of the necessary swatting of sandflies who wish to mass around any warm blooded mammals at the waters edge, getting in their last feed of blood before dark. The change of shift then goes to their cousins the mosquitos, who are not as numerous in numbers but make up for it in cunning. They tend to brush the skin with their long thin hind legs before softly landing, fooling you into swatting the wrong area in the dark. Although the Bay is reasonably calm this evening, it is not the case further out in the main body of the lake which is being affected with a strong southerly. In the fading light I can see white capped waves, endlessly pushing and rolling towards the bottom end of the McKerrow. Short, sharp, deep trough waves which are happily bypassing this sheltered quiet little Bay, just like they normally do.

But something is very odd. The peaceful silence of the evening air is polluted by human voices. I can hear faint voices in the distance which is very unusual for this time of dusk. Most trampers are warmly tucked up in huts by this stage and I know Ian and his friend will probably be inside enjoying a quiet evening tot of whisky prior to hitting the hay. Even more odd, the voices seem to be coming from out in the lake. I soon see the aluminium base of an up-turned dinghy coming into and out of my vision between the rolling waves and guess the situation needs to be checked out further. McKerrow's waters are not warm, an upside down boat obviously heralds problems. Away I head in my cheap little yellow plastic dinghy, out of the calm waters of my Bay to the rough, discovering three men in a bad way, clinging tightly to the outer edges of their upside down boat. The older of the three (not a spring chicken) looks to be in a state of shock, not at all a happy camper, giving me a blank but worried look, while the other two are still quite coherent. With the motion of these deep, short waves, I cannot get them on board without flipping my own little boat as well, foolish to even try. I throw them a rope and tell them to stay with their own boat. I tow their stricken vessel with them still clinging to it the short distance into the calm waters of Jamestown Bay. It was the only wise thing to do considering the conditions. Once ashore I run into the Smith's crib to get assistance. Both Ian and his mate are sitting in the warm, cosy living room and give me, "What the ..." unexpected look as I barge through their door, shattering their quiet evening drink. I give a quick account of events, asking for help and barge straight back out. There is a sense of utter disbelief on their faces at my abrupt intrusion but they soon kick into gear and follow me out. Back down on the sandy beach the older of the three is in real trouble. He is not shaking like the other two but is at that stage of hypothermia where he is not very coherent, just wanting to lie down on the beach and have a little sleep (not good). With the help of Ian and his mate, the exhausted, sleepy mature gentleman is got out of his wet clothes and into the generator shed, to warm up slowly from the heat of the Smith's noisy diesel engine. The skipper of the ill-fated dinghy is still down on the beach, trying to salvage things, which I help him to do. He turns out to be a friend of Evan Brunton who is a local whitebaiter out at Martins Bay. Evan is an interesting character, made in a similar mold as Dale Hunter, being an ex-deer culler, the 'Doer' not 'Talker' type, who spent a lot of time in here over the years. Like Dale I admire his years in the bush and the practical knowledge he has gained from it. It's his dinghy and associated gear we are salvaging out of the cold and now dark waters of McKerrow.

They had been out visiting other whitebaiters, socialising down the Lower Hollyford River. It is what whitebaiters tend to do, that is when they are not feuding between themselves. They had decided to come out into the lake on their travels, coming up the western side then, very unwisely had decided to cut across the deep set waves to the eastern side. All three had been drinking, which is also a standard past-time of most whitebaiters at this time of evening.

Soon all three are out of their wet clothes and warm in the Smiths' little cosy crib in the forest. At this stage two start drinking again with some vigour. The third older bloke comes up to me later in the evening and quietly thanks me in an embarrassed but very genuine way. The other two never said a word of thanks.

Later, in the days that follow, it becomes quite a talking point of the whitebait community, whether they would have survived had I not wandered down to the beach that evening to enjoy a passing dusk. Ian and his friend are certain all three would have died having seen their dire condition. However, down at Evan's camp at Martins Bay, the ill-fated skipper thinks otherwise. I've taken the middle ground and think the skipper would probably have been okay as he was warmly dressed, had a lifejacket on, had been drinking the least of the three and the wind was blowing them all shoreward. They would have beached in half an hour or so. The other two I reckoned though were history, food fodder for bacteria and bottom dwelling eels. They weren't as warmly dressed and were showing very obvious signs of hypothermia. The older of the three was especially in a bad way, even if he had made it back to shore he would have fallen asleep on the cold lake shore gravel never to awake before the skipper could have got assistance from us at Jamestown. That is, if hypothermia hadn't affected the skipper's judgement by the stage he finally got his stricken vessel to land. Affecting logical thought pattern is what hypothermia does very easily when it kicks into gear, it's almost like dealing with a drunk or small child. My guess is he would have tried heading back towards Evan's camp, which is two hours walk away through the rainforest in the dark instead of heading the short distance back along the beach to Jamestown Bay for assistance. But that is just assumption on my part. People do the silliest of things when cold, hypothermic blood invades the brain.

The odds were against these blokes, their senses and wisdom dulled by alcohol, clinging to an upturned boat, in a rough wind swept and chilly lake, in a mainly unoccupied wilderness area and at dusk! The growing religion in me senses the timing of my evening stroll was meant to be. That God had given these blokes another chance to put things right in their lives. But most who don't wish to believe in a Divine presence would probably put it down to a pure fluke of timing and circumstances.

Having failed to bring Jem back to life at his tragic demise in the Pyke, it kind of gives me a small warm feeling inside to know that Ian, his friend and I helped to save at least one life, if not three lives.

THE STORY: My wilderness life ticked on and so did the years but the financial reality was I could no longer afford to live all year round in Jamestown. I had to establish a kind of seasonal approach to my remote lifestyle whereby I came out for three or four months in the wintertime to earn some money to support myself in summer.

My first winter away from the security of my forest hideaway saw a short trip of seven weeks to Western Australia, to try my luck at re-establishing my very tight financial situation. Some quick bucks in the gold mines out in the dry hinterland desert of that very large island. Friends had come back with tales of huge pay packets for those not scared of hard work and remote locations. It seemed very much my cup of tea, as I am not scared of either. I was flat broke and needed some serious capital to keep the project moving forward.

First it was to the garden city of Perth to complete a Shot-firing ticket, giving me the license to use explosives in Western Australia. The theory behind it was that such a ticket would assist my cause in finding work in the mines. This completed, I hitch-hiked out to Kalgoorlie which is about a seven hour drive into the desert from Perth. My main ride was with a maturing, grey bearded gentlemen, very rugged and well-worn in appearance with fresh bandages wrapped around his throat. His truck, equally rugged and well-worn being very rusty and old, smelling of alcohol, stale tobacco and musty old dog which was nestled very happily behind the back seat. He seemed to drink, smoke and talk for the whole seven hours. It was almost comical but sad to hear he had just got out of hospital for an operation on throat cancer. Once in Kal, I found a friend I had met on the explosives course who kindly put me up for accommodation until I found work.

My timing for work was rotten. The day I arrived in Kal the local newspaper had just published that Australia had dumped 150 tonnes of gold onto the world market. So I was walking into a gold town where everybody was just a little nervous about the future and there wasn't much on offer on the job front. However, after some persistence I got a job, which turned out to be only for a couple of days, shovelling mud out of an old tailings dam with long hours and a pay rate not much better than what I could get back in New Zealand.

Kal is a large, seedy and hot town, completely focused around the gold industry with all the sadness associated with it. Miners tended to work out in the desert mines earning very good money for periods of up to seven weeks on and then get seven weeks off. Kal is the centre of the web, so to speak. Miners would return there to play just as hard as they worked. The next main industries of the town are the sale of alcohol and sex. 'Hay Street' is the very well-known brothel road with little cubicle type buildings where the girls seductively sit in the windows, safely marketing their bodies for potential clients to assess from the street through the glass. If a young single bloke had a job in one of the main mines and was both disciplined and goal focused in life, he could do very well for himself. Work for a couple of years, save up a nice wee nest egg, enough to easily freehold a home, attract a wife and establish himself in life somewhere else other than Kal, etc. But if he wasn't self-disciplined he would easily get caught up in the circle of working hard and playing hard. Probably leaving the area, after staying way too long, with nothing to show for the years of toil. No nest egg, no health, a cold soul, a major addiction of some sort and an irritable scratch or worse in his crutch. It's just that type of place.

Next I hitched up to a place called Broome to try my luck on the pearl farms that make the town famous, thinking my aquaculture background would assist in finding a job. I soon found to my disgust that Broome was a tourist town, similar to Queenstown and not the small hick coastal town of my imagination. I spent a night under the stars, sleeping in the coastal sand hills dotted with 'No camping' signs before heading back to Perth.

On my travels to Broome I had a sad experience in a place called Carnavon where I stopped for the night in a back street boarding house of this seedy Western Australian port town. There I meet a really 'down and out' bunch of people, one of whom was a very attractive girl in her early 20s. Blond, blued eyed, almost angelic in appearance with the exception that her young skin was covered in horrible little red welt sores which she was constantly scratching. The truly sad thing was, her time was spent colouring in a child's colouring-in book, her system obviously addicted to some chemical that was rotting her poor brain. She wanted me to take her to the local pub and the style of conversation with her was like talking to a seven-year-old child who wanted lollies but you weren't in a position to give her any. My guess was that she was a broken doll discarded from some mining town brothel to become a plaything for the local drunks in this small coastal town. In her very sad role she seemed happy in her childlike state, doing tricks for a glass of beer. A very beautiful girl lost in life. It seemed everybody at the boarding house had the red welts on their skin and dark rings under their eyes. Eyes showing deep, dark vacancies and souls lost to a major addiction. It all gave me the creeps, an over-powering sense of evil to the place. I left via my second floor bedroom window in the very early hours of the morning after someone tried forcing their way into my room. Leaving town in the dark.

After seven weeks with the odd little adventure thrown in I returned to New Zealand with no extra capital for all the effort. So I went back to stoking coal on the *Earnslaw*, an historic twin screw steamer, a working tourist attraction in Queenstown.

In general, my off-season work tended to be on the TSS *Earnslaw*, stoking black dusty coal into hot fire tube boilers with the likes of Dave, Tim, Jason and Peter as my work colleagues.

Boy, coming out of the bush was always a shock to the introvert system. Social interaction was the toughest, feeling quite out of place in most circles. Dave from on the *Earnslaw* was a bloke with a genuine warm heart, a very intelligent brain and an incredible ability for constant chatter. He would induce me down to the trendy garden bars in Queenstown from time to time to be social, trying to force me out of my little protective shell. I would willingly accept his good company and tried to re-introduce myself into social interaction but the pub scene now felt very plastic and false to me. A couple of years battling away in the wilderness, living off the basics made me see this culture for what it really was, 'false'. Mainly youth addicted to a lifestyle of wine, women and song or, as the old engineer on the *Earnslaw* would say, "Rum, Bum and Gramophone records." Youth fooling themselves that the only things in life that mattered revolved around these short-term pleasures. Having lived such a very frugal existence in the bush, where absolutely every cent I spent was to maintain the survival of my project first, me second, I could not relate to the lifestyle of these people, the money they urinated into the sewage systems of Queenstown, nor their loud conversations where every second word seemed to be, "I". What they spent in one night on party lifestyle essentials (food and alcohol) would keep me in rolled oats for two seasons or cover the cost of one season's worth of ammo. It seemed their whole weekly wage was dedicated to just paying the rent and partying hard. Playing whenever possible with no real long term goals in life.

Back on the smoky old steam boat my frugality became a bit of a friendly joke between my workmates but I didn't really mind because I knew it was not meant in spite. I sensed a kind of respect because of what I was doing and had achieved to date.

Being back out in the real world I started to feel a need to go to church, nothing over-powering to begin with, just a sense that I needed to and in the process to interact with a different sort of people. I found it very tough going. This was forced social interaction with a large group of people, which was a nightmare on my self-induced introvert system. You cannot walk into a healthy church and not get noticed. Walk through a church door and you immediately walk into an intense bombardment of friendly, well-meaning strangers, introducing themselves, vigorously shaking your hand and sometimes inviting you out for lunch or tea in their homes. Each Sunday morning I would force myself along, craving a backseat, out of the limelight of attention. Mini anxiety attacks would rack my system, from sweating palms to pounding heart. Such silly fear was out of all proportion to the situation I was facing. I sensed that something was going on deep inside my soul, something spiritual was happening inside. A war of control so to speak.

As a general grouping of people, they tended to be far more genuine in nature and a lot less self-absorbed than the others sitting in trendy bar gardens. But I felt equally out of place in Queenstown churches as I did in the bars. The churches seemed to me to be a bit over the top and did not absorb introvert bush hermits very well. In hindsight that was not the church's nor the people's fault but totally mine with my lack of any genuine spirituality and an introvert nature.

I felt very alone in Queenstown with the exception of my work mates like Dave (a good friend). I was not able to really assimilate with either grouping, like a half caste neither black nor white, hot or cold, lost between two worlds, feeling alienated to both. But I would never admit it at the time.

Over the years I have developed a healthy dislike to Queenstown's artificial lifestyles. Self-absorbed people tend to be drawn to it like blowflies to rotting meat. I have seen friends and work colleagues seduced and eaten up with the Queenstown party town lifestyle only to be chewed up and spate out a few years later. Normally leaving town suffering broken marriages and relationships, a debt hanging heavy around their necks and kind of broken in spirit.

In these times out of the bush in places like Queenstown, far away from my hard won wilderness home, I would crave my forest lifestyle across the dividing Southern Alps. On return to the security of my bush haven I even got into the habit of kissing the ground being just so relieved to be back in the bush.

I know I was fooling myself, running away from perceived complications of social and spiritual issues as my little lifestyle dream in the forest wilderness fell apart, my faith in the existence of God mushrooming with all the adversity. But that comes a little later in the tale.

Noise was yet another little challenge for me. I have come to love the tranquility of nature's noises and the peaceful, long periods of utter and total silence. Coming back into civilisation it took at least a fortnight or more to establish a healthy sleep pattern. In the quiet wilderness my subconscious was always attune to any form of artificial noise but in town artificial background noises abound, are always there, whether it be the faint hum of a fridge motor in the kitchen or a TV next door or just a car passing on the street in the middle of the night.

THE PRESENT: The static of atmospherics is clattering out Carol's lovely little voice on the HF radio, one has to concentrate really hard to understand her. The brain has to learn to switch off from that background static dross. Once you have learnt that wee trick then you can generally pick up what she is trying to tell you. Unless of course the atmospherics are really bad with a passing electrical thunderstorm or heavy Fiordland rain or even sunspot activity which can at times completely stop any form of communication on the HF, sometimes for days. Tonight, however, the atmospherics are not too bad but there is not much to report. Just the standard chat on the weather, a very regular talking point with people who live in such remote places where nature still dictates the rules and there is nothing else to talk about. We talk twice a week on a Tuesday and Friday nights at 7.30pm. It's normally a very short natter, passing on any messages between myself and my brother John way up in Rotorua who has organised this semi-regular contact with her. John acts as my administrator when I'm in the bush for months on end, away from the phone and mail. He is an older brother, guardian of my outside affairs. As for Carol, she looks after Fiordland Fisherman's Radio in her spare time. A lovely caring sort of lass who keeps a safe eye on those hard working fishermen, tucked away in remote fiords and seas around Fiordland. A women who is much appreciated for her voluntary work.

The HF radio is very old technology in a modern age but it best suits this location, cut off as it is by high mountains from civilisation. HF works on the large radio waves that bounce up over mountains and off the stratosphere, as a result it is very subject to atmospherics way up there that result in constant noisy static in the background. The more common VHF moves through the air on a short radio wave length and tends to be 'line of sight' needing repeaters on high points to relay the messages. It's the type of radio wave your cellphone works on, normally offering very clear phone-like reception with little or no static. Of course there are no VHF repeaters in these mountains, not enough people in this wilderness to warrant such an expense, so it's back to the old HF radio with its noisy static to communicate with the outside world, which is kind of okay with me. If communication into here was too easy then it loses some of its wilderness appeal. At one stage I looked at satellite phone options but they were way too expensive for me to even consider and there was strong doubt about the regular availability of satellites over this quiet, unpopulated part of earth. There is a mute switch on the HF which, when turned on, takes out the static noise, except for the odd short loud burst which sometimes breaks through its control. You flick it on while you wait for the scheduled calls but it is best to flick it off once you start talking as it takes out the first couple of words when you start and only parts of your message get through with it on.

One quiet and still evening I turned on the radio early with the mute switch on and sat down to read, waiting for Carol's scheduled call. Doing so with the sliding door open to the veranda, the insect mesh door closed, as it's a mild and still evening out, a closing of another Fiordland day in the rainforest. It was while reading and relaxing that I heard the distinctive loud crack of a twig being stood on. A heart-pounding sort of noise in a quiet, still forest. Not a bird, as the sound was too dry and heavy. Nor is it likely to be human as they tend to make a constant noise walking in the forest. So it's across to the wood range to grab the trusty rifle then into the pantry for the ammo and quietly back to the sliding door to be greeted with another clear, distinct snap of a yet another twig being stood on, it's very close by. This is real heart-pounding stuff, as this animal would make number two shot from the comfort of my veranda. Tales of easy deer to recite to the jealous.

There aren't many places in New Zealand you can shoot wild deer from your home doorstep and I can barter the hindquarters for some Av gas. Gingerly I quietly slide open the insect mesh, very slowly and stealthily peer out over my veranda hand rail into the tree ferns below, rifle at the ready for a quick shot, looking for the necessary shape to aim at. Suddenly, Carol's loud voice booms clearly and loudly over the HF radio, "Jamestown, Jamestown this is ....., how are you Charlie?" This of course gives me a big fright but, worse still, it terrifies the poor deer slowly ambling quietly through his peaceful forest domain and he explodes off like a rocket. Except for a little colour and movement of his red hide through the ferny undergrowth, I hardly see him, definitely no chance of a shot as Carol's voice scares me as well. I was expecting action and noise from my front, I was not prepared for it from the rear. My nerves are strung tight in this very sudden, short and close encounter hunt, to the extent I'm shaking a little with a touch of dying buck fever in my system. I can't be angry with Carol as she has no idea of what has just happened. I return her call, "Jamestown receiving, guess what .... " and tell her what has just happened but I can't really convey to her the intensity of what has just happened in my quiet little Bay and life.

One day the old romantic but unreliable HF radio will be replaced with a cheap form of satellite phone but that may be a while yet.

Chapter Thirteen

NEPHEWS

THE OUTSIDE BATH is out the back door. It's just a standard model being made of polished fiberglass, white in colour but supported by a West Coast structure of chainsaw milled slabbed Kamahe wood. Very simple and hick in appearance. Its location is not very private so to speak, being easily observed from the back door and anybody wandering up my little bush track, but privacy is not much of an issue away in here. No nosey neighbours to peek over the back fence, in fact no man-made fence at all, just a wee house and bath in a small forest clearing surrounded by natural walls of thick lush rainforest in the wide mountainous expanse of Fiordland wilderness. When it does get used as a bath it's mainly done at night under the stars so, other than an outline of the human form, there isn't much to see.

The bath is not particularly interesting in itself, it having been bought second-hand off a doctor friend way down south in Invercargill, but its tale of transit to this locality is worth a mention. Like all things I have had carried or floated or landed here in this piece of remote wilderness, this bath has a wee story to tell. From Invercargill it was taken up to Te Anau through the green pastoral lands of Southland then into the National Park, up the picturesque Eglinton Valley with its lovely beech forest alley ways, open river flats and mountainous back drops. Then it headed through the snow-capped Darren Mountains via the Homer Tunnel, a hole carved deep through hard granite rock. Out the other side the bath descended down the steep winding road into the tourist chaos of Milford Sound and its floating tourist cafeterias. Then this simple white bath left the road for some boat transport on the Tasman Sea on board Dale Coker's crayfishing boat around the rugged Fiordland coastline with its abrupt mountains jutting straight out of the Tasman Sea. As Dale fishes the coast up from Milford Sound it was no real inconvenience for him. He was keen to be of assistance to Charlie battling away in the wilderness. I met Dale and my bath just on dusk inside the Hollyford Bar. Dale is a very hospitable sort of bloke so I was naturally invited on board for tea and had a pleasurable meal of crayfish, fresh white bread and butter, all washed down with beer. Real, mass produced glutinous white bread, toast sliced that I didn't have to knead, raise, bake and slice myself, with heaps of thick, yellow butter, both luxuries in my little remote world of no fridge/freezer and no regular supplies.

A genuine West Coast restaurant, floating on anchor just inside the shelter of the Hollyford Bar, away from the unpleasant rock and roll of the Tasman Sea swell. I had shot a deer and gave him the hindquarters as a way to say, "Thank you," as I had no money to pay Dale for bringing my bath up the coast. Not that he needed venison as Dale was in the feral deer industry, hunting deer in these hills while I was still spoiling my nappies and he could easily go out himself and knock over his own animals if he felt like red meat for tea. But it was the only way I could say, "Thanks." I had nothing else to give for his service. After being well fed and watered by Dale, I resumed my journey, doing so late in the evening and in the pitch dark. Thus a little adventure ensued as I had to navigate my little yellow boat and new bath from Dale's boat at the Hollyford Bar, up the Lower Hollyford River with its sand bars and submerged trees then into Lake McKerrow and then finally home across the lake to Jamestown Bay, all in the dead of night where I arrived in the early hours of the morning. Not a big thing really and nowhere as arduous or as risky as floating my building materials down the Upper Hollyford in the dark but it does give the reader an idea of the history of my wee bath out back. Nothing is easy in here. Whether it's an outside bath or lounge suit, a bag of spuds or a gas bottle refill, everything small and large brought into this quiet remote piece of New Zealand wilderness involves logistical challenges well beyond the normal requirements back in civilisation. Such wee battles makes one really appreciate the simple things in your world. It helps the development of lateral thinking, patience and persistence which aren't bad quantities to have in life. Although many consider my lateral thinking a bit madcap at times.

The supporting structure for the bath I milled from a tree using a very small Alaskan chainsaw mill given to me on loan by Dale Hunter of Big Bay fame, not to be confused with Dale Coker of Milford Sound. Both fishermen, both interesting characters with interesting and wild histories in this outback wilderness. The thick timber slabs surround the bath so the edges of the timber support the rim of the bath. Kamahe is a nice wood to work with, is very easy to mill and it has nice grains and appears to be a reasonably durable wood. Not a rainforest hardwood like the slow growing and ancient Totara, but neither is it a fast growing soft wood like Five Finger or Whitey Wood. As a native tree it is not used much in the timber industry and I'm not sure why. When freshly cut down, still wet with sap, it splits beautifully for firewood but it needs to be stacked out of the weather before the rainforest moulds and fungus set in.

The water for the bath is heated via an old hot water cylinder perched atop a 12-gallon drum which is used to house the fire. The old copper cylinder has been converted into a simple thermette by placing a single copper tube down through the centre which acts like a chimney and increases the internal surface area to heat the water, similar to the old fashioned fire tube boiler. Being flat broke I couldn't afford the large size copper tubing that was really needed to do the job properly. I had to make do with a much smaller diameter chimney, so it takes quite a while for the water to heat up for a bath. You need to start your fire early and regularly tend it over a three hour period or more before the water in the cylinder has reached the right temperature to soak in. The cold water is supplied via a hose away up the creek. On and off for cold water is very simply achieved by grabbing the PVC hose, undoing a string which holds a kink in the end of the hose to stop and start the flow.

It's not a nice fancy looking tap but it still does the trick very well.

Clients love it, the whole process of lighting a smoky fire and tending it is so different from the instant hot water they are used to getting without any conscious thought back home in civilisation. But equally unique for them is being able to soak in a hot steamy outside bath under a Fiordland night, unpolluted by any artificial light. The stars when not hidden by cloud are brilliantly crisp and clear to see, especially in the frosty still weather of winter. Throw in the sound of a crackling fire, intermittent calls of the Morepork, squabbling possums having domestics, the aroma of Kamahe wood smoke and a glass of cheap port, then it can be very special if you are relaxed enough to enjoy it.

Sometimes the bath is used by clients on dark stormy nights, heavy with the famous Fiordland rain bucketing down, which to them adds another unique experience but this is not my cup of tea. I got that sort of thing out of my system a long time ago. I tend to never relax enough to really enjoy it, unlike my clients.

The novelty of lighting fires, the stars and squabbling possums has long ago worn off. The bath has become a purely functional thing for me. Mainly I use it to soak my bloodied clothes in after returning from a hunt. The process of gutting and carrying a deer carcass home is a very messy pastime as most living things are mainly made up of fluid, copious amounts, the obvious being blood – which means you and your clothes are totally soaked in the stuff as well as your own sweat after several hours battling through the rainforest with a gutted, weeping carcass on your back. It is far simpler and cleaner to just strip off outside beside my bath and throw everything into it to soak for a while, to loosen the blood and gore out from the wool fabric while I pop inside for a hot or warm shower, the water temperature being very dependent on when you last had the Wagner wood range in the kitchen going.

Of course I never do that when I have clientele around, it's a little off-putting for the naive German backpacker from Munich who gets his or her pre-packaged, pre-butchered, bloodless meat in clean, clear, sterile cellophane packages from the local supermarket.

THE STORY: With the materials I had floated down the Hollyford River in the winter of 98 I was able to finish the veranda which, I thought, was one of the last things holding me up from getting the final building inspection from the local authority. Once that was out of the road then I could get that wonderful document called a Compliance Certificate which, after it was issued, meant I could legally take paying guests. But, sadly and typically, other issues developed at the inspection. Head of the list was that my wood range flue in the kitchen was not compliant to the necessary regulations, yet another saga of miscommunication, the story of which is way too boring and frustrating to recite here. Also on the list were other little jobs that needed to be done to satisfy the building inspector. A nice enough sort of bloke, who naturally covered himself by doing everything by the building code, with no exceptions. Just like all building inspectors tend to do, which is fair enough. To help me bring things up to the necessary standard I called on the assistance of my brother-in-law, Russell, who happens to be a builder.

Into the picture comes my lovely sister, Christine, and my two young nephews, Jason and Craig. Jason, being the older of the two boys, had it in his mind to shoot his first deer and this is his little tale of adventure.

Jason had a keen desire to come hunting with his uncle Charlie, to knock over his first deer, a normal enough desire for a boy of twelve. Being a city kid, there were a few things to learn. First the use of the firearm and especially the safety associated to it. Starting with my little .22, I got him practicing reaction shooting which, in this thick forest, is what you have to be good at to knock over your dinner. Not much of an issue when you are hunting open river flats but a very necessary skill in thick rainforest where your prey can be enveloped in the dense forest backdrop in a second of abrupt fanatic flight. I taught him how to bring up the rifle so that it naturally lined up with the target as the butt molded firmly into the shoulder all in the same fluid movement, a trick taught to me by my father. Once he got the gist of that, I threw him into the deep end and put him up to the .308 which, for a young boy is a big step. Like an infant going from his mother's milk to strong coffee. This large calibre rifle has quite a bang and knock to it, completely different to the sedate little crack of a .22. Jason managed the change very well with no fear.

Next was the hunt itself. I didn't want to disappoint him as I knew the reality of him even seeing an animal in the thick rainforest, let alone shooting one, was very remote, so I told him how it was. I explained that deer have a natural sense of survival which doesn't make them hang around to be shot. I explained their ability to hear and smell is far, far superior to humans, ours having been desensitised with civilisation since the need to have acute senses to hunt food to feed has diminished over the centuries. Further, that with a little boy in tow we would have twice as much scent floating on the breeze than just one hunter stalking through the forest. Also to the attentive Jason I explained that we would probably create ten times more noise with two than with one, notifying our hairy friends of our unwanted presence in their secure rainforest domain. As a result of all this the likelihood of getting onto anything was very remote, I didn't want my young nephew to get his hopes up and be disappointed. As with all little boys, and even some big boys, things always appear a lot easier and simpler to do than they really are. I knew this.

So away we headed, me thinking that we won't see a thing, let alone get close enough for a shot. Up the still lake in my little yellow plastic dinghy then we beached it, made it secure and headed into the lush rainforest. My green backyard but not Jason's. A backyard of black supplejack vines, knee deep ferns and fallen decomposing logs to hunt slowly through. Within a hundred metres of the lake, I heard a noise to my right. It sounded like a wood pigeon or even a shy green feathered kaka feeding up in the tree canopy, dropping debris to the forest floor in its care-free feeding process. I had noticed Jason hadn't heard this small background noise and so, obviously wasn't concentrating hard enough to really listen to the sounds in

Left: Nephew Jason with his first deer.   *Right:* Taking some back steaks from nephew Rob's deer on the go – heading up the Kaipo, then over mountains to Milford Sound via Lake Never Never, a trip not for the faint-hearted.

A much older Jason, now an accomplished hunter.

the forest, which takes 100% of your concentration. He needed a lesson, he needed to learn so I brought his attention to the sound, with hand signals, making him change course to follow up on the sound. Only an exercise in my mind to educate him, to get him to attune himself to the forest, liven up his 'un-tuned' city senses.

The thing I forgot was that the season of the Roar was in progress, when the stags are a bit silly, driven by nature to hunt out hinds to mate with. Survival being secondary to that main objective of sex for this short period of the year. Both nephew and uncle were about to have a big learning curve.

I was about five metres behind my small nephew when an incredible little play took place. A play that Jason probably will not forget until his dying day. A stag casually materialised out of the vines, ferns and trees and headed in our direction. Jason between me and the stag. Suddenly the stag stopped within ten metres of my nephew, immediately tense in abrupt realisation that something was very, very wrong in his forest amble. Poor Jason had his rifle up to his shoulder but the reactive shooting lessens were long forgotten and lost in the mists of reality. The tip of the barrel was trembling as buck fever had set into his system, the rifle way too big, the boy way too small, the stress way too great. If I had a camera I could have easily fitted the whole scene into the viewfinder, it was all that close, a memory still etched clearly in my mind. Jason finally let rip, "Bang." The quiet forest was suddenly shattered by Jason's loud explosive shot. I saw a tuft of hair fly as the animal wheeled off to disappear into his thick forest from which he had come. But he wasn't alone, abrupt forest disturbances erupted to either side of us as his unseen harem of hinds also departed the scene in sudden haste. I expected to see blood on the forest floor, a trail to follow to a warm carcass or wounded animal but we were both disappointed to find none. I concluded that the tuft of flying hair I saw was from his thick hairy coat, directly in front of the throat, forequarter area, the bullet missing flesh but slicing close to the skin, shaving off a piece of hair in its path. This was confirmed with a tuft of hair on the ground and no blood. Lucky deer, a very unlucky nephew and an incredulous uncle.

Poor Jason was still shaking from the nerves and stress several minutes after this encounter with nature at first hand. In fact, so would I and most youth at his age have been considering the circumstances. I sat my young nephew down and gave him a chocolate bar to calm his adrenalin induced nerves that were shaking his young stressed system. Round one to the deer but a process of education for both uncle and nephew.

Next was a trip to the head of the lake. Thick podocarp forest over flat, sometimes swampy ground. I was right behind my nephew who, by this stage, had learnt to go quietly but he still had not trained his sense of sight to look through the forest, to pick out the shape and movement of his prey. I sensed that a deer was very close. We were coming up to a semi-fallen forest log with a deer on the other side. I couldn't tell Jason as he was out in front with me behind and it would have spooked the animal to do so. Jason had not seen the animal and would have if he had only stopped and crouched to check the vista from down on his haunches instead of keeping on moving forward. Youthful impatience got the better of him and the mistake cost him the animal which broke off and crashed off into the secure forest. Round two to the deer.

Soon Jason had to go back home, back to school, back to the life of a normal twelve year old and away from here. Away from his Uncle Charlie who has no TV or radio, who heats his water by a wood range, reads his books by candle light, stores his meat in a salt brine and worst of all makes milk from horrid milk powder; a disgusting concept to their young minds milk from powder.

Jason's story is not finished though. He came back in to Jamestown, just a little older this time, still young in the scheme of things but very eager. This time he was accompanied by my older brother John and his son, yet another nephew called Robert. Robert is a very different kettle of fish to Jason. Robbie is a boy raised in a rural environment, schooled in the outdoors by his loving father who, by the way, was the driving force that introduced his younger brother, me, to the outdoors and hunting. Robert's senses are very attuned to this environment so his story is the standard success story. He is a natural at it having had a youth of training his eyes to seek out such game as rabbit and goats in their natural environment. Robbie knocked over his animals, thanks to his father's guiding influence and the fortunate environment his parents brought him up in.

This time around Jason and I went out a few times, saw several animals, even shot at some. There were unwanted learning curves, like an accidental discharge close to our tent camp in the Upper Pyke and the wounding of two animals via gut shots. I had unwisely educated him to place the thin cross hairs on the largest piece of animal in the scope and get the trigger pulled as soon as possible, no time for fancy shooting at close quarters. To Jason this had meant the general stomach area, to me it meant the chest, forequarter area. My mistake, not his. One shot gets a clean kill, the other a slow death. The poor animal can sometimes go for miles before it falls to earth. Miles in this dense forest is a lost animal, unless you have a dog to track its scent, so we followed frustrating blood trails in the forest without retrieval, very bitter disappointments to both uncle and nephew.

The overall tendency for this very keen city-raised nephew was that he was just not seeing the animals, when he did they had already sensed his presence and were on the move which is normally too late to get a round away. Not his fault, just the product of his environment. Like all city kids he was just not versed in seeking out prey or observing nature in a natural setting. Vision schooled at looking at one dimension like a TV screen, not really seeing the trees because of the forest. Anyway, we were probably up to round ten to the evasive deer and zero to the very persistent Jason when, on the last evening just before his departure back to civilization, we decided to go for an evening shot across the lake, the last hunt of the trip. I was beginning to despair that my nephew would ever shoot a deer and I was more following through on duty and love to both my nephew and my lovely sister to give my best to help him by going out this one last time. By this stage I had schooled Jason in the use of my boat, how to find home in the dark on the lake after an evening's hunt, all skills he picked up exceptionally well considering his young age.

So away we headed for the final hunt of the trip. Across the lake on the western shore and Jason was in front, working slowly up an open, rocky creek bed just on dusk, then suddenly he ups and, "bang." The rifle came up to his shoulder and the shot was fired, all in a fluid, well-practiced motion, like a real pro. I was a bit shocked, a stag I had not seen staggered and took off across the gravel and up the creek bank and disappeared into the rainforest. But, this time there was plenty of blood splattered on the ground. Bright, frothy aerated blood, a lung shot, a good placed shot, a killing shot. I was all grins as I looked at Jason who thought the animal was lost yet again because it had taken off into the forest with such pace. I knew better. Jason followed the blood trail very carefully, one blood spot to the next out of the river bend and into the bush edge, concentrating so hard that when he came across his first kill amongst, almost hidden, by the thick ferns in the forest he was almost on top of it before he saw it. It gave him a very pleasant fright. I taught him how to slit the throat to bleed the animal, how to gut, how to prepare the carcass to backpack it back to the boat and then I made him carry it home without assistance, a chore he gladly accepted as the process of a successful hunt includes getting the product back to home. To a place where it is going to be hung, prepared and consumed. In fact, other than giving him some guidance on how to gut/dress the animal, he did everything else, including getting home in the dark, without any guiding lights, using the silhouette of the surrounding mountains against the night sky to work out where my little Bay was on the dark lake, where home was. This deer was completely his own. Taken completely with his own skills.

The little boy had taken on the skills of a man. The knowledge and ability to survive and feed himself, without assistance, away from the softness of western civilisation. When most his age are unknowingly addicted to the comfortable couch, big screen TV and mum's biscuit tin. Weak, soft youth who give up incredibly easily when things get a little tough. But not my nephew Jason.

As for Robbie, the country kid, he's a natural in the outback. He spots animals easily and is deadly accurate with a rifle, all thanks to his country upbringing and his father's loving tuition from a young age. My gut feeling, if Rob was thrown into a similar lifestyle as mine for a few years, this youth would out-perform me in his ability to hunt for his food.

It's Jason's achievement which makes a story that outshines that of his cousin because this city kid was outside his normal environment, he had battled through his city softness having several bitter and frustrating disappointments along the way. Most kids would have given up but he didn't, he stuck with it to a successful conclusion. Who can't respect that? Now that he is older, he is now very proficient at hunting.

My kind brother-in-law, Russell, helped me to get my building compliant with the authorities. Finally, after many battles most cannot comprehend, I got the much wanted Compliance Certificate. The much awaited Certificate was not issued until December 1998. That's three years and three months after starting the building, a far, far cry from my originally planned three months.

Now I could legally accommodate people but, with all the lost time and the never ending challenges, I had lost the commercial initiative in this quiet wilderness valley. In fact, I had lost the edge right back at the beginning with the helicopter misquote and having to float my house materials down the lake. Now, three long and hard years later, when I had finally struggled onto my feet, the opportunity of being the only upmarket lodge in the area was long gone. Those rundown lodges at Pyke and Martins Bay of three years before were no longer run down, they had been replaced and improved and aggressively marketed by the new owners. My theory of being the only upmarket lodge in the valley was a sad and frustrating memory. The owners of the lodge had also invested in a big new twenty-seat jetboat to operate on the lake, things were changing in a big way. I was out of the picture commercially and just had to make do with the backpacker and freedom trampers that trickled off the Demon Trail. A very limited and small market that was just enough to put bread on the table or at least to buy the flour and yeast in bulk to make my own.

THE PRESENT: In the pantry is a white plastic barrel with a red screw lid, kindly given to me by the Smiths so I can pickle my venison in a traditional brine. Brining is a very simple process, being used for centuries to store food before the days of electricity and freezers. To create a brine you just keep dissolving salt into clean fresh water until a potato the size of an egg floats – which, by the way, takes a lot of salt (that is non-iodised salt). You then place your meat in the barrel and keep it submerged in the brine with a large stone so that it doesn't float to the surface. The combination of high salinity and lack of oxygen keeps the decomposition bacteria away. When you come to use it, you need to rinse and soak the meat in fresh water for a while and then boil it. Just like cooking corn beef, except it doesn't taste the same. If you get things right it's not a bad product to eat, especially as cold meat options to meals.

Having said all this I have had a few learning curves (like I always do) with a smelling pantry and rotten, wasted meat. However, time, patience and repetition has taught me a thing or two about brining. Trick number one is to lower the moisture content as low as possible by hanging the meat for as long as you can prior to brining. Never place fresh un-set meat straight into the brine as the resident moisture and blood in the meat desalinates the brine and allows the bacteria to start their horrible little processes. In summer time, situated in a thick and sometimes humid forest with little air circulation, getting meat to set by hanging is not always achieved efficiently and it can go off very quickly. Trick number two, find a big enough rock to hold the meat under the brine as it wants to float. If you don't have absolutely all the meat held under, even a small area exposed to air will put off the whole brine. Trick number three, circulate the meat in the brine from time to time.

Other experiments of preserving food did not always meet with success.

Probably the most notable failure was trying to smoke an eel in my chimney. The eel was a large one as eels go. I gutted him and placed a piece of number 8 wire through his gills, climbed up onto my green roof and dangled him down the flue directly over the kitchen wood stove, near the flue cap away from the main heat, but still in heaps of Kamahe wood smoke. The theory was a 'cold smoke' process as opposed to a 'hot smoke'. Cold smoking apparently preserves the flesh better for storage, but there was still too much heat, even at the top end of the flue, so I ended up with a half cooked eel which did taste okay, but had no preservation qualities to it whatsoever. With eels the main challenge is that they hold a lot of natural oils in their flesh which, in this situation, dripped down into my kitchen fire, creating an unpleasant aroma in the house for a while. Smoking done properly is also a traditional method of food preservation like brining but my little smoking attempt met with little success.

Nothing beats a freezer for storing food. Sadly I don't have one and just have to make do.

Chapter Fourteen

THE TREE OF MIXED BLESSINGS

THE DEATH OF A TREE is an unpleasant, eerie sound in a still, silent forest. Sometimes it is a very distinctive sound, a sharp, loud crack sound echoing through the still forest. Other times its starts as a slow mournful tearing sound as wet timber gives way to excessive weight, building in intensity as the tree breaks through the supporting limbs and vines of its neighbours, finally ending with a thud as the log hits the earth. Many of the trees here are centuries old and for you to be nearby to hear the death throngs as it gives way to gravity and smashes to the ferny forest floor is a rarity. I have heard many a tree crashing down away in the distance. Normally a faint sound, just audible as a disturbance in the forest, but not close. In my forest wanderings I have come across many newly fallen trees, big and small, especially after a storm off the Tasman has ravaged the Fiordland forest. The destruction the trees reap on their downward path creates a great attraction to my friends, my fodder on the hoof, the deer. In the process of crashing through the forest canopy, the tree brings down yummy foliage that is normally out of reach to deer so, when approaching a new light well in the rainforest gloom, it is always worthwhile to slow down and approach with a hunter's caution. You just never know if dinner is quietly feeding nearby or is just resting up nearby with a swollen belly of leaves.

Having finished a cup of tea, I was just leaving the kitchen to head back outside to work on my wood pile, the chosen work target for the day, when I heard the unpleasant sound of creaking, tearing and breaking of very large timber as it gave way to tension. The sound being very loud I knew by pure instinct that it was very, very close. Naturally my body wanted to run, but where? I could not see from where the tree was coming as I was standing in the small hallway between my kitchen and bathroom, surrounded by light cream walls. It was a real dilemma of thoughts, all done in mini seconds, waiting for those cream coloured walls to cave in on me. Multiple sickly sounds followed by the main tearing sound as smaller neighbouring trees in its path gave way to the mightily giant trunk as it crashed its way downwards. Then an even mightier thud as it hit the dark humus of the rainforest floor, sending a mini shock wave through the timber piled foundations of my little forest house and into my feet and body. Shaking the house and me like a bowl of jelly being dumped onto the dinner table.

Sudden relief flooded my system at that lovely earthly thud as there were no collapsing cream walls, no sound of breaking glass or crashing iron. Nothing to indicate a damaged house.

The sight that greeted me as I opened the back door was simply incredible. The main log of a rainforest grandaddy had landed parallel to the back of the house, missing it by a good ten metres. I couldn't see the trunk because of all the associated rainforest vegetation it had brought down with it in a big ugly pile. Basically, from my back step I could only walk four or five metres before I was stopped by an almost impenetrable barrier of vines, broken foliage, limbs and branches from many different trees, the impressive pile reaching up to the same height as the eaves of my house. From up on high, leaves were still floating down to earth as I marveled at the utter destruction, now sitting quietly in my once very tidy backyard. Covering the wood pile I had been working on half an hour earlier.

I have seen the tops of these rainforest giants swaying back and forth, being wind swept in storms raging straight off the Tasman Sea and marvelled at the strength of their massive trunks to withstand such forces of nature and physics. However, on this day it is calm, not a breath of wind, nothing external to encourage it in its final act. Its time was simply up and it fell.

Talk about words coming back to haunt you. This very tree had been a topic of conversation not long before. An interested couple had walked around its base. The lady was a real nature buff and loved these big old Rimus and the way they grew all covered in large twisting vines, supporting mini fern gardens draping down from the folds of large limbs and a dense variety of mosses embedded into the bark. It was all very appealing to her. She was a romantic in business thought, a bit like me, and wanted to start a type of eco-tourist activity with her much older and wealthier partner. She was really keen to purchase the title but her wise hubby on the other hand was the opposite, casting a very logical and critical eye over the tree then asking the question, "What if it falls towards the house?" My answer was that this tree was a podocarp and takes a good couple of centuries just to mature. The likelihood of it ever falling in our lifetime was remote, words I sincerely believed at the time. A short time later I'm standing on my doorstep looking at the very same tree, now lying on the ground having narrowly missed my house. A couple of degrees clockwise at the base of the tree, then the head of this tree would have taken out the corner of my house. Structurally it would have written off the whole building. A very good example of Murphy's Law in action.

Sometimes workloads seem just too big to handle and that was the case with this new mess deposited at my back doorstep. When that is the case it's best not to think about the total workload picture as it sometimes only disheartens you, it may even stop you from ever starting in the first place. The best policy then is just start somewhere, no matter how small, and focus on winning each little battle one day at a time. All I had was a slasher, my father's old-fashioned log crosscut saw and an axe. The first priority was to open up access to the house. That was easy enough. Next step was to start at the base of the giant and work up its wide trunk, which is normally the best way to attack trees, giving clear cutting strokes for the chainsaw at the main limbs branching off the trunk. But that wasn't as easy as it sounds in this case as the trunk was huge and covered in a thick layer of large Rata vines and mini gardens of moss, ferns and rich dark humus, now all in embedded in a mess of other smaller broken trees and foliage on which this giant of the forest had just landed and interwoven itself into. Making it even less easy was, of course, I had no chainsaw as my old McCulloch was dead. A nice little battle for a slasher, axe and an old-fashioned crosscut saw. Instant sweat sort of work to battle on with.

I was making very slow progress, but progress nevertheless, when I had my first visitors after the tree had decided to park itself in my once tidy backyard. Wayne Pratt and friends just made an appearance. Incredible as it sounds but Wayne was the ideal person to first walk onto this scene of Charlie battling away with a large dead Rimu log in his backyard because, for a living, Wayne flies the big Russian helicopters up the West Coast, using them for the logging of native timber such as Rimu. After some introductions Wayne hopped up onto the log and paced out the main trunk, estimating it at approx. five cubic metres of usable timber. It was not economic to bring the machine down for just the one log, not that I could afford it anyway, but he made the offer of bringing in a small Alaskan chainsaw mill to "flitch it up" for me. I didn't really know Wayne at that stage, thinking that such an offer was way too good to be true, being made in good faith but not really expecting him to fulfil it. It's one thing to make such an offer when a tree is lying neatly in some farmer's paddock that has easy access to it but a completely different story when the log is three days walk from the nearest road end. I knew all the costs involved and knew it was just not practical nor logical to expect a complete stranger to make such a generous offer. But Wayne is not the 'talker type' but the 'doer type'. Not the type to make idle offers, as I was to pleasantly discover later.

The demise of this great grandaddy of the forest was to be a mixed blessing for me. It created a huge amount of extra sunlight into my small rainforest clearing. It milled into some lovely timber. It was directly responsible for writing off a helicopter a couple of years later and finally, and the most worrying and distressing of all, it helped create ammo for my commercial opposition to cultivate the Mayor of the Southern District Council. Poisoned seeds sown into a fertile bureaucratic mind.

If I had to choose one tree to come down to give me much needed sunlight, a desirable commodity when you live at the base of a light well in the rainforest, then this Rimu was the one to go. Its massive head blocked off my winter sun from about 3 o'clock. I couldn't take a saw to its huge base as I knew the predatory bureaucracy were waiting in the dark shadows of concrete and glass offices. Patiently waiting like cats to pounce on a mouse for such an action. Plus, of course, I liked the ancient forest giant for its living nature, attractive grandeur and for its many years of age.

However, with its sudden destructive demise came the welcome sunlight with many benefits. The rise and fall of the axe, chopping wood seems a lot more enjoyable when you have sunlight on your back. Sun makes grass grow to attract the timid rainforest deer. Sunlight dries the washing and adds longevity to any building on which it shines. Sunlight lightens the mind of dark worries and is a well-known antidepressant, being very good for the soul.

With the sunlight came rumours that I had assisted its demise, doing so with explosive powergel at its base. It started with gentle friendly ribbing from my part-time neighbour in the Bay. Bill had regularly shown disgust at the level of bureaucracy I had gone through. The story of Southern Health opposing me on the grounds of noise pollution was a story he had me repeat on many occasions to his visiting friends to the Bay. He had been on my back for some time, telling me that I needed to get more sunlight into the clearing, uttering quotes like, "Let DOC stand them back up." He was 100% right. I did need more sunlight but I was very paranoid about adhering to the Scenic Protection Order governing the land which only allowed me 300 square metres of bush clearance per title. Having been through the bureaucratic meat mincer, I didn't want a repeat and rightly sensed that my opponents were just waiting for me to start the chainsaw, waiting to cut me down to size. I did not have the resources to battle the bureaucrats anymore so I wasn't letting Bill's suggestions sway me, even though I sensed the wisdom of his words. The Council had already been in with a tape measure and had left happy enough so I in turn was quite happy to let sleeping dogs lie.

These rumours, however, made me kind of nervous and I took any opportunity to show visitors the base of the tree which had very obvious signs of natural butt rot and no signs of the mushroom effects of explosives in timber.

This red-hearted giant lying in my back yard was worth a few dollars. Heart Rimu in Auckland was fetching $2K a cubic metre at the time, that is if I could get it out to market. Not a viable option to achieve or even consider when the nearest road end was three days walk away. Just too costly to get out. Maybe the timber could be of use for further development in the area? I had silly ideas in my head of building very simple, exposed beam, single bedroom units on the adjoining title. Each unit being elevated up on poles to give a tree top feel, with spiral staircases for access. My guests could have very private and individual accommodation in the rainforest but still use this place as the base facility for dining, etc. Just another madcap dream for a man who has no money. So I looked at my options for this large rainforest giant lying on my property. To begin with, I needed to find out if I could legally mill the log in the first place. After a little research I found that the entity responsible was called the 'Indigenous Forest Unit' based in Christchurch. I rang them, with a sense of dread, expecting to find out that the bureaucracy to mill this log would be nightmarish and not even worth the toll call north. I asked what I needed to do "if" I wished to mill this log. Answer; you need a 'Salvage Permit'. Right, here we go again, I thought. "What do I need to do get a Salvage Permit?" The nice gentleman answered, "Just send me a photo to prove it came down due to natural causes and a copy of the rate demands for the title to prove that the log is on your land and I'll issue you a Salvage Permit." It was that easy. I got my Salvage Permit for the cost of a phone call, a stamp and a photo. No excessive fees, no excessive paperwork, no excessive time and no real stress involved. A step back in time when bureaucracy was a servant of the people to help not hinder their lives.

When I told Bill about getting the permit, he thought me mad. He thought it all was an excessive waste of time on my part, considering the remote location and the log being on my land. "Who would make an issue, way in here?" or words to that affect. My part-time neighbour thought my reasoning paranoid and silly and was quite happy to tell me so on more than one occasion. Bill is an enigma to me being a very good neighbour to have, hospitable and generous to a fault. But he seems to be my complete opposite in every thought or action associated to this little Bay away in the sticks of North Fiordland. I have taken to writing down his quotes about the values of land in the Park. Some are real gems. I sense he is just slowly wearing me down with applied psychology so as to accept an offer from one of his mates. But, on this topic of the fallen tree, I'm going to stick to my guns. I have just worked too hard not to.

Later the manure was to hit the fan but I had covered myself with the necessary paperwork in the form of the 'Salvage Permit' and came out clean in a legal sense but not in a health sense. The resulting stress of yet another bureaucratic battle left me with a bleeding bowel and a very angry mind. It did expose a level of bureaucratic cultivation by the rich kids playing in the Fiordland National Park sandpit that terrified and sickened me. It did bring me to a turning point where I began to realise that this project had eaten me up, in all areas of life, an obsession that would destroy me if I didn't get out. But I will leave that story for later, as I don't really feel like writing about my bleeding bowel motions just yet. There is still some fun and games to be had yet.

Wayne made contact and restated his generous offer, which I gladly accepted. It took Wayne a couple of trips with a little R22 helicopter to get all his gear and mates in from the Hollyford Road end. They had two big, beautiful chainsaws and all the lovely associated tools. It took us one day to expose the trunk and prepare the log for milling, in the process cutting huge side limbs in minutes which would have taken me hours of hard, physical work with Dad's old cross cut saw. The next day they assembled the simple chainsaw mill and had the whole log milled into 8 inch flitches before the day was done. These timber flitches were big beautiful slabs and, to prove the point, Wayne got a bucket of water to wash the middle surface of one of the flitches which exposed in the process a rich red heart timber that this native timber is famous for. Heart Rimu is mainly used for furniture, it makes lovely table tops and is even veneered into thin slices to cover doors. Each flitch or slab was about 300 kgs in weight and it required jacks and crowbars to move them around and stack nicely. Wayne had thought the whole project through and even brought in some liquid wax for me to seal the ends of each flitch, to stop the timber slabs from drying too quickly. Rimu is known for its splitting if it is dried too quickly.

I had some scales to balance with Wayne for all this. He seemed quite happy that his friends could come in and stay, giving them something interesting to do in the process, etc. One of them even shot a yearling stag on an evening stroll but I was still very indebted to Wayne for all he did for me. I was able to balance those scales a little by doing a winter down in Preservation Inlet, Fiordland's southern-most fiord, caretaking at Kissbee Lodge which he had recently bought a part ownership in.

As an exercise to ascertain the age of this giant Rimu deposited into my life, I tried counting the rings in a cut off section. I lost count near the centre of the core at around 300 rings which made it over 300 years old.

DEATH OF A HELICOPTER: I wasn't in the Bay when the copter was written off as I was doing a winter down in Preservation Inlet, looking after Wayne's new Lodge. I heard about it later, directly from the horse's mouth, Dale Hunter. At the death of this very expensive beast, Dale was lying face down in my little creek which feeds down through my wee beach into the lake almost directly in front of my place. Dale was desperately trying to merge into mother earth so as to create the least size profile as the machine's rotors beat themselves to death in the gravel nearby. A pretty terrifying experience when you know anything about helicopters. Probably comparable to being a poor soldier in a World War One trench with the opposition trench being only fifty metres away sending a continuous spray of bullets directly overhead. Not a good time to raise one's head. Knowing only a small section of Dale's life, I'd say he has used up all his nine lives and is well into feline overtime after that experience.

From the milling of the log were some nice timber off-cuts. These were the very first slices with the mill, flat on the milled surface but half rounded underneath from the curvature of the tree, still covered in the distinctive, heavy, flaky and dark bark of the Rimu tree. Dale expressed an interest in one of these large off-cuts and, as I'm greatly indebted to Dale, I naturally gave it to him. A very small thing between friends. Dale in turn gave it to another friend, James Smith.

James Smith is a share broker from Australia who also has one of the few freehold titles in the Park, being directly opposite mine on the other side of Lake McKerrow. He recently had built a nice little holiday home on it. Ever since I had proved that freehold land in the Conservation Estate could be developed under the Resource Management Act, others had gained permission without having to 'notify' their applications, as a result they had far easier bureaucratic roads to travel than I did. Piggy-backing off the rewards of my successful test case. James was one of those and I had absolutely no problems with that as he had been supportive of my application, writing out a submission of support – which I am grateful for. Anyway James and I get on well, we help each other out when need arises, etc.

James is in a fortunate social circle with friends that own helicopters and high country sheep stations, etc. He duly arranged for a helicopter to lift the Rimu slab off-cut from off my patch of wilderness to take it across to his patch of wilderness. These slabs are large and aren't light so the copter was the most practical way to do things. To fly the slab over, it needed to be stropped underneath the machine. Someone, I presume Dale, had the job of connecting the strop onto the hook under the hovering machine. So far so good. The 'copter flew across the lake with my Rimu slab dangling below and dropped it onto James' clearing in the bush. The copter then returned to my side of the lake where it landed on the beach to pick up

Dale. The pilot obviously wasn't planning to stay, just to pick up Dale. This is where it all went to custard. The pilot hopped out of the machine, for some reason I don't know and, in the process, the pocket of his overalls caught on the control collective – that's the gadget that controls the revs and pitch of the rotors above. The machine in turn took off performing a quick hover above my beach. Without a pilot at the controls it soon lost its ability to hover evenly, pitched over and naturally beat itself to death on my little beach. A sight to behold but only from a very safe distance. Dale apparently was not and only had time to dive into the small creek bed. The poor pilot must have known what he had done as soon as he had hopped out of the machine, it being too late for him to recover the mistake. I guess he dived into the nearest cover and probably had a gut-wrenching feeling as he watched and heard a very expensive machine thrash itself to pieces. Years later I'm still finding pieces of perspex in the forest in front of where this accident took place. I even salvaged a smashed rotor and still have it beside my generator shed where it has become a talking point for visitors. Thankfully no one was killed.

From time to time I pop over to James' for a cuppa when he is in residence, which happens very rarely as James is a busy man as most successful men are. Maybe just once a year I'll see him in here. He now has a Rimu off-cut as his living room table. The first time I sat down at it for a cuppa with James he remarked that it had to be the most expensive table top in New Zealand. No doubt it is as a new Hughes 500 helicopter is well over a million dollars to buy.

| Chapter Fifteen | # THE LOST RUBY MINE & WOMEN |

I AM THE YOUNGEST OF FIVE KIDS, very much an autumn leaf. We moved from a southern sheep farm, from the good country life to town when I was only five years old, when most of my brothers and sisters had grown up and left the nest. So I became a soft city kid, spoilt by loving caring parents in their greying maturity and by my grown up siblings. It was big brother John who, in his breaks from university at Otago, introduced his baby brother to the great outdoors, the New Zealand wilderness, helping to establish in me the desire for the great outdoors and that healthy lifestyle that country folk have by pure nature. School holidays were spent on hunting trips for whitetail in very remote places like Lords River, Tikotahi Bay, Port Adventure, Port Pegasus, where the only access was by hours of sailing in the unpleasant Southern Seas regularly battered by stormy cold fronts coming straight off the ice shelves of the Antarctic, sailing around the very rugged and unpopulated coastland of Stewart Island with its dense wind-blown forest and cold swampy inlands. Then on trips in the mainland South Island like deer hunting in mountainous Fiordland, goat hunting in the tussock country of the Skippers, wallaby hunting at Mt Nimrod, Hunter Hills, pig hunting in Marlborough, etc. Trips he didn't have to take a little boy on, but did. All such trips having a profound effect on a little soft school boy from town. This was off the trails, learn to navigate and camp in the forest recreation in true wilderness that most just don't get to experience. Anyway, John organised a couple of adventures while I have lived here in Jamestown Bay over the years that are worth noting for the record. Trips which also introduced his two sons and others to some great adventures in Fiordland.

Probably the most memorable was the 'Lost Ruby Mine' adventure. Brother John is a qualified geologist and did his thesis in the Red Hills, north-east of here as the crow flies. His close friend Roy Johnstone, also a geologist, had been involved with mineral exploration in the Red Hills during the 1970's so they both knew the lie of the land. Both now had boys of similar school age so a trip was a must do, to introduce their young sons to a very interesting part of Fiordland that few have ever heard of. A character building trip to burn off some puppy fat.

Now to describe the Red Hills is reasonably simple. This remote, small section of the mountainous Southern Alps is very mineral rich, the ultramafic rock specifically has a high iron and magnesium content. Because there is so much of the red stuff trees don't grow in the thin soil, the steep hillsides are mostly barren of vegetation. From the distance the rocky terrain appears red in colour, quite spectacular in the rising and setting of the sun hence the obvious name Red Hills.

There are no roads or even recognised tramping tracks into this interesting part of New Zealand, it is mostly pristine wilderness.

To add further interest to this specific adventure, I need to recount in brief, a very interesting article written and published in the Otago Witness back in 1897. An interesting read for the long skirt ladies and the grizzly bearded gentlemen of the day. It recounts three very tough miners who discovered rubies in Fiordland and established a mine. One got murdered, the other two up-sticks and flee. They end up selling their precious rubies in Amsterdam around 1896, the location of the mine kept a guarded secret. It's a very good read and most will probably conclude it's purely a tale of fiction, a bit too far-fetched and dramatic to be true. However, this is where the printed tale gets super interesting because, back in 1897 when the article was printed, most of the country west of the Southern Alps in Fiordland was still relatively unexplored, the Red Hills specifically unknown to the readers of the day. The descriptions given by the writer (one of the miners) of the terrain and access to it are pretty accurate, knowledge only a person who has actually trodden the area could give such an account of. Plus, of course, the area is very rich in minerals, not something then known at the time.

With this very old tale my brother John and his friend Roy were able to add a little spice to the trip for their sons. A Fiordland trip to a very remote unknown part of New Zealand wilderness to find the Lost Ruby Mine and of course to visit me, the weird Uncle Charlie battling away at Jamestown Bay who would accompany them on this adventurous task.

John and his son, Robert, Roy and his two sons, Aaron and Tim, my nephew, Jason, and I flew by helicopter into the Red Hills over the standard spectacular mountainous Fiordland scenery. To a location I'm not going to describe to the reader but one both John and Roy already knew well from their earlier times as geologists in the area. We set up an idyllic tent camp beside a little mountain stream and set about exploring and, "Yes," within a very short time in a rocky outcrop shown to us by Roy, we found gems but, to be honest, they were only garnets and of a very low quality but still very exciting stuff for little boys and for me. And for the reader, "No," we never found the Lost Ruby Mine, it's location a secret of the dead, not that we really looked hard for it as John and Roy already knew the area well and had never found any evidence of its existence. But anyone who knows Fiordland well also knows that man-made evidence can be easily destroyed by nature, slips and floods, swallowed up by the pure extremes and huge expanses of this wild place and this has been done in a very short period. The Lost Ruby Mine was, however, a great excuse to stimulate young active minds for a Fiordland adventure and it did just that. This trip was memorable to me for a number of reasons. A mighty storm hit the next day as we broke camp and headed down off the tops, very exciting stuff descending steep mountainous country in a stormy tempest with a torrential downpour typical of only Fiordland. The heavy rain made the ground underfoot unstable with rocks regularly tumbling dangerously down the steep mountain beside us with flashes of lightning and heavy cracks of thunder overhead as we descended and raced off the mountain for cover away from the dangers. A wet, unpleasant night in the forest as we couldn't cross a storm-fed stream and, when we did the next day, it was a very hairy river crossing. Boys and men linking arms and supporting those who lost their footing, stumbling on submerged boulders in the raging torrent, what an experience for the boys, even I had my heart in my mouth with that river crossing. A lovely calm night at an old mining camp, its buildings still standing on the flats. A separate shed still had the drilled rock core samples from the 1970s. A tidy pit toilet privy was of interest with three walls and a roof, completely open to the front with a spectacular postcard view of the rugged mountains across a beautiful little stream as you sat and pushed out the unwanted byproducts of backpacked tramping food. Next day we headed out via the Upper Pyke Gorge, my nephew Robbie taking what I thought was an impossible shot at a hind, way down in the deep gorge and across the river, wondering inside my incredulous head why he should even bother in taking such a silly shot and even if he got it how would he retrieve the meat. But I was wrong on both counts as young Robbie is a superb shot, well trained in marksmanship by his father. An incredible shot with his father's old .303 BSA that resulted in Rob's first deer which he dropped at some distance and downhill, difficult shooting. Robbie and the young crowd on this trek went on to successfully retrieve the meat by backtracking up the opposite side of the gorge the next day. We spent two very pleasant nights camping at the Durwood Pyke confluence where we found our food drop and dined very well around an open fire. After leaving this idyllic little camp we had an easy walk out to Big Bay for yet another comfortable night in the DOC hut but where the associated smelly pit toilet was so full that any solid dropping turd would splatter your lily white behind if you foolishly chose to use it, which I didn't, opting instead for the clean comfort of a sterile bush setting. Next day heading south along the remote West Coast beach to Dale Hunter's little hideaway. Dale wasn't in residence but he had given his okay to use it. We encountered a very mis-mothered (farming term for a lamb lost from the ewe) German backpacker who was very irate that the bush track between Big Bay and Martins Bay was overgrown "dangerous as you might get lost" and "you shouldn't use this track without a GPS"! A bit of a giggle in my mind considering the untracked, unmarked wilderness we had just covered. How could one get lost in the bush on the coast with the sound of the sea always on one side and the steep terrain of the Sarah Hills on the other? Big Bay is always north and Martins Bay is south. But he was a product of his environment, a European city kid wanting a New Zealand wilderness experience on his pre-conceived terms of wilderness, always expecting well-formed graveled pathways in the rainforest and DOC markers every twenty metres and getting neither, which was really putting his head into a tail spin. True New Zealand wilderness doesn't come with man-made tracks and a dry hut every five hours, just the very opposite. The following day we headed around to Martins Bay and up the Lower Hollyford track back to my little rainforest home. Quite an adventure for all concerned, thanks to my big brother John and his good friend Roy.

There were other trips, like coming down from Jacksons Bay via the Cascade Valley, over the mountains and back into the Upper Pyke Valley then home via Big Bay, all of them great fun, full of challenging adventures and all character building stuff for the boys in tow. Good memories with great people.

WOMEN: Some say that when God created the heavens and the earth and all things contained within them, that with each passing day his level of design got more wondrous, more spectacular than the preceding day to climax in a design perfection with his last and final creation, that of a woman. Kind of has a ring of truth about it as, when one studies the inner and outer essence of a woman and the true beauty of womanhood and motherhood, then the female of the species is indeed a wondrous thing to behold. However, for a single celibate, introvert male living in the remote wilds of Fiordland the presence of a woman can be utterly nightmarish at times. Creating aching testicles, sleepless tortuous nights with unwanted hard throbbing aching pieces of anatomy and a very drained exhausted body during the day. No amount of cold showers or bromide in your tea seems to work when there are feminine pheromones floating around my wilderness domain.

No story about life in the wilderness as a celibate hermit would be complete without making some mention of the age-old male challenge of celibacy and the few women who passed through my life and rocked my celibate boat.

Many males reading this tale may think that my wilderness lifestyle would attract healthy, young, free-spirited, free-loving women in their droves and jealously conclude that I never lacked obtaining female comforts, but that is simply not the case. Yes, some very beautiful, single women of very healthy exquisite forms did pass through on their global travels from time to time. Yes, some were even the earthy, free-loving, hippy types of young boy's dreams. Yes, I did fall in love at the pure sight of many of them. But I am simply way too shy to exploit any real advantages this wilderness lifestyle gives me. I was also brought up in a conservative manner with a deep respect and love for the females in my life, my mother and sisters are very special to me, so activity exploiting or seducing a woman to solely meet my physical needs and nothing else felt inherently wrong. Unless of course the women in question literally threw themselves at me, which did happen on very, very rare occasions much to my surprised delight at the time but, sadly, there is always a price to be paid for such tussles of passion.

When it comes to women my theory is quite simple and kind of in line with old-fashioned conservative wisdom but out of line with modern mainstream liberalism of today. Men and women were designed to act and think completely differently to each other but those differences are not a reason for division, the disease of the modern relationships, but for a unique togetherness. Designed to operate perfectly together as a functional unit, as a husband and wife, man and women, friend and lover. A nut and a bolt look completely different in appearance but their true purpose only works when used in conjunction with the other, made whole together. A woman's wants are completely different to a man's wants. Female brains are naturally geared towards finding security in a relationship, whether its physical, financial or emotional, she needs to know that when she has kids to love and cherish that there is a rock secure protector and provider of such things in her family life, her brain is wired like that, wired to be naturally maternal, naturally loving. Whereas a man's brain is wired towards meeting his basic physical needs and the reality of day to day protection and provision for his family, making money. His need in a relationship is that his body is being looked after (food, sex, sleep) as he gives it over to a lifetime of labour to supply the protection and provision necessary for the fruit of his loins and the love of his life. So, by nature we think differently, want different things, act differently but are made whole when we work together. I'm guessing the loud, gay liberalist will hate that simple reasoning but their main domain is the city, the quiet and conservative wilderness isn't their cup of tea, which is okay with me.

Then there is the spiritual aspect of male-female relationships that very few now accept or believe, that with the intimacy of sex there is somehow a deeper spiritual connection associated to true lifelong love and commitment. Of course, most who now don't believe in a soul or spiritual context of life will take this as utter rubbish, the dribble of a simple bush hermit polluted by a conservative upbringing but it's what I know to be true.

In essence there lies my big problem with women. On those very rare occasions a woman does start flirting with me and desire is activated, the blood starts pumping below depriving the brain of oxygen which causes all that conservative wisdom to be conveniently forgotten, passion and lust simply takes over with an all-consuming vengeance beyond all reason then, sadly, when the short term passion is spent, it is replaced with a guilt deep down in my soul. A sense of sadness that this is not the way it is meant to be. If the woman chooses to hang around it becomes a horrid circle of lust then guilt, over and over again until I can find a way to break her hold on me, normally by running a country mile. In many ways I crave true love and commitment, a binding of souls for the long term. I know that will never happen if a relationship is started only by sexual desire. Sadly, that is the common path of today, the accepted norm. When once it was friendship then courting, with the odd barn dance and maybe a stolen kiss thrown in over time to explore compatibility and commitment for the long run, now it's get blind drunk and laid with a complete stranger as quickly as possible. Once the passion is spent, the relationship tends to dissolve and for many the real problems and sadness begins, especially for the poor, bewildered girls who have yet to click that lust-based sex for a man has absolutely no emotional connection or content for them at all. It's just a basic physical need like thirst or hunger that needs to be satisfied, nothing else. Normally he has instinctively lied through his teeth with sweet words of false love to get that very basic need met.

To be a true celibate, you have two basic options. One, cut your testicles out with a razor sharp knife, or two, hide away from all contact with healthy single females. Obviously running a backpackers lodge on the Hollyford track avoiding healthy single women is an impossibility, nor is sacrificing my precious silk purse enclosed gonads on the celibate's altar of self-mutilation a viable option either (I like the concept of having children one day) nor do I have the testicular fortitude for such drastic and painful action.

Having said all the above I have had the odd feminine encounter. Not always of my own making but sometimes I wasn't always the innocent party either. All of which I do regret, but can't undo.

For a short while there was a very unique woman that did share my life here in the wilderness. A relationship based on convenience and companionship for both parties at the time, not one of any true love. She was not a stunner but nor was she ugly either, just a very pretty plain Jane, not her real name of course. She didn't have the desirable vase shape that modern society craves with its lovely long, shapely legs, narrow waist and dainty breasts. She was short in stature with an hourglass shape. Not the polluted hourglass shape of the western world with all its gluttonous jiggles and wobbles, folds and flab, the obvious byproduct of modern processed foods and our standard couch-bound lethargic lifestyles but the truly breathtaking hour glass shape of a distant time when women tilled the fields, walked to market and only ate the healthy produce of the land. Hers was a well-defined feminine perfection and although she lacked any real fat on her petite figure from her rib cage down she was still well endowed with copious amounts of fat cells, well positioned and proportioned in watermelon sized breasts. When naked, a state she was not at least inhibited by, she was a sight that made your insides literally contract for want, a perfect design of creation. She loved the wilderness lifestyle, was physically and mentally tough, definitely not a soft women but a real pioneer women not scared by the challenges of life in the bush. Some may say she was perfect for me and my chosen lifestyle but although we were friends, we did not love each other and the longer I enjoyed her company in my bed the more guilty I felt. I told her this but she didn't really care, for her it was just convenient, 'fun,' and plainly told me so. The whole love, spiritual, moral side didn't seem to bother her at all, which for a lot of men would be perpetual Christmas time for them but not for me, it only seared my soul over time. Other than our love for the wilderness lifestyle and simple companionship, we were poles apart in many, many ways, the relationship doomed to fail. She was, however, an incredible woman in many aspects. For a while she did possum control for DOC in Fiordland which is not as romantic as it sounds. It was tough, messy work even for a bloke, the rigours of the untracked Fiordland bush not a gentle place to live and work in. She was a rare gem of tough womanhood in a modern world of soft womanhood, probably more suited to life a hundred years ago than today with all its many plastic feminine facades. My conscience couldn't let the relationship continue but boy it was incredibly hard to turn that free-flowing tap off when it felt like I had spent most of life dying of constant thirst.

The Smiths once jacked me up with a women who I instinctively knew was trouble with a capital T and I did my utter best to avoid her but she was a true feline predator and knew when to pounce, climbing into my bed in the middle of the night after I had some drinks at a party (the Whitebaiters Ball) orchestrated by the Smiths. Desperately wanting and weak, the basic male in me was unable to repel the obvious conclusion. It was like asking a starved bee not to land on a nectar rich flower. Stupid, silly me, nature couldn't but help take its course, but once the deed was done I had instant and utter regret at my actions. It is amazing that when there are no genuine feelings or love involved, how a simple physical act of release for a male can make his mind go from uncontrollable lust for a woman to disgust in a few short seconds. The female honeytrap had been sprung and sadly it took a while to extract her claws in my life, she was that sort of girl and silly me knew it was so right from the outset. In hindsight I wished I had listened to my gut intuition and went and slept under a log in the bush that night.

A young hippy German girl with quite a sad countenance and piercings in unusual places once made life unexpectedly interesting and very awkward one night but she was gone the very next. I had huge, conflicting emotions watching her walk away down my little rainforest track, the male part of me desperately wanting her to stay, the other logical, wiser side of me filled with huge relief she wasn't hanging around. Two polar opposites binding for a very brief confusing, exhausting interlude. Guessing that the introverted bush hermit with his skin and bones stature was way too inexperienced in the ways of a woman, too inept for her liking. Both of us mixed up people looking for love in all the wrong places and I'm guessing that both of us were a little sadder for the sudden, unexpected wilderness romp in my rainforest abode, no real good came from it. She ended up living with Dale at Big Bay for a while which took my head quite some time to get used to.

Then there were women who I never ever laid a hand on but who I fell in love with all the same, simply because they happened to be the only women who happened to pass by and stayed a day or two, their feminine pheromones drifting on the Fiordland breeze driving my poor celibate mind nuts. The lovely, Christian nurse from Auckland, beautiful both inside and out, the attractive journalist from the States who did an article on me for some State-side magazine, the blonde, blue-eyed American scientist of jaw dropping beauty who the Air Fiordland pilot proudly bedded down at Martins Bay but who, much to my utter amazement, started writing to me of all people for a while. None of whom I even got to kiss, nor made any real advances towards out of shyness and respect for my opposites. They still had a dramatic effect on my poor celibate system all the same, purely because they were single, healthy women tramping the Hollyford with easy friendly smiles for me.

A tale of a very scared Japanese girl is worth noting. There is absolutely nothing seedy or inappropriate about this little feminine yarn either. It was autumn, a quiet time in the Hollyford Valley, hardly anybody in the area. I discovered her down at the Hokuri Hut in my lonely forest wanderings. I knew as soon as I opened the hut door that something wasn't quite right. She was terrified to the extent she become quite clingy at the thought of my departure. One should never leave a damsel in such obvious distress so I offered to take her back to my place for the night and to arrange a flight out of Martins Bay with my old SSB as soon as a flight was available, an offer she grabbed without hesitation and with a great deal of excitement. The reason she was so scared was that she had never in her life been subject to such complete solitude or had been so isolated. Quite naive on her part really, probably thinking the Hollyford Track was a bit like the other tourist tramping highways, like the Routeburn or Milford tracks with their huts filled every night to bursting capacity and people constantly passing each other on the well-trodden, idyllic forest trails during the day. She had started the Hollyford with the expectation of meeting people along the way, but to her surprise hadn't done so. With each passing night in the DOC huts along the way (Hidden Falls, Lake Alabaster, Demon Trail Huts) she became a little more disconcerted until the prospect of a fourth night and day of not seeing anybody had this little petite Japanese girl sitting in a cold, dark, musty DOC hut very worried indeed. The sudden appearance of a skinny bush hermit in bare feet, thread bare clothes with a rifle slung over his shoulder had actually made her day. To put things into context for the reader, people from Asiatic countries are very used to having copious numbers of people around them from birth to death, it's just the way things are in very populated countries, the standard norm for them is to have wall to wall people in their daily lives. Thankfully not for us. To experience such isolation and solitude was a very new experience and defiantly not to her liking.

After her departure back to civilisation the story didn't end there, however, because within a few weeks, she was back at my door with another Japanese girl in tow, a friend. Not something I had expected at all after all the previous drama. My wilderness hospitality had obviously had an effect on her and she was now excited to share the uncommon experience with a friend. My problem now was how to feed these unexpected guests. There was no meat hanging so away hunting I went with two petite Japanese girls in tow, a very new experience for all parties involved. I was not expecting to get anything because of the very noisy company and our combined scents but, surprisingly, I did. I shot a hind and fawn beside a small creek, shooting the fawn because it wouldn't have survived by itself. There was shocked silence, blood drained faces and gaping wide open mouths as they watched me slit the throat of the still kicking hind to bleed the meat, then gut and quarter the warm steaming carcass in the cool evening, autumn air for carrying back. Never in their city sterile lives with grocery bought, cellophane covered, bloodless meat, had they ever witnessed such a sight with all the associated blood and gore in abundance which is common to the killing of any animal for eating. The sudden dispatch of the hind and its cute little Walt Disney Bambi look alike, complete with beautiful spotted coat, introduced these Japanese girls to the harsh realities of survival in the wilderness, a scene that has played out for thousands of years around the globe as people kill to eat and feed their kin, a scene now foreign to city born folk. Up to that point there had been a constant foreign chatter, it was now replaced with just a stunned silence except for that very peaceful, clean sound of a forest brook bubbling over partly submerged rocks. I now had meat to feed my guests which they seemed to really enjoy eating that evening.

That, in short, is a brief look at the celibate life and my battles in the wilderness over the years, definitely not a romantic novel at all and probably a huge disappointment for male readers expecting copious tales of seedy encounters with free loving hippy girls. That domain belongs to a certain gentleman around at Big Bay and he's not one for showing off, the complete opposite.

I do have women friends, a school teacher in Wanaka is one but there is absolutely no expectation of anything else inappropriate. She is just a good friend of the opposite sex and still is today. She is fully aware of my male shortcomings.

I can honestly say that I regret all my past sexual relationships and I have a deep desire to find a true partner in life. A good wise women, caring and gentle but who won't drop her knickers in my or even her weak moments of want. Least not until I can put a wedding ring on her finger. Then I can enjoy the natural pleasures of marriage without the guilt, boy that will be a real treat in life. Sadly, until this wilderness lifestyle has run its course, that is very unlikely to happen.

POST-NOTE (2017): For the reader's interest. Years have passed, I am now married to a drop dead, gorgeous Christian girl of beautiful exquisite form and great genetic and parental stock, ancestry dating right back to the raping and pillaging period of the Vikings. Bronwyn is her name. A very maternal woman with a very loving, caring and incredibly wise spirit whom I love deeply. An extremely rare and priceless gem of a woman, a unique discovery, the sort of woman I had no right in finding and marrying but did. She hadn't dropped her lovely lace knickers for any man until our wedding night; hard to believe but true. She has since blessed us with two very healthy, happy children and life is very good in all regards. She has made my incomplete life very complete. Boy, I wish I had controlled my passions and married her a lot earlier in life. God didn't intend a weak male like me to be celibate but, in hindsight, I probably was way too immature in my youth to do any wife justice so God's timing with Bronny was perfect as always. It was Bronny's idea for me to dust off this old manuscript and get it published.

Advice to my precious children on the topic of sex and finding a mate (just in case I'm not around to explain it when the time comes): Sex should not be something to be treated casually and lightly; it is designed as an enjoyable, essential part of life with lots of benefits for mind, body and soul within the boundaries of a loving and committed marriage. Outside of marriage it tends to become a very cheap commodity with no real meaning nor hold any real, long-term fulfilment. It may be great fun at the time but ultimately you will end up jumping from partner to partner trying to seek unrealistic fulfilment, only to end up very lonely carting a lot of sad emotional baggage and guilt around in life.

To my Son: Don't make the same mistakes I did, keep it in your pants. Don't be fooled by your testosterone. Those extrovert, bubbly, flirting bombshells boiling

My lovely wife and kids.

At Old Miners Hut, above Upper Pyke Gorge.
From left: nephew Jason, brother John, Aaron, Roy, nephew Robert and Tim.

over with simmering sexuality may have your head and groin doing uncontrolled and delirious somersaults, but the depth of their attentions is only limited to short-term pleasures and not lifelong companionship. They bore very easily when not having fun and flee to greener pastures when times get tough, they are trouble with a capital T.

Always be aware of a woman's vanity. If she has heaps she will have a hidden selfish spirit and will be hard to please long term – run a country mile. See how she treats the males in her family; if she treats them with love and respect you are onto an absolute winner. A happy woman, especially in adversity, is a trophy girl. She will make life's bumpy road a pleasure to share; don't you dare let her escape. An easily angered women is unhappiness in the making; avoid her at all cost. A woman who likes cuddles will keep the marriage bed warm and fulfilling; avoid the cold-fish types for they will be dry wells in a parched desert. Finally, a woman with the same values and attitudes as your own makes marriage an easy road to travel.

To my beautiful Daughter: Lust is not love. Until he puts a ring on your finger don't be sweet-talked into dropping your knickers; all men are expert liars when the blood is pumping to their nether regions. Don't be fooled by the sweet words of false love they will issue forth. Men with big egos are simply selfish brutes in disguise; keep a wide berth from them. See how he treats his mum and sisters. If he loves and respects them then, once the 'honeymoon stage' is over, he will treat you the same. A man who laughs in the face of adversity is worth holding on to, whereas one who angers easily is one to avoid; he will only bring you sadness. When attracting a mate, a woman's happiness is her best cosmetic and it helps to keep yourself in good shape. Finally, no man is perfect but one who strives to maintain moral integrity in all things will stay true to you alone. Plus it helps if he happens to be rich.

Now kids, for the actual mechanisms of sex, refer back to Mum.

Post-note finished, now back to my yarn.

Chapter Sixteen

BLOOD

OUT FOR AN EVENING'S POACHING. It's a lovely little spot across the lake, easy to access, easy to hunt and normally results in an animal. An easy animal, if the rainforest clearing has been well rested from human activity, if the hunting conditions are right and if the owner is not at home because this little clearing is on freehold land, not National Park. The owner lives overseas, offshore most of the time, a nice sort of bloke who only visits his very private hide-away in Fiordland a couple of times each year. He has built a lovely wee home inside a substantial bush clearing. A once overgrown clearing that Dale and I helped to bring back into order a couple of years back, doing so with chainsaw, fire and sweat. Our noisy and smoky endeavours helped to re-establish this nice wee clearing in amongst the Podocarps. No need for secrecy there as it's very much out of sight and mind of the bureaucracy. Not like silly Charlie who made himself a target by doing everything correctly, openly and honestly.

Anyway, the evening or morning poach involves a short boat trip across the lake, a very short walk through the rainforest, then a very cautious approach as you come close to the clearing's edge. The approach for the poach is normally done very, very slowly, every step well placed with intense concentration so as not to land on any loud, cracking twig on the forest floor. Your heart is always pounding hard in your chest, it pulsates in your eardrums, seemingly so loud that any deer for miles around must be able to hear the unusually loud beat. Sometimes you can just sense something is there in the clearing before you even see it and buck fever starts to kick in. On the forest edge the vista slowly opens onto a nice clearing of two to three acres with an equally nice wee house sitting in the middle of it. First, a double check that no-one is at home sitting in the living room or, if it's early morning, that no boots are on the veranda or any other similar signs of habitation. Once I have confirmed no one is in residence, I move very slowly until I can reach a spot where I can observe most of the clearing and wait for dusk to approach. Sometimes my timing of arrival is just perfect, the closing of another quiet and still Fiordland evening with an animal or two already out in the open, away from the security of their thick, rainforest home. Quietly feeding but always very alert. I prefer them close to the bush edge, it means I don't have to drag them far to gut. Obviously it's not good form to leave the guts, head and shanks in the middle of my neighbour's clearing, just in case the owner or his friends arrive for a visit before the maggots and nature has had time to work and hide the evidence of my poaching activity. If the animal is small, I will simply pack him or her the short distance to my boat and then I'm home in no time.

I have never yet poached this clearing and found the house inhabited, mainly because they always arrive with a great deal of noise, just like the Smiths next door. The noisy mechanical sound of a copter or jetboat will notify me that the owner or friends are now staying in my little poaching spot. On those occasions this little clearing is no good for poaching but it's always good for a cup of tea and a social natter, normally about the very petty Martins Bay politics, which is almost always vice driven. The jealousy of the 'have nots' versus the greed of the 'haves'.

Once the humans depart this poacher's Eden, taking with them the meat eating scent of their carnivorous diets and their overtly loud day to day noises then the deer, my dinner on the hoof, will start to graze again in this peaceful little rainforest clearing where the grass and poaching is good.

The owner, I guess, knows full well my antics. We have both done each other enough neighbourly favours to call each other friends. I don't abuse this resource, only poaching his block when I really need to get an easy animal, when I'm hungry or have guests arriving and there is no fresh meat hanging under the veranda. I may only shoot five or six animals on his clearing every year. The rest I knock over in my own forest back yard. On rare occasions I poach on the freehold clearings down at Martins Bay. Where it's like hunting in a farmer's paddock, especially mid-winter when no-one has been around for weeks, if not months.

The really funny thing is when the short whitebaiting season kicks in and I observe others poaching my little spot (as one character regularly does) I get a little jealous and grumpy! Such is the very small world of a bush hermit.

A MEMORY. Sickly, bright, splattered like a dropped can of shiny red paint against the clean white of my toilet bowl. Fresh and warm, red and fluid versus the cold sterile, snow white porcelain. There is something very clinical about fresh blood on a white surface. It sends a cold shiver to your spine. It creates a mental image of hospitals and death. A draining feeling of one's own mortality. Chilling contrasts in an unpleasant memory.

I stare down, knowing I should feel an emotion of some sort, be it concern, fear, uncertainty or even sadness. For it is my blood splashed against the white sides and seeping slowly downwards, staining the water below like red ink. But, there is absolutely no emotion! Nothing. Not even surprise at the pure quantity of blood. It seems impossible to pass so much blood and yet still be standing. Here I am staring down into my bloody toilet bowl, surrounded by my cream-walled bathroom in the middle of the New Zealand wilderness, totally empty of emotions, utterly burnt out in mind, body and soul, casually thinking, "well this is my fate." All my many battles, all my unwanted learning curves, all the never ending hard work, all the stress, it all has accumulated to this. The realisation it has all been for nothing!

My mindset is that I am going to die, death by a consuming bowel cancer seems to be my chosen path and I don't care. I've been literally eaten up and destroyed by my own selfish and foolish dreams, destroyed by the vice of my foolish pride of 'not giving up' when I should have. Destroyed by my own greed and jealously, destroyed by the utter unfairness of a bureaucracy prostituting itself to my larger commercial opposition. And I have no emotions to it all except for a seemingly resignation to my fate. The fight at this point of time is all gone.

The lack of emotion, whether it's joy or sadness, is the classic sign of depression. A burnt-out soul driving his rusty old wreck of a body down a road of no return.

THE STORY. It had started well over a year before. Nothing major, just a little blood, nothing to make a song and dance about. In fact I thought it to be just a minor fissure from around the anus. From time to time it would go away but it would always come back, just a little more pronounced than the time before, until I came to the point in time when there were regular, clockwork, explosive gushes of hot blood from my bowels into a cold, white bowl.

I was recovering from yet another bureaucratic shock which had been the worst to date. After all the battles to do this project by the book, after all the ridicule by my part-time wilderness neighbour for crossing all my bureaucratic 'T's and dotting my bureaucratic 'I's, I had a letter from the top bureaucrat herself. The Mayor of the District Council, threatening me with disciplinary action under the Resource Management Act.

It had all started with a rate increase by the Council that pushed my rates up to $1200. As I was just surviving on very meagre finances, and that's the under-statement of the book, this new burden was going to really hurt, like a sharp stick in the eye. I was not getting any extra services, in fact I wasn't getting any services at all, nor had there been any council services like roads, rubbish collection, libraries, etc. in here ever. So paying rates for non-existent services hurt in the first place, let alone being subject to a massive rate increase, it was grossly unfair. My part-time neighbour in the Bay, Bill, challenged me to act, so I wrote to the Council, asking Bill's advice on the draft and was encouraged to post it, in the raw, which in hindsight I should not have done.

I knew it would have little impact if it was thrown in with the rest of the council affairs at some council meeting, just another letter amongst many, so I posted it to the home address of each councillor which I hunted up out of the local phone directory. Clearly stating in bold, large text, the word, "Help."

The plan worked, my letter wasn't overlooked but the response was shocking in its implications. The top bureaucrat herself wrote back and the message was crystal clear. Shut up about the rates or I will take you out. Bureaucratic blackmail at its sickly worst delivered with silky, smooth words but the threat was obvious. I was shocked and spitting tacks.

There was worse to come as events unravelled. Not only was this a clear example of bureaucratic blackmail by an uncaring bureaucrat keen to push through rate increases at the expense of small remote ratepayers but, within a short time, it became evident that bureaucrat cultivation had a part to play in a drama to take

Charlie's little enterprise out of the rich kid's sandpit. This National Park of New Zealand was the playground of the big kids, no small poor kids allowed, especially ones that started from next to nothing.

I received her letter on site and was totally floored by the threats of 'Disciplinary action.' I had expected fairness and consideration from the Council whose motto is 'People First.' My concerns were very genuine and I had thought I put my case very well. I hadn't expected blackmail from the Local Authority in my wildest dreams. It seemed so immoral, so wrong, so very unjust.

I went into fight mode. Dark, angry thoughts which produced very silly, dark, angry plans, plans of a sick and depressed mind pushed to its very limits. The worst plan of many though was to march into a council hearing, cover myself in petrol and make myself a dying public torch to expose an uncaring group of bureaucrats bent on pushing through a rate increase. Pure madness on my part to even think such thoughts but at the time my project in the Fiordland wilds had consumed me through years of endless battles and stress.

I flew out of the wilderness with very dark thoughts in my heart, formulating plans of attack. First was a visit to my solicitor Rex, my solid anchor in a stormy sea. Rex read her letter then, in a very calm, professional manner, gave good sound advice to choose winnable battles and back pedal. He then refused to charge me for his time stating, "This sort of treatment shouldn't happen." He was obviously disgusted at her response but was wise enough to know it wasn't worth a battle for his client and friend. He convinced me of the same with wise words. His professional manner and sane advice calmed my self-consumed, dangerous thinking, it brought logic back into the equation.

My next visit was to the DOC head office for Southland which happens to be across the road from Rex's little office. My sleeves rolled up, still angry at the circumstances but no longer so mad or sick in mind to do anything really stupid. I had guessed that the source of information about my offences the Mayor had listed in her offical letter was from DOC. It seemed only logical. However, DOC had given me no warning about any of these issues, which all seemed very weird. Since I had gained all the necessary consents, permits, permissions, etc. we had had a reasonably good relationship with each other, at least I thought so. So this development had caught me totally by surprise. I was ready for action as I stepped out of the elevator doors into the DOC offices. I aimed for the top bureaucrat, the 'Regional Conservator' but he was away, so the 2IC was next in line. The wind was very quickly taken out of my sails as absolutely no one had any idea what I was talking about! I was totally floored, expecting words of conflict but was offered hands of peace, soft words and terms. "Soft words pacify anger," – wisdom from old King Solomon. The appropriate compliance people were called into DOC's little windowless conference room and clearly denied that they, nor anybody else in DOC, were responsible for giving the Mayor the information used in her letter. They explained that procedure had to be followed with an investigation undertaken and documentation completed... and there was absolutely nothing on file. The top man (Dave) from the Te Anau office which administers Fiordland National Park was visiting the Invercargill office at the time. In fact Dave took me aside after the meeting, looked me in the eye and stated words to the effect, "Charlie, if we (DOC) were the source of this information I would have heard about it." He was very genuine and I clicked that both he and the DOC people I had just been talking to had no reason to be lying. He quietly went on to suggest, in hushed breath, that maybe someone else had something to gain by giving the Mayor the impression I was the naughty kid on the block.

Then the 'penny dropped.' The mayor had not sourced the information from another bureaucracy such as DOC or the Regional Council nor from any policing agency from within her own bureaucracy but from a private source who had her ear and stood to win if I was taken out of the picture. A private, commercial entity.

It didn't take a rocket scientist to nut out where she got the information from. The words of her own letter gave the game away. "After a recent visit to the area I was informed..." She had been in Fiordland opening a new private, commercial lodge owned by some very wealthy New Zealanders. She was their guest to be wined, dined, accommodated and, as it turned out, successfully cultivated by people who stood to gain the most if I was not operating commercially in the Park, their sandpit. She had been wined, dined and accommodated by a person who had written a submission of opposition against my project, right at the very beginning of my resource consent process. She prostituted her bureaucracy to the wealthy. She actioned this letter without getting all the facts and was doing it with complete bias to one side. She actioned her letter direct from her mayoral office to one of the smallest, remotest businesses under her governorship, using bureaucratic blackmail to achieve her aim and exposing in the process that she was subject to cultivation. Of course that was all assumption on my part. All the pieces were beginning to fit the puzzle but I had no real evidence except her own written words, "After a recent visit ..."

This quiet but growing assumption was confirmed months later by a visiting councillor, from within her very own council. He was a guest and friend of my neighbour Bill in the Bay. Bill, as per normal, was being the natural host keeping all his guest's glasses full of alcohol which has a great tendency to loosen tongues. Later in the evening I was helping with a fry up of steaks out back of Bill's little bach. Just me and the friendly councillor who actually is a nice, down to earth guy of healthy Southland farming stock. While cooking the meat on Bill's gas hot plates, he casually brought my little problem into the conversation. I had learnt through damage to my tender ego to hold my tongue and listen more than talk. There is old wisdom in doing this, there are times when it's best to keep your mouth shut. "Even a fool is thought wise if he keeps silent, and discerning if he holds his tongue." Proverbs 17:18. And I can be a pretty big fool at times. He casually asked me if I knew where she (the Mayor) got the information used in the letter which had rocked my whole existence to the very core. I wanted, needed to hear my assumptions proved by an outside source. I needed to justify the dark, angry, inner thoughts against this unjust bureaucracy so I shrugged off a half truth and said, "No, not really." He then proceeded to confirm my assumption, "It was .... of course," in a very matter of fact tone, as if I was pretty silly to have not nutted out who the source was all by myself.

Here I was doing everything by the book, I had gone through a nightmare procedure under her Council to obtain a 'Fully Notified' Resource Consent for land use, a 'Fully Notified' Resource Consent for septic, I had adhered to the guidelines of the 'Scenic Protection Order' administered by her Council, to then watch a person who opposed me during the Consent process purchase and redevelop two lodges in the area, both with capacity far larger than mine, and doing so without the 'Notified Consent' procedures that I had been forced to go through with my much smaller lodge, developing them outside the guidelines that her Council had made me strictly adhere to. Then, to rub dirt into my nose, she opened these competing lodges, giving them her official blessing, doing so with much positive media and in the presence of important people like a local MP and Head Conservator. Then she gives me the coup de grace with a kick to the head when she uses her high office and position of power to imply that I am the naughty kid on the block, doing so with information supplied to her by the very people who have accommodated her. Commercial competitors who stood to gain for me to be perceived as being in the wrong by her Council. She acted on this information with complete bias to their side, without checking out all the facts.

It was sickening in its utter unfairness, sickening in utter hypocrisy, just outright sickening. Her letter exposed firstly bureaucratic blackmail and secondly an abuse of her power, it favoured the strong to take out the weak within in her dominion.

What made it worse was that I couldn't do anything about it. I couldn't work any harder to solve this one. I just had to roll on the ground and take the bureaucratic kicking I didn't deserve. My solicitor's advice was to go to the council compliance people, drop the rate issue and back out of the battle, which I did.

All the points she had raised, with the exception of one, were reasonably easy to defend to her compliance people, simply because she had not done her homework. The veranda balustrades were a classic of the left hand not knowing what the right hand was doing within in her own authority. The bush clearance was covered by the wonderful salvage permits that my neighbour Bill had repeatedly told me I was silly in getting.

The total unfairness of the situation though was hitting me very hard. The perceived thinking in New Zealand is that our bureaucracy is just and fair. Authorities administering our affairs with no bias to who is big and who is small, no bias to who is rich or who is poor, no bias to who is friendly with the right bureaucrats and who is not. But that misconception is simply not the case. At least not in my situation.

The stress, anger, jealously, greed were all accumulating up to a point of time which saw me staring down into a bloody toilet bowl in the middle of nowhere, totally beaten by a woman who allowed her position of power over me to be used. I was not angry at the man who gave her the information. He had operated completely within the scope of the law, however the cultivation of a top bureaucrat who should be impartial and fair in such things was breaking me, turning my poor bowel into a bloody mess of ulcerating, weeping sores and my soul into a dark, self-consumed place.

I was stuck away in the wilderness with an advertised season to complete and not a bean in the bank to go back into the real world to gain assistance, to mend my leaking body and bitter mind. All I could do was battle on with what I had in the Fiordland rainforest and find ways to survive, which is exactly what I did. Getting up to some very silly antics as you will read in the next chapter, but also meeting some really nice people.

THE PRESENT: The old hand-crank diesel Lister is thumping quietly away in the background, a very distant sound muffled by the rainforest as I have built a very small punga generator shed and situated it away from the house, hidden by the old podocarp giants. The exhaust which makes a majority of the sound is also muffled by a 12-gallon drum which is then surrounded by river rocks inside a 44-gallon drum which does not look a pretty picture but works quite well. This little generator, although old and archaic in design, runs off the smell of an oily rag and has been super reliable. It doesn't need a charged battery to start each time which is a big plus when you don't run a generator enough to charge a battery anyway and, because of its equally simple design, is easy to fix when things do go wrong which isn't very often. Nine times out of ten it's a fuel problem easily fixed. Simplicity in the wild for such things is the key to long term survival when one is poor.

I feel I should end this chapter on a more positive note as most of it has been about my weeping bowel and angry soul which probably isn't everybody's cup of tea to read about. At present the bleeding is managed in some degree by huge suppositories in bad times and mitigated the rest of the time with a better diet with a far larger green intake than in previous years. The dark, angry soul and self-consumed attitude is slowly changing for the better.

To end this chapter and maybe lighten the mood I'll tell the reader about some of the people I have met and who have stayed with me over the years in my wilderness homestay in Fiordland. There are a whole spectrum of people from all sorts of backgrounds but, in the main they have been really nice people to get to know. Some of them have been very interesting in character as it takes a special kind of person to make the effort to explore places like this.

Some short descriptions :

Friends, Nick and Penny. A lovely, married couple with big hearts and a practical 'can do' attitude. They have been working for Hollyford Track Ltd at Martins Bay in the company's guided walking seasons for a couple of summers so far, one as a cook, the other as a jetboat driver. As a result they have become very

Happy guests having fun in my outside bath.

On the beach at Jamestown Bay – me, friend Nick (centre) and
a staff member from down at Martins Bay Lodge.

good friends to the extent that Nick, a builder by trade, has helped me to build a large, open, insect proof conservatory out the back of my little bach. This is a big plus in Fiordland, especially when you want to be outside but away from the persistent sandflies and their annoying bite. A great place to hang a deer carcass so you can skin and dress the meat away from the equally annoying blowfly and its associated foul brood of maggots. Or just a nice place for a midday meal in summer surrounded by tall podocarp rainforest. I will always have an open door policy for Nick and Penny, good friends.

There is a lovely couple, English imports to New Zealand now living in Te Anau. Retired seafood restaurateurs from Saint Ives, they have come and stayed with me as paying guests more than once over the years. Repeat clientele is always good business and they are always great company to accommodate and entertain.

However, the weirdest person experience to recount to the reader was the visit of a North American transvestite, which was a major fright for a very straight and traditional southern boy to digest and still is. Not something you expect to see in the wilds of Fiordland. His arrival up my little bush track was completely unexpected. He was tramping the Hollyford by himself and had booked a night via my brother John prior to starting the three day trek. Because I had missed my radio schedule with Carol I didn't know of his booking. Thankfully I had plenty of venison to feed him with and the house was in order to accept guests, however, his sudden arrival and unique appearance had me completely caught off guard. In description he was a huge man, not in the sense he was overweight, as overweight people can't manage walking three days in the wilderness to get somewhere, especially navigating the likes of the Demon Trial with their day to day needs packed away in a heavy pack on their back, but simply big in his frame, a very tall and solidly built man. There his masculine appearance stopped utterly, much to my shock and horror. He had shaved legs and was wearing very tight leotards, the sort young peach bottom women wear to gym classes. He had breasts which I supposed were hormone induced but by far the weirdest part of his appearance was his hair. He had half his head completely shaved like a skinhead, the other half had long hair with a ponytail down his back. Once I recovered from this sudden shock to my system, I set about making my paying guest at home the best way I could. I did him my standard fare of a venison back steak, being prime cut meat which I marinated in ginger, garlic, red wine and honey. He polished it off very quickly and then asked for a repeat, saying it was the best meat he had even eaten. Basically eating the complete back straps of a yearling which would normally feed four. My frights from this unexpected guest were not yet complete because, just on evening he found a lone humble bumble bee trapped in his bedroom ensuite. Bouncing out to me in the candle-lit living-room with a very feminine prance, hands held high, limp wrists flying and literally yelling in the best feminine voice he could master, "There's a bumble bee in my bathroom," repeated twice for effect. Once I recovered from that whole visual assault on my poor traditional senses (a large framed man, wearing leotards, with breasts, acting like a women and very distressed over a small insect) I then dealt with the

Upper Kaipo Valley.

offending bumble bee and by doing so noticed he had all female toiletries neatly on display, the sort of things most seasoned female trampers would not burden their back with. Needless to say I slept very poorly that night and even placed a wooden wedge under my bedroom door. He never tried anything inappropriate and other than his confused gender and scary appearance was a nice sort of person. I discovered through standard homestay chit-chat of complete strangers that he was a successful record producer from Canada. My guess being that he was also a very wealthy man traveling the world and not at least worried about the effect his transgender appearance had on people. Especially a conservative bush hermit in the remote wilderness of Fiordland.

Chapter Seventeen

BANGS IN THE NIGHT

OFF SEASON FROM MY WILDERNESS HOME. I was lying on my stomach, exposing my lilywhite, skinny butt to the surgeon, a Mr Ngai down in Invercargill. He had a probe of some medical description up my back side having a jolly good explore at the inner workings of my poor, weeping bowels. Not a glamorous position for me to be in. Normally the whole undignified situation would have been made even more embarrassing for me because he had a very attractive nurse in attendance with him. Attractive women always drive poor introvert, bush hermit's inner workings into chaotic turmoil of unsatiated wants but I didn't really care anymore. My pride, ego and over eager libido had evaporated like early morning mist on a soon to be sunny day in the Upper Hokuri flats. She could have been Miss New Zealand and wearing only a pink ribbon in her hair and I wouldn't have really cared. To her credit, she made the situation a little lighter in mood with a well-timed joke.

Suddenly there was a very abrupt, intense pain from my innards, something I wasn't quite expecting. My surgeon had just taken a sample, without telling me, but I guess that was the best way to do it. This sampling business didn't bode well in my head, why had he taken a sample? It was obviously a part of me because of the pain, obviously a growth in my bowel with nerves in it which shouldn't be there. I had expected that there would be something unpleasant growing, unwanted and unloved in my bowel, the sampling process just confirmed my suspicions.

Mr Ngai stated in a matter of fact tone, giving nothing positive or negative away, that he needed to send it away for testing. Okay, that I knew was necessary as well.

Back I went to Queenstown, stoking on the *Earnslaw*, winter time again, off season from my wilderness home. Working myself into the ground, hating the plastic tourist town with its equally plastic fast-living lifestyle but part of me enjoyed my work mates. I was slowly becoming a little more used to the church going than I had previously. Dave as per normal was looking after his bush hermit mate.

The results came back in so it was a two hour drive back down to Invercargill. I was ready to hear the worst, in fact I kind of expected it. "Benign," stated Mr Ngai. Now silly, simple me didn't really know what that meant. "Does that mean it is cancerous or not?" "Ooooh," it's not. Well that's one out of the bag. Still, what was causing all the blood, equally important though was how to stop it? The surgeon and the doctor both had different theories on the cause. One said it was probably, "Overwork and stress," the other said, "It's probably poor diet." After all, I had had years of living on red meat, tin and dry goods with very little or no fruit and vegies for long periods. Fruit and vegies are super important to our diets. My wilderness lifestyle experiment with no freezer to store food and helicopter re-supplies only done every six months had its down side. In a way I reckoned both surgeon and doctor were right, overwork, stress and poor diet had been a standard part of my existence since this project started and even a bit before. Time was getting close for a change in life. Doctor and surgeon told me I needed to start looking after myself a bit better as there is a tendency towards cancer in this sort of situation, the next time the growth in my blood weeping bowel may be cancerous. Mr Ngai prescribed me some huge suppositories, the size and shape of short fat Cuban cigars. I showed one to one of my stoker work mates and there was huge mirth as these things aren't small items to be putting up one's backside. The laughter was great to hear, after all I had been through it wasn't cancer and I could enjoy the joke and enjoy the fact they found humour in the whole situation.

THE STORY CONTINUES. I had tried so very hard to do everything by the book. I thought I had succeeded, fought the good fight and could stand securely on all the bureaucratic procedures, consents, licenses and permits, I had battled through to live and work on my own piece of wilderness. Now, however, I was faced with the cold, stark reality of how things really are with NZ bureaucracy. Abundances of money and influence had far more effect on major bureaucrats at the top of the management tree than actually doing everything by the book with the petty bureaucrat swinging around in the lower branches. At the end of the day adhering to all the laws, rules and regulations was a poor second place to wining, dining and accommodating the ego of the right bureaucrats. I was never in the position to have the money nor the influence to play this game. It seemed so wrong, so unfair, so unjust. Yet this was the way it was.

My respect for the local authority simply vanished.

Although I was getting a little sicker in mind and body, I had no choice but to keep battling forward, even be it ever so slowly. I adopted the local policy, as repeatedly encouraged by my part-time neighbour, Bill. It was time to become a little more cunning in my approach at managing my affairs at Jamestown. If a tree was on my land and was affecting sunlight, I dealt with it. I didn't tell the Council, I didn't tell DOC. In fact I didn't tell anybody, I simply dealt with it, as quietly and as quickly as possible although, in the process, I still made sure that I had some legal correctness to my activities.

The Scenic Protection Order that the council was making me and not others adhere to stated only 150 square metres of 'bush clearance per title'. My lawyer Rex brought to my attention the definition of the word 'clearance' and argued that the word meant total removal of vegetation to create a 'clear' area, a bit like a lawn or paddock. Therefore, on this premise, one could still top a tree or even take out a whole tree, if you left the sub-storey vegetation, the ferns and bushes underneath. It could not be deemed to be 'bush clearance', at least not in a technical, legal sense.

More like managed gardening of the forest on your own land. This was very much my cup of tea as I could top trees affecting my sunlight but still leave the forest feel of my property and, in theory, do it legally.

Due to my previous treatment by bureaucracy I sensed I would not be dealt with in a fair manner if I placed such a proposition to them. A couple of years earlier I would have chosen that as the correct and only right path to follow, without even a second thought, but not now. I opted for the more cunning and stealthy approach to survive. If found out, I could always fall back on the legal definition of bush clearance. A new approach to life in the wilderness.

Stealth in this case meant explosives, powergel and cortex. The effect in theory looked more natural in appearance. A blown, shattered tree trunk looks more like the result of natural causes to the unsuspecting, unknowing eye than the obvious straight lines of a chainsaw cut.

I embarked on another series of learning curves. The concept given to me by my part-time neighbour Bill was to drill a hole in the trunk and place a stick of powergel into it and "bang." It sounded simple enough but, in reality, it didn't work that well. Firstly I couldn't find a big enough drill bit, second I had to slit open the plastic wrapped explosive plugs and force the grey product into the hole and, thirdly, these were Fiordland rainforest trees covered in vines, mosses and all sorts of other growths, so establishing a drill hole straight into the core of the tree, at the right place, was not as easy as it sounds, especially when perched high up in the tree working a hand brace and bit while tied to the tree, normally in a very awkward position, balancing on a branch or wedged in the fork of a tree, or hanging in a very uncomfortable harness. It all got a little Mickey Mouse.

Having the time with a lack of other options bred persistence in the wilderness, so I soon refined the whole process. The main change was not drilling one hole and charging it with a single stick of powergel but drilling a series of far smaller holes and charging them with homemade explosive charges. These little self-made charges were simply manufactured by cutting short strips of cortex and taping them tightly together to form mini-explosive plugs that fitted very snugly into a hole of my largest diameter drill bit. Cortex is basically an instantaneous fuse made of high explosive called PETN. Cortex doesn't have filler product in it like powergel, just concentrated explosive so, when confined, it has a far bigger bang per weight than Powergel. Each hole drilled into the trunk was connected to the next with a single piece of cortex then connected to a single number 8 detonator and safety fuse and I was set to go.

The preparation of the tree would sometimes take days. A factor probably more associated to my failing, bleeding body, lacking in normal energy levels than the actual workload involved. First I had to work out the amount of tree I wanted to top to get the optimum angle of morning and evening sunlight. This was achieved through simple dawn and dusk observations of the tree silhouettes and shadows as the sun started and finished its day. Next I had to find a safe way to get up and down the tree. Normally I would start using a ladder for the base. From the top of the ladder I would then very slowly and carefully climb up, through the branches and rata vines, attaching ropes along the way and securing them to my harness. This first climb was a little hair-raising at times, at least until I had some ropes secured at the top then it was reasonably safe. When I reached the desired height I would then drill my holes by hand with the old hand operated brace and bit, a 'pass me down' tool of my father's. I would load the holes with my little made up explosive charges, connect them all with cortex before finally setting up the detonator and fuse. Safety fuse burns very slowly but I wasn't relying on this, so was working with good safety margins with fuses that took several minutes to burn. They were still very short in length therefore had to be set alight while I was still up in the tree, hooked up in my harness. When all was ready I would abseil down out of the tree, ensuring I had a clear and quick escape route down through the branches, vines and tree ferns. Next I checked that no one was in the locality by darting down my little bush track and hopping into my boat, shooting out of my sheltered Bay, into the centre of McKerrow's waters where I could clearly observe the beach both north and south to ascertain that there were no trampers on the local section of the Hollyford track. Then, straight back up the track, climb back up the tree, light the fuse, abseil down and hide behind a stout looking moss and vine covered tree, away from the action, with my stressed heart pounding in my chest like the poor thing was wanting to break out through my rib cage to freedom. Waiting nervously full of pent up adrenalin for the thunderous bang, hoping I didn't have a misfire, hoping the vibration would not take out my windows, hoping no trampers were in ear shot, hoping I would not have a hung up tree, tangled up high and hence dangerous to clear.

Boy, what a noise it created. Using powergel and cortex below ground is one thing, the sound in general is muffled, absorbed by dirt, but the noise above ground is a completely different story altogether. Open to the air waves it goes with a deafening and loud crack, the explosion echoing and thundering around the valley and through the rainforest for several long seconds.

I never had a misfire, never lost a valuable window and never had a suspicious tramper query the big bang down in the Lower Hollyford Valley but I did have a few hung up trees, not crashing to the forest floor like they should have but caught up high in the branches, forks and vines of other trees. Of the whole process this was by far the most dangerous part, climbing back up and nutting out the best ways to deal with the offending tree tops hanging a couple of storeys above the ferny forest floor.

After a while I got a little paranoid about the possibility of a passing tramper hearing the bang. I could argue that it might have been a rifle shot and from a remote distance most people could easily be confused with the difference, I decided against not chancing this possibility and decided to wait patiently for a stormy, rainy night. If anybody was at the Hokuri hut and did awake to the sound, they would think in their sleepy, dreamy state of distant thunder rumbling in the forest clad mountains. They would never think it was some weird bush hermit, paranoid by an evil, unjust bureaucracy, blowing out the tops of rainforest trees at night. So, on a stormy night I hopped out of bed in the very early hours and lit the fuse with some difficultly as rain and wet flints on lighters don't always go well together but, once the safety fuse was ignited, it was on its way. (The hess and tar covered safety fuse even works under water so it is a sure product for this sort of endeavour in wet environments.) With the fuse lit there was then a dark, wet and very hurried abseil out the forest tops to find appropriate shelter from the chaos I was about to cause on this part of my rainforest domain. I waited out the big bang, dried off the soaked body and hopped back into bed but never slept, my system too full of adrenalin and a huge curiosity to see what the effects my antics and hard work had accomplished. Waiting impatiently for the budding, dawning light of the following new day.

It worked out well but I only did that once. I went back to climbing and cutting by hand, normally with the old hand crosscut saw but sometimes with a chainsaw, which was a dangerous act to behold and would have given kittens to any OSH inspector if he had ever seen it.

With the trees topped the work did not stop there, it had just begun. Up the tree the evidence looked like natural causes and was very unlikely to be the subject of any close inspection but it was a completely different story on the ground. Anybody with a little experience with explosives could tell by the shattered, splintered trunk or equally evident chainsaw cuts what I had been up to. With the aid of Dad's trusty old crosscut saw yet again I would cut it into manageable sections, drag out the cut or blown section of tree and burn the evidence. The heads of some of these trees were huge, being heavy and green with leaf, all full of wet sap, so these bonfires took some getting going. However, when they finally did get a good heavy firebase, the heat and energy would burn even wet wood and green leaves but would also create huge amounts of white smoke, billowing high up into the air. Any plane flying in the National Park would be drawn to this oddity in a wet rainforest and that's not what I wanted. So around mid-afternoon I would start with some dry fire wood from under my house, which doesn't generate very much smoke, and get a good strong base to my fire. Just on dusk I would pile on the green branches, creating large bonfires in the Fiordland night that no-one except the Moreporks, possums and I could see. I would tend the fire throughout the night and by morning would have most of the smoke-causing greenery gone. Sometimes these clear up jobs took days to do. At this stage I was always nervous of discovery as the evidence of my handy work was lying on the forest floor for all to see and I would work hard to get rid of it.

One afternoon I got a little impatient. I hadn't heard a passing plane nor any passing trampers for some days and presumed that I had the area to myself and it was going to be okay to start burning the greenery a little earlier than normal, saving me an all-night fireside chore and get me a few more hours of extra sleep. I worked on the assumption no-one would be flying at this time of day as it was late in the afternoon and they would run out of daylight to fly home back to civilisation over snowy Southern Alps. Unless of course they were heading to Martins Bay but I hadn't heard anybody fly into Martins Bay for some time. I took a little gamble and started earlier than I should have. But, patience is a virtue, a very old and wise proverb. I should have waited an hour as no sooner had the thick, wet greenery started pushing a huge, straight column of dirty white smoke skyward than I heard the dreaded sound of a plane and, sure enough, it deviated off course to circle my large column of smoke in the sky to check out what was happening below. Murphy's law at work. No doubt cameras were clicking away as the plane flew on the short distance to land at Martins Bay for the night.

Within a very short time the trees would naturally bush over the damage I had inflicted. The surviving lower branches got extra life-giving sunlight and as a result sprouted forth new, vibrant growth. In a way it was pruning with cortex. Nobody new to my little forest clearing in the Fiordland noticed anything unnatural about the tree skyline. The exception of course being those who knew what my clearing size was like prior to my tree-topping activities.

I got at least a couple hours of extra winter sun as a result. A process that would need to be done again in ten years' time, if not much sooner.

THE TREE THAT WOULDN'T FALL OVER. My little piece of wilderness in the National Park is situated on the corner of Lake and Bay Street. Streets surveyed off in 1870 drawn with ink on vellum but never formed. They are only 'paper roads', existing only on paper, never on the ground. No cars or trucks or bikes have ever used these roads. It's virgin rainforest, just vines, ferns and century old trees with only birds, possums and deer to transit through and over what man has drawn as roads on pieces of old goat or pig skin 130 years earlier. The interesting thing of note is that although these roads have never existed as the real thing, they are in fact still seen as 'legal'. A fact I confirmed from the District Land Registrar early in my bureaucratic battles.

My trusty solicitor brought to my attention a law which states that as a land owner you have a legal right to keep your road frontages clear of vegetation. An interesting concept. I was aware of a land owner in the Park, way down Preservation way, who used this law to clear roads in the forest but I was just a little different in the fact that I liked my forest surrounds. Yes, I cut down trees here in the wilderness, yes I topped surrounding trees but that was for very practical reasons. I saw no reason to clear the roads adjoining my properties, I was here because of the forest surrounds. I was here because of the wilderness. I saw no reason to clear fell the roads, I was not in suburbia, nor did I want to be. But this law gave me a small legal edge as I could take out the odd tree or top the odd tree to give either sunlight or view.

By this stage my opposition were using their jetboat to transport people along the lake, bypassing the Demon Trail, to deposit their clients at Jamestown to see where people had tried to exist a century beforehand, their guides giving them a historical rundown on the failed township with its sad history. These tourists would then walk along the lake through the podocarp forest to their lodge at Martins Bay. These guides began to show their clients my place in their passing, many of whom came in for a look and sometimes even for a cuppa, my little wilderness endeavour of interest to them. Showing their clients my rainforest hideaway was though bad business on the part of the guides. Their clients very soon noted that my place was a lot better and far, far cheaper than where they were staying. To counter-act this, a new policy was started by my opposition which simply meant that after a visit to Jamestown they hopped back onto the jetboat and were transported down past my place, instead of walking passed my front gate, to the bottom of the lake where they disembarked and walked the last hour through the easy going forest to their lodgings. The problem this had of course was the growing number of freedom walkers opting to use the jetboat service to avoid doing the dreaded 'Demon Trail'. This meant that in bypassing my front gate in effect it reduced the number of people discovering my little forest hide away lodge. In a business sense I could see why they made such a decision.

I needed more exposure. If the freedom walkers could simply see my place from where the jetboat disembarked and embarked them on the beach in my Bay, potentially that would make them curious. A good thing which may have a spin off. More people wanting to walk from Jamestown Bay to Martins Bay and in the process check me and my little accommodation facility out.

I figured that if I knocked out one of the lakeside trees it would create a small glimpse of my place from where they landed people on the sandy gravel beach.

The obvious tree was an old, large beech leaning well over the beach with a nice hollow and semi-rotten trunk. Being on my road frontage I had the legal fall back of 'keeping my road frontage clear of vegetation.' Secondary was the hazard the tree presented to anybody parking their boat on the beach in front of my place, a common occurrence, but wisdom said deal with the tree on the quiet and only use the legal fallbacks if it became an issue.

I had three sticks of powergel left. Having to live such a frugal existence and to get the absolute best out of the limited resources at my disposal, I decided to place just one stick into the hollow, rotten core of the tree, thereby save the other two sticks for other opportunities. I waited for the next flood when McKerrow's waters were up above the gravel beach and lapping around the base of the tree, invading the forest. This way I could drag the tree out of my little Bay into the centre of the lake and let wind and nature deposit the evidence of my mischief far away from my beach frontage. Out of sight, out of mind.

A day dawned with the perfect flood conditions to proceed. I placed the stick of powergel into the hollow trunk, packed it tightly with sandbags to get the optimum effect on the trunk, checked no-one was in the locality and lit my tar-covered safety fuse and hid myself behind a moss encrusted tree to await my new view of the lake and, incidentally of course, for potential clients to see my little lodge.

"Bang." The forest shook with the concussion of blast waves vibrating through the dense rainforest, echoing loudly once again off the surrounding hills. But there was no follow through sound of a tree crashing and splashing into the muddied flood waters of McKerrow. On inspection I was horrified to find the tree still standing but, worse still, on the lakeside of the trunk facing the beach, obvious for all to see, was a massive hole with a mushroom effect of shattered and splintered white wood blasted outwards. Shattered wood for all to see sticking out against the green and grey old trunk. Obvious to anybody walking along the Hollyford Track directly in front of my place. This was not good. I had to do something. My next step was to place a second stick under the root system at the back of the tree. "Bang." The second explosion rocked the surrounding forest and my ear drums. Still the strong old beech tree stood. In panic I placed my last precious stick of gel deeper under this very resilient tree that refused to drop. A third and final explosion rocked my peaceful forest domain and still this very stubborn and resilient tree was still standing. What a complete and utter stuff up. I should have used all three sticks together under its base instead of being so frugal, so Scottish, with my supplies. When doing my blasting course in Western Australia we had learnt the technique of blasting tree stumps and I should have stuck to that instead of trying to use the rotten core of the tree to save on my limited supply of explosives.

What a predicament to be in. With the large hole blown in the tree it didn't take a rocket scientist to nut out what I had been trying to do. I had to act before the flood waters dropped, before I lost the opportunity of removing the evidence from out in front of my place in this wee forest Bay.

By this stage I had another chainsaw, joint ownership with Bill. The last resort option was to cut down the tree, which I did but the massive tree splashing into the flooded lake didn't end my troubles. The very stubborn tree only partly floated, the weight of greenery had caused the tree to partly submerge, the heavy large upper limbs rested on the lake bottom which made it impossible to tow away with my wee boat. I had to cut off some major limbs to get the thing floating. What a nightmare. A chainsaw doesn't work under water so it was out with Dad's trusty crosscut saw to try and cut off some of the large limbs, a massive task. Soon I was very wet, working in the lake, sometimes up to my armpits. I got very cold, very miserable, very exhausted. Then the worst possible thing that could happen, happened. Around the point came the opposition's jetboat full of tourists. I was caught in the act. A large native tree lying in the water directly in front of my place, me battling away trying to get it to float properly before the lake dropped and the opportunity would be lost for its removal. The tourists disembarked across the Bay and disappeared into the forest with their guide to check out the remnants of old 1870 Jamestown.

There was nothing for it but to carry on with the battle, get the tree afloat and out of the Bay before the flooded lake dropped too much, a process that happens very quickly once the rain stops. Finally, after hours of much frantic work, I got the main log free of the bottom and floating. Towing my large moss-covered nightmare out into the lake for the wind to carry all the evidence away and deposit on some far away shore.

This tree, however, was to have one final dig at Charlie. The next day I found it high and dry, resting on the beach directly in front of the Hokuri Hut, deposited there by the falling lake. Of all the miles and miles of remote shore line on this long narrow wilderness lake for this log to end up on, with all its obvious chainsaw cuts, it had to choose a very small section of shoreline directly in front of a DOC hut as its resting place.

On the upside of the whole equation I talked to Nick who was skippering the tourist jetboat on the horrible day of my failed tree-felling attempts and he said that the no one on board really noticed my activity across the other side of the Bay. They thought it was all just a normal activity, away in the sticks, at the ghost town of Jamestown Bay. A passing interest for them to look at then get on with their tour. Even Nick thought I was just removing a fallen tree from my beach frontage, a tree he thought had come down through natural causes.

In hindsight I wasn't doing anything illegal. The trees were on my own land or on my legal road frontages but at the time I had developed a very unhealthy paranoia about the council connection to my commercial opposition and this had infected my thought patterns in a very negative, unhealthy way. It was a paranoia out of all proportion to the whole situation. Paranoia that drove me to climb high rainforest trees and light fuses on dark, stormy nights. Easy to say now but I would not have admitted it then. My nocturnal activities, in my head, was my way of surviving against an unjust bureaucracy and keeping my venture going forward by good old-fashioned hard work and persistence.

This paranoia though, whether it was sound or unsoundly based, was not mending my bleeding body.

A SIDE STORY. Dale's little place at Big Bay is quite an interesting piece of dirt to visit. He is my closest full time neighbour so to speak but it takes about five to six hours walk to get there. So don't be fooled into thinking he is just a gentle amble away through the rainforest.

Anyway, Dale has lived there for thirty-five very interesting years. His little hick house with its outside bath and drift wood door handles is very basic in design but is very functional for his lifestyle. It is also very close to the sea. Dale's practical wisdom made him choose the very best and most sheltered place on that piece of wild west coastline, facing the sunny north but completely sheltered from the predominate weather and seas. He is so close to the sea in fact that, at high tide, it's only about twenty metres to his front door.

My tale of using explosives to achieve an aim would be incomplete if I didn't tell the reader about Dale's antics with a whale on the remote West Coast. A dead whale washed ashore directly in front of his house, which is a major problem because decomposing whales stink for months as they rot away. Not a good thing to have sitting at your residential door step.

First he tried cutting up the whale into manageable pieces with a chainsaw but this soon proved to be a waste of time. No doubt it clogged the chainsaw and covered the operator in a mist of rotten whale blubber. So next came the powergel which did the trick. His only problem then was that chunks of blubber, big and small, covered everything in the surrounding area, including his little hick house and associated out buildings.

Not the sort of problem that one gets in town.

| Chapter Eighteen | # SLOW ENLIGHTENMENT |

THE PRESENT: Deep Cove, Doubtful Sound, Fiordland National Park. It's been two years since I sold, leaving my hard-won wilderness home and that tranquil little half-moon shaped bay with her pristine still waters, presiding over many memories, both pleasant and dark. I'll leave describing my present occupation and location (Deep Cove) for later in the chapter as it will take a couple of pages just to explain. There are still plenty of fresh memories and messy notes to refer back to. Before I complete my wilderness tale gone wrong, I had better, however, first set the stage for the reader about finding in this lush, temperate South Pacific rainforest, a genuine faith in God. Not the luke-warm faith of my youth with a free entry card to heaven just in case it was all true. Insurance policy type of false faith. This is a real and unshakable belief in God's existence. It will help explain my life's turn around and the unique tales yet to be associated to selling my special wilderness home of seven years. Some may find the next couple of chapters uncomfortable in a spiritual or personal belief sense as most cringe at the pure mention of the topic. If that's the case, you have that wonderful God given choice of 'free will' not to read them, especially if you feel your worldly sensibilities are likely to be offended or challenged. Free will sets us apart from just being created robots, free will is an essential part of having a soul. We have the choice to read or not to read whatever we want, to believe or not believe whatever we want, that solely is your choice. However, by not reading them, it will make some of my decisions and actions in the last chapter totally and utterly incomprehensible for you to understand. So maybe don't read the last chapter either.

SLOW ENLIGHTENMENT: There are many secular theories why one starts to believe in God. Sociologists, psychologists and the wisdom of common man will have many varied opinions on the topic.

Looking at my little story of woe, they will probably cite a variety of causes. Some may blame depression, that in my self-absorbed opinion my world was falling apart, that I would naturally turn to God. Take to the false and short lived emotive highs of some happy clappy charismatic church as a way to break out of my depression. Maybe they would say it was because my bleeding, weeping body was constantly whispering to my subconscious mind that I was not immortal. That with the finality of dying no one is truly an atheist. When the time comes for our little candle to finally extinguish itself for ever, we deeply consider such things. Then again they may say I was outside of the normal conditioning effects of modern society with no TV, radio, nor regular human interaction to recondition my mind to modern, accepted norms of the world. Norms that say a genuine belief in God is no longer appropriate in our modern educated western world, which loves the 'everything goes' loud liberalism of today and hates old- fashioned, quiet conservativism of the past. Some may say it was because of my surroundings, being immersed in nature's best. Encompassed by scenic snow-capped mountains and engulfed by lush emerald rainforest. Nature's incredible beauty making me see God in the complex design and purpose to it all that in the Darwinian opinion of modern educated man doesn't really exist. Design and order that is just a figment of my over-active imagination. Others may say that the remote solitude and immense stillness of the wilderness would force me to try and find companionship in a God. Or even the amazing coincidences that arose when I called out to God for help, or put me in just the right place at just the right time to be of help or even save others. Maybe they would all come to a consensus and say it was a combination of all of the above.

Personally I know that there is a bit of truth to all of the above. It is very hard to fully describe the inner sensation or feelings of personal faith to another person. Or of the situations where I felt the eerie presence of something either very good or very evil. Or of situations where I had the 'free will' to choose a course of action which either gave me an inner peace that I was doing the right thing or the complete opposite of inner turmoil when I chose the wrong thing. All very hard to explain to those who don't accept the existence of a soul or of a spiritual context to life. However, if I had to choose just one of the non-spiritual options listed above as a driving force in my ever growing faith in a God and Creator, it would be seeing the complex order, design and purpose in the nature that surrounds me. A line of thought that blossomed when I started to read about the taboo fields of the sciences that supports creation. A growing field of science that points away from the standard accepted theory of evolution. A theory which in essence says there is no need for a God.

God and Science are not spoken about in the same breath; some academics say it's very naughty to do so and get passionately angry about it. To most in our modern western society God is now deemed completely and utterly illogical, a phantom of ancient myths and fables. Story-telling of the Bible reserved for the simple-minded folk and the uneducated – not relevant to the modern age of the enlightened world. A bygone superstition of previous generations. The other is logical. Science is all about proven facts, solid foundation for the intelligent, educated, modern man to base complete rock solid faith in. Never the twain should meet. Not comprehendible to even consider it. You're mad, weird, unsound of mind to even think the two can mix. It's like mixing oil and milk, no good ever comes from it.

However, being outside of the conditioning of modern society, stuck in my self-imposed forest and mountain prison with its rocky high walls of mountain, snow and ice and the tall bars of ancient, twisted rainforest trees, locked away from the wisdom of enlightened man, I did the socially unacceptable thing. I started reading by flickering candle light about the science that supports creation as opposed to evolution. It's not as mad cap as one would imagine, of twelve thousand scientists surveyed in the States, in excess of two thousand believe that life was created as opposed to evolved. The book 'Cosmos, Bios, Theos: Scientists Reflect on Science, God, and the Origins of the Universe, Life, and Homo Sapiens' was written by no less than sixty notable scientists, including twenty four Nobel Prize winners. One of the contributing authors, Yale physicist Professor Henry Margenau concludes, "There's only one convincing answer for the intricate laws that exist in nature, ... that creation is by an omnipotent omniscient God." So science and God can be talked about in the same breath and is done so by some very reputable scientists to boot.

Many pages of rough order notes did ensue in my manuscript to justify my transition from mainstream, follow the crowd, evolution believing acceptance to a creationist, describing in detail such things as the 'Second Law of Thermodynamics' (or Entropy) a well-known law of 'Operational Science' that, in a biological sense, means the evolution of the very first cell by 'random chance' without any physical or intellectual input is a mathematical impossibility. The super complex DNA programming even in the simplest cell (equivalent to libraries full of ordered text) just couldn't happen by random chance, it needed intelligence to program it in logical order. It's like saying heavy hail stones falling from the primeval sky, landing very hard and randomly on an exposed computer keyboard over millions and millions of years, went on to produce from some miraculous self-produced printer the complete works of Wilbur Smith purely by random chance. Then, somehow, all Wilbur's many novels started to self-replicate or print out all by themselves (without the original computer and printer). That still doesn't describe the mathematical odds necessary for the very first simple cell to self-create (or evolve) its own DNA program. You may think that sounds absolutely nutty but basically that is what the theory of evolution is saying about the biological evolution of the very first cell (life). That logical, programmed, ordered genetic instructions (DNA) in the first living cell all happened by complete and utter random chance. This is just the tip of the iceberg for scientific evidence pointing away from a very debatable theory of 'Historical Science' (evolution) and pointing towards creation. However, I received friendly advice to remove the content due to the utter boredom it would create for most mainstream readers. If you are brave enough to explore this very controversial topic further then a good DVD to watch is "Unlocking the Mystery of Life" presented by a number of well-respected scientists from several fields of academia.

Why is all this important to a Charlie slowly rotting away in his self-imposed rainforest prison? Simply because it proved an existence of a God and offered a way to bring me back from the edge of the abyss where I had been standing, sick in mind, body and soul.

Where I was willing to fight the evil bureaucracy to the bitter end, climbing rainforest giants to top with a chainsaw and lighting tar and hess covered safety fuses on dark, stormy nights to blow over trees with powergel. Where my pitiful weeping body was saying, "Enough!" When you are down and out, dark and angry with depression, working yourself into the ground and living a self-absorbed life, finding a genuine belief in God tends to turn your world upside down. For some it happens very quickly, like a sudden break from a lifelong addiction or the sudden peace in a life of turmoil and stress. For me it was slow going. My silly pride and headstrong arrogance battling the foregone conclusion.

I already had a luke-warm belief in Christianity since childhood. Its boundaries, its morals seemed an invited system, refined over centuries to keep order and love in society. When societies embrace Jesus' teaching, the base Christian philosophy of love and forgiveness, they seemed to flourish but when they move away from it, society seems to fall apart. Look at the history of Western civilisations, look at the per capita statistical data here in NZ just on violent crime. Take the ultimate crime, murder. Fifty years ago there were maybe two or three murders a year making the national news for months on end. Fifty years ago most people in New Zealand went to church and believed in God, most believed that their actions in this world were accountable for in the next. That a moral code had a purpose to hold society together. Now most people don't believe in God or the basic moral code of the Bible, we have four to five murders a month. The severe break-up of the family unit which is glue that holds society together is yet another indicator of a declining, dysfunctional society as we move away from the old biblical morals and the quiet conservatism of our forebears and actively embrace the loud, free and easy liberalism of today with the 'no rules' and 'everything goes' mentality. Everybody living for themselves, their selfish wants and their basic desires and not for their family, community or society. All resulting in huge social problems which are not getting better but will get worse and worse, just turn on the telly.

I thought I was a Christian in my youth. You deemed yourself to be a good Christian by keeping good moral conduct and by doing good deeds for others from to time to time. Going to church seemed to be a prerequisite. You didn't really have to believe in God, just pretending to was just fine. Artificial Christian versus genuine faith.

I got a big fright when I was introduced to the concept that science could prove God's existence real. An existence far more logical than evolution, a theory I had just accepted as fact without thinking deeply or logically about it. Darwin's theory kills the belief in God for the majority. When you look at all the misconceptions tabled about the Bible and you find out just a little of all the evidence behind the Bible, you naturally side towards the God of the Bible as the Creator. It's then a short step to accepting Jesus Christ as your Lord and Saviour. From that step of faith (if genuine) comes a real sense of growing peace and a spiritual awakening beyond the scope of science, or my words, to explain. Don't be fooled into thinking that step means you are perfect, far, far from it. I am most definitely not, never have been with loads of dark dirty secrets hidden in my guilty past, nor will I ever be perfect in the future under my own power. In fact follow Christ's teachings and you soon discover that you cannot earn your salvation by being perfect or doing good works and never ever will. That is the largest misconception ever, that Salvation is somehow earned by doing good works, a concept which is not taught by Christ, nor found anywhere in the Bible. Loving your neighbour and doing good works are clear Biblical instructions but have nothing to do with your actual Salvation. Your Salvation is a totally free gift, available to all. All it requires is a genuine faith in God and two very basic requirements from you, first a genuine repentance of sin and second a clear verbal acceptance of Jesus Christ as your Lord and Saviour. The rest is God's pure love with a free gift of Grace from him. All beautifully simplistic. In fact the Bible puts it very simply in Romans: "If you confess the Lord Jesus with your mouth and believe in your heart that God raised him from the dead, then you will be saved. For it is with the heart you believe and are justified, but it is with your month you confess and are saved." There are no hidden additions or agendas in that simple verse saying you must attend a specific church or denomination to be saved, be a good person or give all you own to the poor. It's all about your Faith and God's Grace, not your works and deeds. No other religion or faith offers such simplicity of action, such security of salvation or such inner peace as Christianity.

That is enough of the stuff most will consider the religious ramblings of an idiot. Before I go back to my romantic wilderness story gone wrong, which still has a bit to go wrong, I'll better describe my present location.

THE PRESENT: Deep Cove, Doubtful Sound. Have I escaped the Fiordland wilderness, that very seductive mistress of my life? "Nope." I write these last concluding chapters still inside the National Park but not from my remote and secluded Jamestown Bay, instead from Doubtful Sound, New Zealand's largest Sound. Still in a remote setting in most people's minds but to me this is civilisation, not true wilderness like my home Bay. For starters, I have a gravel road to my front door, a very steep, twisty road which cuts through the majestic rainforest and the rugged snow-capped Southern Alps via the Wilmot Pass. This mountainous, scenic road connects the West Coast flowing catchment areas to East Coast flowing catchment areas and by doing so this road also gives me access to Lake Manapouri on the Park's eastern boundary. At this beautiful Fiordland lake filled with her many bush clad islands there is a regular boat service out of the Park boundary and into the modern world most accept as normal. I now have a regular flow of electricity via a mini-hydro plant in the local stream out back. I have a freezer, fridge, even a microwave and incredibly a TV, pure luxuries in life for me. Most amazing of all is I have a phone via a satellite. More incredibly still, there are people galore coming through my life. Heaps of them, twenty to thirty new faces every three to four days. The introverted bush hermit and his past lifestyle has had a shock to his system, a well overdue change for the better.

I find myself in the employ of a Charitable Trust in Doubtful Sound, looking

My lovely Bronny (future wife) – Wilmot Pass Road, Doubtful Sound.

My sign on Hollyford Track, trying to attract customers.

after a very old and rundown hostel set up to cater for the educational needs of 12 and 13 year olds in the form of school camps. It's been going near on forty years and serves a huge social good for the Southland and Otago communities. There is a saying that most people under 40 in Southland have been through Deep Cove Hostel. The pay is poor but I accept that as a natural aspect to working for a charitable cause where cash flow is always a battle to maintain. The kids that come to camp tend to stay for three or four nights. For most this is their first introduction to an environment like this. Mostly pudgy city kids used to home comforts of soft couch, processed food and paying homage to the household idol, the TV, definitely not used to temperate rainforest nor the accompanying sandflies and rain. The focus of the Trust is not on adventure like most imagine such remote school camps would, it is education based, mainly conservation related, working closely with DOC. The kids get out into the outdoors doing marine studies on the Sound and learning about ecosystems in the forest. My job is probably best described as a caretaker, come warden, come manager. I keep the place operational for power, sewage, safety, maintenance and paperwork, etc. It suits my practical background of 'Jack of all trades, but master of none' and my Scottish background of making things work with limited resources (shoe-string budgets). I let the teachers do the educating, that is their gift, definitely not mine. My job here varies hugely in workloads. Sometimes I am pushing many barrows at once, rushed off my feet both day and night trying to keep many parties happy all at the same time while trying to keep a very old infrastructure operational. At other times I am pushing nothing. The feast-famine circle of the wilderness has followed me even to here.

Doubtful Sound is a very majestic sort of place, in some ways much more scenic than its famous cousin Milford Sound which is the main icon on the tourist viewing agenda in the South Island of New Zealand. The geography and geology here in Doubtful differs from my old stomping ground in North Fiordland. Whereas my old surrounding mountains had much gentler curves and slopes, here everything is deep glacier carved U shape valleys with the rainforest in a permanent battle with gravity just to cling on to the steep valley walls. Where the battle is lost to gravity there are very impressive cliffs of granite towering vertically for hundreds and hundreds of metres up into the misty mountains. At regular intervals these bare rock cliffs have equally impressive waterfalls cascading straight down into the green velvet forest valleys or the cold blue sea below. The rainforest here is denser, wetter and chillier than my old home in North Fiordland. The trees are similar with podocarp giants still dominating the forest scene but here in mid-Fiordland there is a lot more rain, coming in literally bucket loads, averaging six to seven metres a year. As a result there is an over-abundance of mosses of every type. From the long stringy moss that hangs off the thick podocarp branches like green wispy, torn lace curtains to rolling, bumpy, green carpets of water-laden spongy moss on the forest floor, postcard scenery at every turn of the head. Sadly, just like at my old home, the forest is also deadly silent, slowly dying, a ghost forest with silent echoes of beautiful bird song long lost. Most have no idea of the ecological disaster taking place here and throughout Fiordland and if you don't live in it, most don't really care. This dying rainforest is DOC's testament to their bureaucratic and academic failures best hidden from the public. (The old Charlie still has to put in an opinionated dig –sorry.) I dearly love my forest and the limited bird life that it still retains so it's very hard to shut up on the topic.

Deep Cove for me is the people now in my life, people that are associated to the Hostel, the Trust and the Sound, people that are helping shape my new life. There are Paul and Bob, my bosses, both ex-teachers with hearts of gold and personalities as separate as chalk and cheese. Bob is an outright extrovert. He is famous for his ability to articulate a great deal without actually getting to the point, to the wonderment of those listening, especially me his employee awaiting a clear instruction to action. He is equally famous for his mischievous wind ups with many a fond story being told of his antics and fun mayhem, which both kids and accompanying adults love. Paul on the other hand is the complete opposite, a very quiet and wise instigator who has a huge heart to serve community. He is an anchor in a stormy sea as things do not always run easily for charitable trusts. He has been on the Trust 40-odd years, a founding member. He is also on several other Trusts as well, working incredibly hard for little or no reward, thanks or recognition. Paul is literally an unsung hero in the Southland Community, knighthood material. There is Frankie and Paul each taking a seven day shift at being my only neighbours here in the Cove. Each takes turns in the Sound skippering the Real Journey's tourist vessel. Like Paul and Bob their personalities are also chalk and cheese. Paul is a caring sort, of quiet temperament and personality, very reliable to his employers. Frankie is a hard-working, mince no words, roll up the sleeves, doer sort. Although complete opposites in personality Frankie and I have struck up a sort of friendship as we have similar outdoor interests. Frank is well known for his huge artwork pieces made from driftwood logs, sourced directly out of the Sound in his spare time, normally with an adventure or two tied into their retrieval from the sea in these remote fiords. He has incredible mental toughness that few have, running local mountain tracks in hours which most take days to walk. He is also known for calling a spade a spade, when sometimes it's more polite or politically correct to call it a shovel, not a person you cross verbal swords with. There is Ron, the local sea kayak guide with the good looks of a healthy, ageing surfy and a laid-back mellow character of an unselfish spirit. There is Nigel who operates a small tourist trip operation in competition with the big kids on the block, a David and Goliath commercial battle where he survives against the odds. Nigel goes out of his way to help the Charitable Trust whenever it has need, which is quite a lot. Nigel is a real battler and doer as well and I respect him for it. I have been down a similar road with similar battles which I didn't get on top of like he has. There are many others but if I was to focus on just one character it would have to be John Carter.

Johnny is an import from England and is the local DOC educator for the kids at the Hostel. Not the standard bureaucratic health and safety English import we all know, wrapping us all up in silly cotton wool thinking of the old home country, slowly destroying the practical can-do, pioneer spirit of our colonial forefathers, but just the nice genuine English gentleman type of gentle temperament. When I first met Johnny I wasn't sure how to take him. His affection and passion for people, kids in particular and for New Zealand conservation in general, I considered way over the top, just an extroverted act to get by in life as extroverts tend to do. But the more I got to know him, the more I realised my first, off hand estimation of him was incredibly wrong. You couldn't get a more genuine caring sort of bloke with a deep and genuine passion for both people and conservation. He really ruffles my growing faith, but it is very unintentional on his part. My faith dictates that I should love others, it's one of those important Biblical principles for a Christian to try to follow as just part of day to day life. But, by human nature, I only love those who love back, such as family and friends. I sometimes find it difficult to love people in general, it's not what a Christian should admit to. Johnny on the other hand does love everybody that comes into his arena of influence. He doesn't have a malice bone in his body, which for a male is truly a rare thing. That, of course, humbles me deeply in a spiritual sense and probably helps me grow.

His passion for conservation is a credit to him. It's an infectious passion that rubs off on the kids and the parents that come to camp. They go from lethargic, bored city kids to energetic converts to conservation under his endearing tuition. He is always talked about with a smile by the adults and teachers who have exposure to his unorthodox teaching style but the kids learn by it. Once he got 25-odd kids to carrying a bucket each full of water part way up the Hanging Valley track which is quite a climb through temperate rainforest in the hanging valley raising above and behind the hostel to the south. A walk that sometimes involves using both hands to grab thick tree roots like a ladder as you climb up the very steep bush track. Of course the kids thought this endeavour utter madness but also a great deal of fun. None had full buckets by the time they got to the top. Johnny then gave a lesson to the bemused group of kids and bewildered adults with the lush ancient forest as his school room and moss covered rocks as chairs about how rain clouds full of stolen water comes off the Tasman Sea, hits the rugged mountains of Fiordland, rises and condenses, losing its moisture as rain, hence a rainforest on the western side of the Southern Alps and dry beech forests on the eastern side. A lesson not easily forgotten by the kids. Another time he gutted a possum I had freshly killed to show the eye-popping city kids the differing organs in the body and explained what each shiny, slimy organ did in the body. He regularly takes kids on bio-diversity work trapping and killing stoats, rats and possums which would give the liberal city raised educators kittens to even consider as an educational activity for their political correct, risk adverse, cotton wool thinking. He is probably the best walking, talking public relations rep. DOC has for 'Joe Public.' Sadly I sense he is too passionate for his bosses and has way too much practical sense for DOC. Like me he has a real passion for 'practical conservation', of getting out there onto the ground, getting one's hands dirty and bloody, killing the introduced species to save this special forest ecosystem.

His good looks, his endearing, caring, happy spirit and his very articulate tongue makes the single female teachers go a little gooey for him. But John never exploits this male advantage as a large portion of males would do given half the chance. His true love in life is his lovely wife Carolyn and he's not shy letting others know how special she is. She is his life, sun, moon and stars.

It's time to stop nattering about my friends and job and get on with the story.

HOW TO DISPATCH A POSSUM: To finish and fill the page, a wee note on how to dispatch a possum caught in a gin or leg hold trap. Part and parcel of living in the NZ wilderness and conserving the New Zealand environment is knowing how to kill a possum caught in a trap. I have watched an inexperienced bloke make a very poor job of it which caused an unpleasant death by hammering away at the poor thing as it bounced frantically around on the forest floor trying to avoid the poorly aimed blows. With all things practical, there is a technique and with a possum in a trap, the technique is reasonably simple. Possums are nocturnal, once caught in a trap, they tend to ball up during the day, least until they hear you approach, then they try to distance themselves from you by trying to drag the trap away, normally caught by the front paw until the chain securing the trap is pulled up short, exposing an easy bushy tail to grab very quickly with your left hand. Quickly, but not forcibly, pull the possum tight on the chain, the possum being in a horizontal position and parallel to the forest floor. This means that those horrible sharp, tree climbing claws can't rake at you, nor can angry teeth bite you. This position also gives the hammer in your right hand a very clean efficient back swing, across and along the length of the spine at the back of a now reasonably still head. Quick and painless, if done right.

Another trick for re-setting the trap for the next night's work, is to bleed the dead possum a bit over the plate of the re-set trap. Simply hang onto the tail and dangle the possum directly over the trap and do a short vertical cut to the throat so the blood drips down onto the plate or trigger of the trap. Being omnivorous, possums love the scent of blood. It makes a very easy additional lure to the one you have already used on the now re-set trap, a trick taught to me by a North Island possum trapper.

Chapter Nineteen | TIME TO DEPART

THE PRESENT: Deep Cove, Doubtful Sound. Since selling my wilderness rainforest home, the book writing endeavour has very much taken a back seat. Now it's time to conclude the tale and maybe get on with life.

I have very mixed emotions reading what was written over the years, it brings back very vivid memories and mixed emotions. It makes me feel a little uncomfortable at times. It's not because I miss the wilderness lifestyle, which I do, nor because the memories of injustices still hurt just a little, small dying embers deep inside being extinguished in both time and forgiveness of a slowly growing faith, a work in progress. However, the main reason I find re-reading it a little hard is because my present attitudes and beliefs have changed so much from when I first put pen to paper almost nine years ago, under that candle perched atop a wine bottle in the remote Fiordland rainforest. The Charlie of the present is a very different person to the Charlie of then. Some sections seem so very dark now, so full of dark, opinionated anger that reflect poorly on how I now view life as a confessing Christian. Should I re-write it all, should I water it down for more palatable PC consumption by the reader who may be family and friends? Do I leave out the stories about the injustices thrown into my path with all the resulting challenges and the self-consuming anger? If I do so, how do I explain the reasons for having to float my house down a remote lake in the Fiordland wilderness? How do I explain the seven years of constant battles, of a wilderness life with no money, surviving with a pioneer lifestyle that most will find utterly incomprehensible in the modern age of welfare and free lunches? How do I justify the need to blow over giant rainforest trees with powergel on dark, stormy nights? How do I explain the sick bleeding body, the sick mind and dark angry soul? How do I explain finding a genuine belief in God, seeing his design and purpose in nature? I simply can't without being dis-honest to the whole tale. So it all stays, warts and all. The best I can do is leave out names of those on whom this story will or may reflect badly, hence the use of the pseudonym names from time to time.

MY STORY CONTINUES, back to Jamestown Bay. I have hit rock bottom. I seem to have been here before, more than once, calling out to God because I have tried everything possible to fix things myself. No matter how hard I have tried and battled over the years, here in the still expanses of Fiordland's immense rainforest, I just can't seem to get on top.

The last time was years before, with the little episode of the sunken boat, with me on my knees on the Demon Trail, in a situation where I was completely and utterly stuffed. My precious life savings in building materials spread around Fiordland between a flood prone delta, my little Jamestown beach and the Hollyford airstrip. My bank account emptied by a helicopter pilot's misquote and my own foolishness. My boat sunk, resting on the lake bottom at the Demon Trail Hut and me, burnt out, physically and mentally at my absolute wits end, on my knees unable to even shed a tear.

Now a few years later I am forced to humble myself yet again, all my pride, ego is thrown aside and I'm back on my knees. It's a real cry of despair, still without the much needed tears.

I cannot recall what brought me to this rotten state, but I do remember that it's night time and I'm in the candlelit living-room of my very hard won wilderness home. I am totally and utterly sick of all the constant challenges and the accumulating years of battles, they seem never ending. There is no light visible at the end of this dark tunnel for me. My body is still weeping regular gushes of bright blood and I am constantly tired. A body drained of its energy rich iron being flushed regularly down a toilet bowl, rich nutrients to be absorbed by my dense rainforest surrounds, making strong prison bars of those tall strong, vine covered podocarps that imprison my home and life. I have become desperately lonely, a nightmare for a natural introvert. My sick, self-centred mind seems to daily explore the options of ending things. Imagining bitter, twisted endings to convey a martyr's message to the evil bureaucratic world to avenge myself of their unjust management, catering to the rich at the expense of the poor. Some final straw, now forgotten, has brought me back to my knees yet again. I challenge God to give me guidance, "What should I do?" I open my Bible at complete random, a new habit in my growing faith. The very first verse I read by the flickering candle hits me like a ton of bricks. I was expecting some comforting words, maybe promises of a better future from up on high. I felt I was owed it, being my due. But I go from self-indulged, self-pity and remorse to utter shock. The words seem to bounce out of the page at me, the printed text of the verse seems larger than the surrounding text which seems suddenly unreadable. The verse I read at random after a prayer of guidance is this, "Arise and depart, for this is polluted and will be your sore destruction."[1] It sends cold shivers up and down my spine. These aren't words of comfort or a promise that all my hard work would be made all worthwhile. This was the complete opposite, this was a warning and a very severe one at that. "The word of God is sharper than any double edge sword, it penetrates even to dividing soul and spirit, joints and marrow: it judges the thoughts and attitudes of the heart. Nothing in all creation is hidden from God's sight. Everything is uncovered and laid bare before the eyes of him to whom we must give account."[2] A loving God had made it clear to me that the path I had put myself on only had a bitter end, a conclusion not of his making but completely

1   Micah 2:10
2   Hebrews 4:12-13

My very hard won wilderness home, that I was told I could not build.

Charlie now a different man on a charitable house build North Nalawi, Africa,
and absolutely loving it.

my own. That all this I had achieved in the wet, dense rainforest of the Fiordland wilderness was absolutely nothing to him. It only glorified me, my large stupid male ego, my silly pride, not him. To the All Seeing and All Knowing it personified all my vices and my dark, angry soul. He had paid the ultimate price in blood to forgive me my sins, yet here I was unable to forgive the perceived injustices/sins against me. It made me a hypocrite in my new found faith. For some we have to "work out our salvation with fear and trembling." I guess I'm one of those. Very few modern, happy clappy preachers teach this Biblical aspect in their feel good sermons, it's more the domain of bygone and almost extinct 'fire and brimstone' style preachers. But that's not to say it isn't relevant in today's world or for people like me.

I knew exactly what he meant about my wilderness endeavours being polluted. It has been said that, "Every mans conscience is the custodian of his destiny" I've been no saint and at the beginning of this project I had done something that had severely pricked my conscience in a moral sense, but maybe not something that everyone would be concerned about in today's world. Our conscience is a very individual and personal part of us and is, I believe, often God directed, if you let it be. A husband and/or father may do things unbeknown to the rest of the family, initially with a very guilty conscience but the more he does it the less guilty he feels, until one day he finds his actions have spoilt a good family life or even destroyed it beyond repair. Ignoring your conscience is a very dangerous thing, the continued dulling of your conscience to justify wrong action will ultimately have sad consequences. Anyway I had conveniently thrown the skeleton of my actions into my deep inner closest to forget forever. Now, years after the event, it had caught up with me and I knew with utter certainty that this very stupid action had polluted it. Just like a very old festering wound that never really healed then suddenly it goes septic, poisoning and polluting the whole system. Nothing is hidden from above. If you are not accountable for it in this world, you definitely will be in the next.

My lukewarm faith, my pride, arrogance and ego couldn't quite accept this scary instruction. Was I really expected to walk away from seven years of hard work, away from my hard won domain in the wilderness of Fiordland which I love. My answer was, "Nope, can't be," not after all I had gone through. Maybe it was just my over active imagination, a fluke of random chance combined with my own weak mind so I dis-regarded it for a while, a long while in fact. But, with each passing day and week and month, those scary words didn't go away, they seemed to ring louder and louder in my soul. A branding iron that wasn't cooling down with time, instead it was heating up to sear my conscience deeper and deeper. You can't constantly battle, work, bleed and have such deep dark thoughts as I had and expect to have a positive ending. The instruction clarified and solidified, it became crystal clear in my mind. If I stayed here, I would die. I was working my mind, body and soul into the grave. 'Sore Destruction' means just that. Looking back I now realise it was a very clear instruction based on love, true parental love from a caring Father saying very clearly to a child, "Continue touching that stove and you will get burnt." It was time for a big change in life, time to stop battling, time to move out of the wilderness I love, time to sell up the dream. The decision was made.

Now the old age challenge of coming up with a selling price. Bill, my part-time neighbour, had a strong opinion on the subject and had done so ever since I had known him. It was only worth $200,000, re-enforcing that line of thought whenever the opportunity arose. Once, when working for him, he glanced over towards a brand new tractor he had just purchased and stated casually, in a matter of fact tone, "You know that is worth more than your place," meaning Jamestown. I had learnt a long time ago not to rise to such baited comments as I would only lose any verbal contest with this very intelligent and articulate man. Another time when alcohol had control of his tongue he stated, "If you ever get over $200,000, I'll write you out a cheque for $10,000." I might be slow of speech, lacking the ability to formulate my words quickly, but I'm no fool and sensed his real motivation, read it like an open book. Making such a comment was an alcohol induced attempt to get me to sell to his friend, who happened to be in the room at the time. A Queenstown gentlemen very keen on purchasing land at Martins Bays. Bill wanted to keep his playground in house to his social circle of friends. The fact he thought he could do that at the expense of my life's work only strengthened my resolve to stick to my guns.

Anyway, I knew my place had to be worth much more, but how much more was the real question. I had been down this road seven years before. Freehold titles of land are a very rare commodity in a National Park, whether it's in New Zealand or across the globe. There were no real recent sales to give guidance in establishing a price. I had to basically grab a figure out of Fiordland's still air. So, once again, I got down on my knees and asked God for guidance. Once again I opened my Bible at complete random, and yet again my eyes landed straight on the verse in the book of Numbers that seemed to bounce out of the page. Moses had done a census on all the men that could bear arms wandering around in the wilderness after leaving Egypt. The final tally of Moses' census was "603,550" and my eyes fell onto that verse. Most will probably laugh reading this, but I don't really care, it's water off a duck's back. I challenge you to think about the odds of opening the Bible at complete random and reading the very first verse your eyes rest on. Literally out of thousands and thousands of verses dealing with everything from history and prophesy, law and life, sin and love, then out of all those hundreds of pages and thousands of verses have your eyes fall only on a single verse that happens to have specific reference to a large figure, large numeral. The odds are stacked heavily against you. Just try it.

So my selling price became $603,550. Not a bad sort of price but a little hard for real estate agents to get their heads around the $3,550 part. When dealing with such large figures you tend to round figures up or down to the nearest thousand or even tens of thousands. Personally I would have liked the figure much higher but that was just the old greed in me trying to kick back in. Life was changing, I was beginning to follow Christ and not my own inner vices driven by selfish wants of the past.

The season ended. I was very resigned to the fact I had to leave and sell up. I started stoking on the TSS *Earnslaw* yet again. And started to try and sell my wilderness property yet again. My final battle of my project and, like all battles with this project, it wasn't an easy process.

I was utterly and totally flat broke, nothing new in my life. When you have no money and your target market is very limited, dealing with the upper end of the society where the rich kids play life, it gets very expensive to advertise in the likes of upmarket fishing, hunting, outdoor recreational magazines. Everything I earned went towards food and board and the advertising of the property.

I thought it wise to keep trying to run my little wilderness as a business until the property sold. It turned out this was not such good wisdom. It took me a long time to sell and I was forced to run yet another season, in a very Mickey Mouse manner.

A visiting journalist visited and did a two-page Saturday feature with one page entitled, "Going Bush" on Jamestown history, me and my battles building, floating materials down rivers and lake, etc. The other joint page was entitled, "Paradise in Fiordland." It described the wilderness property for sale in the Fiordland National Park, stating an asking price of $750,000 taking on advice from agents to have some wriggle room to negotiate my bottom line of $603,550. This great article with its lovely colour photos put me on the map in the mind of the general Southland and Otago public. Up to that date I had kept a reasonably low profile when I could.

Now all the romantic tyre kickers come back out of the woodwork and I had inquiries galore. Mostly they were all just that, romantic tyre kickers, dreamers a bit like myself. No story of a quick sale to recite here. My wilderness property did not sell which left me in the horrible situation of nutting out how I was going to keep my advertised season running while awaiting a buyer and not have to go back into my wilderness home to live, which part of the old me craved deeply to do. The plastic life of the tourist town was like bitter bile in my mouth but to return to my wilderness lifestyle would be returning to eat my own vomit in a spiritual sense. It would be disobeying a clear command from God. A kind of test of faith.

It was now that my friends Nick and Penny down at Martins Bay Lodge came to my rescue. Although they had absolutely no idea of the spiritual predicament I was in, probably incomprehensible to them like it would be for most people, they did, however, know of my poor health and challenging money issues and suggested a solution of sorts. They had friends from up Canterbury way, a retired farming couple, Allan and Ruth Bell who happened by chance to be strong Christians. A lovely couple who were spending their retirement traveling around helping people in need, doing so in very quiet and unassuming ways. Very much in line with Christ's teachings on loving your neighbour. This situation had a feeling it was meant to be, a form of inner peace about it so I asked Nick and Penny to test the waters with them to see if they wanted to come in and work my advertised season for food and board only, which was all I could really offer them, I had nothing else. And they did.

Now the story took a real twist of interest. I flew in to show Allen and Ruth the ropes. While doing so I had some very interesting and unexpected visitors.

UNEXPECTED VISITORS: One Howard Paterson (no relation) and his entourage of Queenstown's who's who have just wandered up my little rainforest track off the Lake. I hadn't heard this lot arrive and am caught a little off guard. Normally money people are associated with the noise of jet boats or copter rotors in the great stillness of the Fiordland wilderness, but not these characters. I've been out-foxed by them as they have coptered into Martins Bay and walked here. The silent, stealthy approach of predators.

Weird how life all works out. Years ago it was Sir Tim Wallis who was published in the 'Rich list' as the South Island's richest man, now his financial star has fallen somewhat from the media listings of the rich. That grand accomplishment now belongs to Howard Paterson standing before me, firmly shaking my hand and drilling me with direct eye contact and a confident, friendly smile. Both Sir Tim and Howard being very blessed in life with astute minds for business, both men taking time out to humble a poor man (me) battling away with his little project in the New Zealand wilderness. Howard, a typical man of success, takes a five minute look around my property, likes what he sees, marches up to me, with forceful direct eye contact again and says in a clear confident voice, "If you are willing to negotiate on your price, we can do a deal here and now." An agent had told him my bottom price. I of course say, "No," my price is my price, it's set in stone. He says fine. Then Howard smiles again, changes the topic completely and explains that his entourage of Queenstown's who's who have arranged to stay at the Smith's crib and he was wondering if he could spend the night here at my little establishment while his rich friends stay at the Smiths. I say, "Sure." I sensed my flat refusal to negotiate my price had just presented him with a little challenge that men of Howard's stature thrive to take on and he wanted more time to work on me.

I find out, in the course of the conversation, that there is indeed a helicopter servicing their little play trek in the wild, bringing in the food and alcohol that accompanies such people. Howard then invites me to join them for food and drinks later in the evening.

The others depart down my little rainforest track heading towards Smith's, expensive Scotch, fancy cheese and tasty crackers while Howard stays behind. It's just the two of us and now comes the dreaded question, "Charlie, how come you have such an unusual asking price $603,550?" Boy, I knew someone was going to ask me that question but not Howard Paterson of all people, not here in the rainforest with me in thread-bare Warehouse jeans with skinny knees on display through denim worn holes, standing bare foot in my forest backyard. How do you explain that I had sought divine guidance from above on the selling price? How I opened my Bible at complete random and the first verse I read was Moses' census of the tribes of Israel, 603,550. How do you explain that to the richest man in the South Island, in a modern age where reference to God is definitely not cool, a major social turnoff in most conversation? But I did, doing so in an embarrassed sort of way, expecting ridicule or even a short, uncontrolled laugh but I got nothing of the sort, just a very deep, serious look and a very startling comment. "Charlie, do you know I have a degree in Psychology and a degree in Theology and I fully understand." I was a little shocked. I had become very accustomed to Bill, my part-time neighbour in the Bay, ridiculing me on my price and presumed Howard would do the same. Both men being blessed mentally, socially and financially. But what I got from Howard was a feeling of respect that appeared very genuine. He understood that at this time my price was set in stone at $603,550. Nothing more was ever said on that topic.

The little story doesn't end there. After a nice evening of eating food and drinking wine, etc. that only the financially blessed can afford to eat and drink as standard fare (which I also enjoyed), Howard and I headed back along the little beach of Jamestown Bay in the dark then up to my little log hideaway, elevated on the old lake terrace in the rainforest. Howard grabbed some books from my growing library, some of which I note are on creation science, then bids me good night.

Now, I am very aware of my hard won surrounds. I don't really sleep properly until all my guests have put out their bedside candles and my little log house is plunged into darkness, the Fiordland nocturnal stillness having descended on my wilderness home. Anyway, I note the candle light emitting from under Howard's bedroom door (my room is adjoining his). I sleep with the door open, just in case I need to attend to the fire of my kitchen range or a guest. Howard's bedside candle burns all night, Howard didn't sleep all night, nor did I. I presume he just read and read and read all night. In the morning I was floored yet again by my daily random Bible reading. "The labour of a poor man is sweet, whether he has a lot to eat or not, but the abundances of a rich man will not suffer him to sleep."[3] Of all the verses to read that morning it had to be that one, with me accommodating the richest man in the South Island and him by all appearances not sleeping a wink. It's a verse that has stayed in my mind ever since.

Howard and his entourage of Queenstown's social elite duly depart by helicopter. They didn't arrive in my little wilderness Bay like rich people normally do but they certainly departed the way the rich normally do.

Much later I heard Howard had a very sad ending. He was by himself in a Fiji resort room and happened to choke to death on a potato chip of all things. He didn't die old, nor do I guess did he die a happy, contented man either. We come into this world with absolutely nothing and we certainly leave it with absolutely nothing. Pretty humbling stuff for those who wish to think deeply on it.

I had by this stage well and truly gotten over any jealously of these rich kids. I had socialised enough with them over the years to note how plastic their lives really are. Their many inner vices sometimes far out match the poor man's singular vice of jealously.

Another interested party of note, who I didn't actually meet, was Viggo Mortensen who played Aragon in the 'The Lord of the Rings' fame. The real estate agent showed him around my little rainforest home in the Fiordland wilderness but obviously it wasn't his cup of tea.

---

3   Ecclesiastes 5:12

A SALE TO A CENTRAL OTAGO PROPERTY DEVELOPER is negotiated. A nice, down to earth bloke who informs me he doesn't want to run my place as a commercial proposition but to keep it in part as a legacy to pass on to his family and future generations. Kind of a wise line of thought for the ex-school teacher come Central Otago property developer. It's a deal that almost falls over when final settlement isn't made on the due date. However, after a little more negotiation and the fact both parties felt honour bond to make the deal work, a settlement is finally reached.

A long story but, at the end of the day, instead of getting my $603,550 I got a deal which ends up at $810,000. So it's worth letting God do His thing. And, boy, tractors must be getting very expensive down on Southland farms. Yet to see Bill's promised cheque.

OUT OF THE WILD: To come out of the wilderness took a bit of doing. It wasn't just leaving a beautiful physical location that chewed up seven years of my life. It was leaving behind all the inner rubbish that had polluted my being. The arrogance, the ego, the pride, the greed, the jealously and especially the self-consuming anger. It took time to digest all this change in my life. I had to let go of seven years of constant hard work, seven years of endless challenges and battles, bleeding and sweating, depression and loneliness. Seven years of building up a dream in the wilderness from literally nothing to only find that my dream fulfilled had come with a huge cost that I never, ever envisaged. It was also time to forgive.

Do I miss the quiet peace, the immense solitude, the encompassing stillness of the Fiordland wilderness? A definite and huge, "Yes." Do I miss the simple lifestyle of evening candles and a simmering kettle on a wood stove, of using an axe and rifle as normal daily tools, of sharing a cheap port with complete strangers beside a drift wood fire on the sandy Jamestown beach under the Fiordland stars? Again a huge, "Yes." Do I miss the ancient rainforest with its slowly disappearing birdlife and quiet wandering deer? A very sad, "No," simply because I am still living in Fiordland, still watching its sad demise.

I polluted my own project. It was no longer the lifestyle, nor was it Fiordland the physically wilderness location. The project became a consuming anger at the injustices, it became my ego to achieve what others said I could not do. Both drove me to extremes in mind, body, soul and action. Had I stayed it would have totally consumed and ultimately killed me. A certainty of fact.

Now, to end this little tale of mine on a positive note, I feel much wiser from the seven year experience. Only a fool does not learn from his experience. My three years of bleeding has stopped. My mind has mostly cleared of selfish, sick, dark thoughts. Things are far from perfect. Nor am I perfect, nor will I ever be, a Biblical fact. But I know I'm forgiven and loved by a caring God all the same. A God that designed and created an incredibly beautiful world and ordered universe for us to live in. A God that gave us a free gift of salvation (life after death) through the very simple act of accepting his son Jesus Christ as our Lord and Saviour. I still feel like

Above: My beautiful Bay. *Below:* Enjoying God's wonderful Creation – the wild Earth (Lake Never Never).

a fish out of water at times away from my quiet wilderness Bay, but out of all the adversity, I have found a certainty of faith and a slowly opening path to spiritual fulfilment that is a free gift, available to absolutely anybody, saint or sinner, whether rich or poor, young or old, it does not matter. All it takes is a genuine faith and the guts to humble yourself to get it.

For the non-spiritual sort reading this tale, the New Zealand wilderness will be forever a part of me to my dying day and, "Yes," there is also a little pride in having achieved what most said I could not do.

Two small pieces of advice. Choose your dreams in life very, very carefully. Nut out the right priorities because you may just succeed. If you haven't chosen wisely then you could end up in a wilderness of your very own. Maybe not a physical wilderness of misty mountains and deep green forested valleys like mine was, but a wilderness nevertheless, one that will totally consume you if you let it and maybe even destroy mind, body and soul.

Learn to forgive and love. It may happen quickly or take years and happen slowly, but the art of forgiving and loving others will certainly lighten the load in life's journey.

ACKNOWLEDGEMENTS

Thank you to Geographx (for supply of maps),
Doug Wing (for editing) and Ellie van Empel (book design).

Cover photo: *The Southland Times*

Made in the USA
Middletown, DE
03 September 2019